D1298672

BOOKMARK

BOOKMARK

BOOKMARK

BOOKMARK   **BOOKMARK**   **BOOKMARK**

TO MARKET, TO MARKET
Home Again, Home Again

The Junior League of Owensboro
presents
a collection of Kentucky recipes
with a grateful tip of the hat to its friends.

The Junior League of Owensboro is an organization of women committed to promoting voluntarism and to improving the community through the effective action and leadership of trained volunteers. Its purpose is exclusively educational and charitable. The Junior League reaches out to women of all races, religions, and national origins who demonstrate an interest in and commitment to voluntarism.

Projects supported and sponsored by the Junior League of Owensboro, Inc. include, but are not limited to, the following:

Hospice
Kids On The Block
I'm Special
After School Enrichment Program
Leadership Owensboro
Boulware Center
American Heart Association
Kentucky's Speakers Bureau
M.A.D.D.
ODC Literary Council
Owensboro Area Spouse Abuse
    Shelter
Rape Victim Services
Musicians In The Schools Program
Green River Long-Term Care
    Ombudsman
Big Brother/Big Sister
Girls' Club Teen Program
Rolling Heights Family
    Development Center
Just Say No

Red Cross
Girl Scouts
Volunteer Connection
American Cancer Society
Small Wonders
Encounter-Hands On Museum
RiverPark Center
Cliff Hagan Boys Club
Parent Resource Center
The Girls, Inc.
"The Kids are Making It"
Adolescent Pregnancy
    Prevention Program
H.L. Neblett Center
Owensboro Area Museum
RiverPark Center Children
    and Family Programming
Hospitality House
CASA (Court Appointed
    Special Advocate)

First Edition

First Printing:	September 1984	10,000 copies
Second Printing:	May 1986	15,000 copies
Third Printing:	December 1988	20,000 copies
Fourth Printing:	December 1993	10,000 copies
Fifth Printing*:	December 1993	20,000 copies
Sixth Printing*:	February 1994	36,000 copies

(*Southern Living® Hall of Fame edition)
by
The Junior League of Owensboro, Inc.
Post Office Box 723
Owensboro, Kentucky

All rights reserved including the right to reproduce this book or parts thereof in any form, except for the inclusion of brief quotations in a review.

Library of Congress Catalog Card Number: 84-81147
ISBN-0-9611770-0-4

Copies may be obtained by writing to **To Market, To Market,** P.O. Box 723, Owensboro, KY 42302, or use order forms at the back of this book.

Table of Contents

To Market, To Market

To market, to market,
To buy a fat pig;
Home again, home again,
Jiggety-jig.

To market, to market,
To buy a fat hog;
Home again, home again,
Jiggety-jog.

To market, to market,
To buy a plum cake;
Home again, home again,
Market is late.

To market, to market,
To buy a plum bun;
Home again, home again,
Market is done.

Introduction

To Market, To Market...Home Again, Home Again. This beautifully illustrated cookbook picks up where the nursery rhyme leaves off. Filled with tempting selections, it will help you take your groceries from the kitchen counter to the dining table. It offers regional cookery at its best, with recipes especially chosen to bring back memories of the past and to create memories for the future.

Owensboro, located on the Ohio River, is the third largest city in Kentucky. Its best cooking reflects the warmth of the South and the bounty of the Midwest. It also includes some strictly local specialties. Bourbon, for which Kentucky is famous, is used not only as a beverage, but also as an unexpected flavoring in meat dishes, breads, and desserts. Barbecue, a favorite throughout the South, finds its local expression in mutton, carefully smoked and basted.

All good cooks make creative use of foods they find in abundance. Because fresh vegetables are available so much of the year, we use them often. **To Market, To Market** contains a large and tempting array of ways to prepare them. Since many Kentuckians are avid hunters, we have included a variety of ways to cook such standards as dove, quail, duck and venison, as well as the more exotic bear, elk and rattlesnake.

To Market, To Market includes not only a collection of carefully tested recipe favorites, but also many features useful to the beginning cook and the gourmet alike. Bookmarks will help you relocate special selections. An assortment of menus will help you to put together memorable meals and festive occasions. Much loved and frequently requested recipes appear throughout the book.

The Junior League of Owensboro is proud to present **To Market, To Market**. We enjoy good food and good company. Our book will guarantee the food. The rest is up to you!

Original
To Market, To Market
Committee

General Chairman: *Sylvia Jones*
Recipe Chairman: *Hadley Harrington*
Design Chairman: *Katie Shively*
Finance Chairman: *Mary Ann Medley*
Editing Chairman: *Marifaith Barr*
Sustaining Advisors: *Lucy Dawson, Sharon Kurtz, Sarah Purdy*
Office Manager: *Beth Best*
Marketing Chairman: *M'Alys Bowen*

Susan Bartlett
Leah Berry
Barbara Bittman
Marsha Burton
Gail Crowe
Joyce Edwards
Debbie Hayden
Marian Hutchinson
Cindy Iracane
Barbara Jarvis
Kathy Kirk
Gail Kirkland
Lane Langford
Sue Carol Lawson

Susan Mayes
Nancy Malone
Ann Meyer
Anne O'Bryan
Anne Padgett
Judy Peters
Iris Roberts
Jan Ann Scott
Lyllis Shrewsberry
Jo Anne Skillman
Lana Snellgrove
Peggy Stemle
Debbie Taylor
Harriett Whitaker

Cover design and illustrations by Katie Cox Shively

Contributors and Testers

Becky Altman
Bernard E. Alvey
Jo Ann Alvey
June Anderson
Wanda Anderson
Clara Ashley
Jo Ann Augenstein
Linda Bachman
Yvonne Bailey
Katrina Baird
Biji Baker
Bill Baker
Mary Dixon Baker
Trib Ball
Nan Barber
Nancy Barnard
Bill Barr
Marifaith Barr
Mary Rose Barr
Susan Bartlett
D Ellen Basham
Christa Beemer
Jenna Bennett
Vicki Bennett
Janet Berry
Leah Berry
Beth Best
Jeannie Bittel
Barbara Bittman
Shirley Bivins
Barbara Black
Pam Blackstone
Ruth Blakeman
Nancy Blewer
Karen Boeyink
Lois Booker
Faye Booth
Jill Bothwell
M'Alys Bowen
Vicki Bowen
Mary Carlyn Bristow
Jane Brockman
Gaynelle Brown
Freda Browning
Edna Bruce
Mrs. Marshall Bruner
Patsy Bryant
Janet Buddemeyer
Mary Bunning
Sue Burgess
Charles Burton
Marsha Burton

Linda Bushong
Linda Byrd
Mary Cabell
Mrs. George Cabell
John Calhoun II
Nancy Calhoun
Karen Callis
Nelda Callis
Brenda Carpenter
Debby Carpenter
Judy Carrico
Susie Belle Carson
Marty Cary
Jean Chapman
Nellie Chapman
Debbie Clark
Mona Clark
Sandra Cohron
Gladys Coin
Pam Collignon
Kay Cooper
Minnie Lou Covington
T. C. Covington
Hattie Jane Cox
Jeanne Cox
Katie Cox
Patsy Crady
Vivian Craig
Gail Crowe
Martha Curry
Anne Damron
Arlene Damron
Judy Daniel
Allene Darnell
Gregory Daurelle
Betty Lee Davis
Mary Davis
Beverly M. Dawson
Lillian Dawson
Lucy Dawson
Marie Dawson
Mildred Day
Wilma Lee Day
Ruth Ann Dearness
Violet DeLacy
Betty Delker
Bill Delker
Jane Delker
Sheila Depp
Sue Draper
Mary Ann Drumel
Rita Dutton

Mrs. Louise C. Eagles
Janet Ebelhar
Gerald Edds
Joyce Edwards
Bev Erwin
Nancy Eskridge
Joyce Ann Evans
Corrine Fay
Jan Fay
Jane Fisher
Susie Fister
Margaret Fitts
Mrs. K. Flinn
Connie Ford
Donna Ford
Dot Ford
Joan Ramey Ford
Lisa Fowler
Lee Fulton
Peggy Gleason
Kelly Goetz
Gloria Goodaker
Becky Gordon
Dorothy Gore
Jennifer Green
Lexie Greene
Betty Greenwell
Ann H. Greer
Linda Gregorian
Maureen Hackett
Fay M. Haddell
Stacy Hagerty
Cecille Hammond
Marie Hancock
Carole Harreld
Beth Harrington
Hadley Harrington
Larry Harrington
Bonnie B. Harris
Pam Harris
Joan Hartman
Patti L. Hartz
Jack Hatfield
Judy Hatfield
Mary Havelda
Alice Hawes
Benjamin W. Hawes
Janice Hawes
Debbie Hayden
Larkin Hayden
Mary Michael Hayden
Myrna Hayden

Mrs. W. T. Hayden
Sally Helwig
Jennie Hendrix
Edna Hicks
Julie Hidgon
Dorothy High
Ila M. Hight
Janice Hill
LeGrand Hisle
Mrs. Morton Holbrook
Peggy Howard
Josh Howes
Karen Hubbard
Judy Hughes
Marilyn Hunsaker
Marian Hutchinson
Ann Ingling
Cindy Iracane
Hazel Izor
Betty Jagoe
Gayle Jagoe
Barbara Jarvis
Helen Jarvis
Beth Johnson
Beverly B. Johnson
Bonnie Johnson
Buck Johnson
Joyce Johnson
Ruth I. Johnson
Sallie Johnson
Suzanne Johnson
Ginger Jones
Gerry Jones
John W. Jones
Julie Jones
Sylvia Jones
Louise Kahn
Flo Keeley
Ann Murphy Kincheloe
Kathy Kirk
Gail Kirkland
Mrs. Martin E. Knott
Diane Koch
Betty Kretman
Bobbi Kubik
Sarah Jane Kuntz
Jane Kurtz
Sharon Kurtz
Bill Langford III
Lane Langford
Louise Lashbrook
Carroll Laswell

Contributors and Testers, cont.

Evelyn Laswell
Sue Lawson
Martha Lee
Judy Lockhart
Diane Loucks
Marna Loucks
Louisa Lovett
Mary Lovett
Janice Lowrey
Brenda Lowry
Linda Lynch
Mrs. Geraldine Lyons
Diane Mackey
Kathleen Madauss
Jackie Maddox
Nancy Malone
Gerry Mann
Mrs. J. E. Martin
John E. Martin-
   Rutherford
Mary E. Mattingly
Arthur Marx
Karen Mayberry
Susan Mayes
Elsa Mazanec
Mrs. Kenneth McClure
Sue Roberts McCulloch
Gladys McGayer
Carolyn McKelvey
Ann McManus
Carol Medley
Charles Medley
Kathy Medley
Mary Ann Medley
Mary Medley
Marilyn Mercer
Ann Meyer
Janet Meyer
Paddy Miller
Joyce Miller
Marilyn Mills
Mrs. Gene Mobberly
Mildred Moe
Carol Moore
Judy Moore
Barbara Moorman
Robin Moorman
Mary Moran
Elizabeth Morgan
Ann Moseley
Helen Mountjoy
Claire Neal

Lucy Neal
Anita Newman
Susan Niehaus
Anne North
Grace North
Suzette Nunley
Anne O'Bryan
Nina O'Hearn
Joyce Orrahood
Joe H. Overby
Linda Overby
Marilyn Pace
Anne Padgett
Jane Pantle
Rick Park
Sallie Parker
Mary Pate
Judy Peters
Mona Pierce
Sally Plain
Alex Poore
Ann Powers
Anne Poynter
Linda Preuss
Mary Proctor
Sarah M. Purdy
Wanda Raley
Wanda Reid
Elaine Restad
Ann Reynolds
Becky Reynolds
Ethyl Reynolds
Virginia Reynolds
Karen Rhoads
Janice Rice
Charlotte Richeson
Cecilia Richmond
Mary Alice Riherd
Dee Riney
Iris Roberts
Mary Roberts
Sherry Roberts
Joan Robertson
Margaret Robinson
Judy Roby
Judy Romans
Mrs. James Rush
Peggy Ryan
Marijane Salmon
Jane Sandidge
Pat Satterwhite
Margaret Schertzinger

Jan Ann Scott
Jenny Sears
Dorothy Seitz
Bill Sequino
Cyndee Sequino
Judy Settle
Mrs. Stanley Settle
Kate Shafferman
Martha Shafferman
Marti Shattuck
Jennie Shaver
Anne Sheriff
Katie Shively
Robin Shively
Dorothy Shockley
Lyllis Shrewsberry
Mary Silvert
Wymma Sima
Kathy Simmons
Vivian Simmons
Jo Anne Skillman
Brenda Smith
Diane Smith
Terry Smith
Lana Snellgrove
Barbara Speaks
Mrs. Billy Staggers
Judy Staggers
Peggy Stainback
Beverly Steele
Peggy Stemle
Jan Sterett
Carolyn Stevenson
Jane Stevenson
Norma Jean Stone
Gloria Strehl
Trisha Strother
Charlotte Sturgeon
Joan Sullivan
Eleanor Sutton
Janet Suwanski
Peggy Swan
Alma S. Talbot
Beverly L. Taylor
Camilla Taylor
Carol Taylor
Debbie Taylor
Judy Harreld Taylor
Lucy Taylor
Margaret Taylor
Mrs. Richard Taylor
Glenda Thacker

Jennie B. Thomas
Judi Thompson
Mary Ann Thompson
Edwina Tinius
Laura Threlkeld
Mary Traxel
Annie Belle Triplett
Susan Truitt
Penny Trunnell
Deborah Tucker
Penny Turner
Susie Tyler
Jeannie Underhill
Marian Vasterling
Ann Waldrop
Tom Waldrop
Stella Walker
Nancy Hocker Ward
Barbara Warren
Jane Warren
Kim Warren
Bonnie Washington
Diane Watson
Marye Watts
Kay Weller
Susan Wells
Annette Wetzel
Harriett Whitaker
Julie Whitford
Vernile Whitmer
Gayle Wible
Suzanne Willis
Ann M. Wilson
Betty Wilson
Gay Wilson
Jo Wilson
Marian W. Wilson
William L. Wilson
Lynn Witherspoon
Roberta Witherspoon
John A. Witherspoon, Jr.
Karen Woodward
Kathy Woodward
Roddy Woodward
Nancy Worth
Ann Yager
Mrs. John Yager
Jean Yewell
Sandra Young
Lynda Youngman
Patsy Yunker

Beverages

Beverages

Hot Spiced Tea

Yield: 12 to 15 servings

Nice to serve for brunch.

12 cups water
2 sticks cinnamon
1 teaspoon whole cloves
3 family-size tea bags
¼ cup lemon juice
1 can (6 ounces) frozen
   orange juice concentrate
1 cup sugar

1. Tie spices in a loose bag of cheesecloth.
2. Place spices in water and bring to a boil.
3. Add tea bags, and steep 5 minutes.
4. Heat juices and sugar in saucepan. Add to tea.
5. Remove tea bags. Let mixture simmer 5 minutes. Remove spice bag.
6. Keep covered. Serve hot.

Hint: 6 regular tea bags may be substituted.

Citrus Iced Tea

Yield: 1 gallon plus

3 family-size tea bags
1 gallon water
1 can (6 ounces) frozen
   orange juice concentrate
5 lemons or 10 tablespoons
   lemon juice
2½ cups sugar

1. Boil water and pour over tea bags in container.
2. Steep 10 to 15 minutes.
3. While hot, add orange juice, juice of lemons, and sugar.
4. Stir until all sugar is dissolved. Refrigerate.

Grace's Iced Tea

Yield: 1 gallon

Delicious thirst quencher!

1½ cups sugar
1 cup white grape juice
¾ cup instant lemonade mix
½ cup instant tea
1 gallon water

1. Mix all ingredients.
2. Serve over ice.
3. Garnish with mint.

Hint: Some may prefer to increase the amount of sugar.

Made In The Shade

Yield: 4 servings

Lemonade at its best!

1 cup sugar
1 cup water
½ cup fresh lemon juice
4 cups water or soda water

1. Combine sugar and water in small saucepan. Cook 3 to 4 minutes until sugar is dissolved. Cool syrup.
2. Mix lemon juice with syrup and store in refrigerator.
3. To serve, add water or soda water to lemon syrup and pour over ice.

Hot Cranapple Punch (Microwave)

Yield: 7 cups (6 servings)

Deliciously simple!

1 quart apple cider
3 cups cranberry juice
   cocktail
2 teaspoons brown sugar
3 sticks cinnamon
½ teaspoon whole cloves
½ lemon, thinly sliced

1. Combine all ingredients in 3-quart heatproof bowl or pitcher.
2. Microwave on High until hot (about 10 minutes or 160°).
3. Remove spices with slotted spoon.

Red-Hot Cider

Yield: 20 cups

The fragrance from the perking pot makes this doubly delicious.

1 gallon apple cider
1 bottle (28 ounces) ginger ale
2 sticks cinnamon
28 whole cloves
1 cup red cinnamon candies

1. Mix cider and ginger ale in 34 cup percolator.
2. Put remaining 3 ingredients in basket of percolator.
3. Cook until candies have melted.
4. Serve hot.

Summertime Cooler

Yield: 4 servings (3 cups)

Appeals even to those who don't like buttermilk!

1½ cups chilled buttermilk
1½ cups chilled orange juice
1 tablespoon lemon juice
6 tablespoons sugar

1. Whip all ingredients in blender until smooth (about 30 seconds).

Fancy Fruit Freeze

Yield: 16 servings

2 cups sugar

3 cups water

1½ cups frozen strawberries

1 can (16 ounces) crushed
   pineapple

2 bananas cut into small
   pieces

6 teaspoons lemon juice

1 tablespoon frozen orange
   juice concentrate

Ginger ale

1. Boil the sugar and water.
2. Add remaining ingredients to the sugar.
3. Freeze in a 9 x 13-inch pan until serving time.
4. Combine ¼ of frozen fruit mixture with 2 to 3 ounces of ginger ale in blender until thick and smooth.
5. Serve in a stemmed glass.

Hint: Substitute rum for ginger ale for an interesting variation.

Sunshine Punch

Yield: 20 servings (16½ cups)

Just mix, chill, and serve.

1 can (12 ounces) frozen
   orange juice concentrate

3 cans (12 ounces each) water

1 can (46 ounces) pineapple
   juice

1 quart ginger ale

1 can (6 ounces) frozen
   lemonade concentrate

1. Dilute orange juice with water.
2. Add remaining ingredients.
3. Chill.

Winter Wine

Yield: 8 servings

Keeps you warm and cheery on snowy days.

4 to 5 sticks of cinnamon
2 teaspoons whole allspice
1 teaspoon whole cloves
Peeling from ½ orange (outer
    orange peel only)
½ cup sugar
½ cup water
1 bottle (750 ml.) sangria

1. Put first 6 ingredients in pan and
   boil until sugar is dissolved and
   mixture is thickening.
2. Stir in wine.
3. Reduce heat and simmer at least
   15 minutes.
4. Serve hot.

Claret Punch

Yield: 9 quarts

6 cups sugar
Juice of 10 lemons
5 quarts chilled claret or
    burgundy
1 quart brandy
10 sliced oranges
1 can (15 ounces) drained
    sliced pineapple
2 quarts chilled champagne
1 quart chilled soda
Prepared ice ring

1. Dissolve sugar in lemon juice.
2. Add claret, brandy, and fruit.
3. Let flavors blend in refrigerator
   for 2 or 3 hours.
4. Pour over ice ring.
5. Add champagne and soda.

Welcoming Wine
Yield: 22 servings

A wonderful way to say hello.

1 can (6 ounces) frozen
   orange juice concentrate
1 can (6 ounces) frozen
   lemonade concentrate
2 cups cold water
1 fifth (750 ml.) white wine
1 cup orange liqueur
1 bottle (28 ounces)
   carbonated water
Ice
Orange slices

1. Place frozen concentrates in punch bowl or large pitcher.
2. Stir in 2 cups of cold water.
3. Mix until smooth.
4. Stir in wine and orange liqueur.
5. Add carbonated water and ice.
6. Stir gently.
7. Top with orange slices.

Cranberry Sparkle
Yield: 6 to 8 servings

A real crowd pleaser!

3 cans (6 ounces each) frozen
   lemonade concentrate
2¼ cups cranberry juice
   cocktail
3 cans (6 ounces each) rum
7UP, optional

1. Mix first 3 ingredients.
2. Freeze for 24 hours, stirring occasionally.
3. Serve by spooning into glasses.
4. Pour 7UP over mixture if desired.

Hint: Vodka or gin may be substituted for the rum.

Yellow Bird

Sit back and relax!

1½ ounces white rum
½ ounce crème de banana
3 ounces pineapple juice
3 ounces orange juice
Fresh pineapple to taste

1. Blend and enjoy!

Summer Slush

1 can (12 ounces) frozen
   orange juice concentrate
1 can (12 ounces) frozen
   lemonade concentrate
2 cups brewed tea
1¾ cups sugar
7 cups water
2 cups vodka or Kentucky
   bourbon
7UP

1. Pour first 6 ingredients into
   container and freeze.
2. Spoon into large wine glasses.
3. Pour 7UP over slush mixture.

Hint: Place orange slice or maraschino cherry in bottom of glass.

Bloody Mary Mix

Yield: 8 servings

Spicy!

1 can (46 ounces) V-8® cocktail vegetable juice
11 ounces beef broth
1 teaspoon horseradish
¼ cup lemon juice
¼ teaspoon hot pepper sauce
2 tablespoons Worcestershire sauce
Salt
Black pepper
Celery or lime, optional

1. Mix first six ingredients together in large pitcher.
2. Salt and pepper to your taste.
3. Set in refrigerator overnight.
4. For individual servings, mix with 1½ ounces vodka if desired. Serve with stalk of celery or lime slice.

Kentucky Mint Julep

Yield: 1 serving

100 proof Kentucky bourbon
Simple syrup
Mint Leaves
Crushed ice

Simple Syrup

1 part boiling water to
2 parts sugar. Stir until dissolved.

1. Place 3 to 4 mint leaves in julep glass.
2. Add crushed ice. Press down with spoon to bruise leaves.
3. Add 1 ounce bourbon and ½ ounce simple syrup; stir well.
4. Pack glass with crushed ice and fill with bourbon.
5. Garnish with mint leaves.

Hint: Traditionally, this is served in a frosted silver mint julep cup.

Family Holiday Eggnog

Yield: 20 servings

A great family tradition!

6 eggs, separated
¾ cup Kentucky bourbon
¼ cup sugar
2 tablespoons powdered
   sugar
1 quart milk
2 cups whipping cream
Dash nutmeg

Day 1

1. Separate eggs — save whites for the next day.
2. Beat the yolks until lemon-colored.
3. To yolk mixture, slowly add bourbon.
4. Slowly add regular and powdered sugars.
5. Add milk.
6. Beat mixture at medium speed for 5 minutes, cover with plastic wrap. Refrigerate overnight.

Day 2

1. Beat egg whites until stiff.
2. Fold into Day 1 mixture.
3. Beat cream until peaks form; add nutmeg to taste.
4. Pour over mixture. Ladle and serve.

Long Island Tea

Yield: 2 servings

Sip it slowly!

1½ ounces gin
1½ ounces vodka
1½ ounces light rum
1½ ounces tequila
2 ounces Daily's cocktail mix
4 ounces cola

1. Mix ingredients in pitcher by stirring with spoon.
2. Serve over ice in tall glasses. Garnish with lemon wedge and sprig of mint.

Velvet Hammer

Yield: 2 servings

Smooth!

3 ounces vodka
2¼ ounces white creme de
   cocoa
4 large dips vanilla ice cream

1. Mix all in blender.
2. Serve in frosted glasses.

Spanish Coffee

Yield: 1 serving

Ole!

¾ ounce coffee liqueur
¾ ounce almond liqueur
1 cup coffee
Whipped cream

1. Pour liqueurs into the coffee.
2. Stir and top with whipped cream.

Expresso Mocha

Yield: 32 servings

Great for a cold winter night!

1 cup sugar
1 cup instant coffee
4½ cups instant powdered
   milk
½ cup cocoa

1. Combine all dry ingredients.
2. When ready to use, mix 3 tablespoons with ½ cup boiling water.
3. Rum or brandy may be added if desired.
4. Garnish with whipped cream and sprinkle with cinnamon.

Hint: This is a nice mix to put into containers for little gifts at Christmas and other special occasions.

Almond Liqueur

Yield: 8 servings

This makes a special Christmas gift!

1 cup light brown sugar
⅔ cup water
1½ cups vodka
1 tablespoon almond extract
1 teaspoon vanilla extract

1. Combine sugar and water and bring to a boil, stirring constantly.
2. Lower heat and simmer 5 minutes.
3. Cool to room temperature.
4. Add vodka and extracts. Mix well.
5. Bottle and store two weeks in a dark place.

Coffee Liqueur

Yield: ½ gallon

3½ cups water
4 to 5 cups sugar
6 teaspoons instant coffee
1 fifth (750 ml.) brandy
2 vanilla beans split open or 2
    to 3 tablespoons real
    vanilla extract

1. Bring water to a boil and add sugar and instant coffee.
2. Stir in brandy.
3. Add vanilla. Stir thoroughly and enjoy.

Hint: If vanilla beans are used, observe the following: After splitting beans open, place into ½ gallon jar and pour mixture over them. This must stand for 10 days. If vanilla extract is used, you may drink immediately.

Christmas Punch

Yield: 25 servings (18 cups)

Takes the color and tang from the cranberry.

1½ cups cold orange juice
3 cups cold apple juice
6 cups cold cranberry juice
2 bottles (28 or 33 ounces
  each) very cold ginger ale

1. Combine the three juices in advance and chill.
2. Add ginger ale just before serving.

Hint: Add a semicircle of orange slice to each cup for garnish.

Frozen Lime Delight

Yield: 12 servings

2 cans (6 ounces each) frozen
  limeade concentrate
6 cans (6 ounces each) water
1 can (46 ounces)
  unsweetened pineapple
  juice
½ cup sugar
1 pint (500 ml.) white rum
Mint

1. Mix first five ingredients in large container.
2. Freeze for 6 hours, stirring every hour.
3. Pour into tall glasses.
4. Garnish with a sprig of mint.

Hint: This mixture keeps forever in the freezer.

Appetizers

Appetizers

Beef Mexicale Dip

Yield: 24 servings

For lovers of the hot and spicy taste.

3 tablespoons butter

3 tablespoons flour

1 cup milk

1 jar (8 ounces) pasteurized
process cheese spread

1 pound ground beef

Tomato sauce (to moisten)

1 can (4 ounces) green chilies

Chili powder

Cumin

Garlic salt

1. Melt butter in top of double boiler. Add flour and milk; stir with wire whisk until thickened. Add cheese and stir until melted.
2. Brown meat in skillet. Drain fat. Add enough tomato sauce to moisten.
3. Add chopped chilies to meat mixture. Season to taste with chili powder, cumin, and garlic salt.
4. Combine cheese and meat mixtures. Mix well.
5. Serve warm in chafing dish with assorted corn chips for dipping.

Superb Shrimp Dip

Yield: 2 cups

Dramatize by serving in a sea shell.

1 can (10 ounces) shrimp (or
use fresh shrimp)

¼ cup cocktail sauce

Dash garlic salt

2 teaspoons lemon juice

3 to 4 drops hot pepper sauce

8 ounces cream cheese,
softened

3 tablespoons salad dressing

1. Drain shrimp. Coarsely chop half the shrimp and set aside.
2. Using blender, combine remaining shrimp with all other ingredients.
3. Garnish dip with chopped shrimp. Serve with potato chips.

Hint: This keeps well in refrigerator for 24 to 48 hours.

25

Creamy Crab Dip
Yield: 2¼ cups (12 servings)

Microwave in minutes.

6 tablespoons butter or margarine

¼ cup chopped onion

1 clove garlic, minced (or use ⅛ teaspoon garlic powder)

2 tablespoons chopped fresh parsley

2 packages (3 ounces each) cream cheese, cubed

1½ teaspoons Worcestershire sauce

¼ teaspoon hot pepper sauce

⅛ teaspoon salt

12 ounces crab meat, drained and flaked

1. Microwave butter 45 seconds on High.
2. Add onion, garlic, and parsley. Cover with plastic wrap; microwave 3 minutes on High.
3. Add cheese cubes. Microwave one minute on High, stirring once.
4. Stir in Worcestershire, hot pepper sauce, and salt. Mix well.
5. Fold in crab meat. Microwave 2 to 3 minutes on High until thoroughly heated.
6. Serve warm on toast points or with bland crackers.

Kentucky Bourbon Spread
Yield: 2 cups

It's unique, not to mention spirited.

8 ounces cream cheese

4 ounces bleu cheese

5 tablespoons butter

1 clove garlic, minced

1 tablespoon olive oil

Dash hot pepper sauce

Dash Worcestershire sauce

Salt and pepper to taste

3 tablespoons Kentucky bourbon

1. Soften cheeses and butter. Mix well.
2. Add remaining ingredients, stirring in enough bourbon to make a spreadable paste.
3. Refrigerate 24 hours.
4. Serve with crackers. Add more bourbon if spread appears too stiff.

Tex-Mex Dip

Yield: 12 to 16 servings

This deserves a standing ovation!

2 cans (10½ ounces each)
   jalapeño bean dip

3 medium avocados, ripe

2 tablespoons lemon juice

½ teaspoon salt

¼ teaspoon pepper

1 cup sour cream

½ cup mayonnaise

1 package (1¼ ounces) taco
   seasoning mix

1 bunch green onions with
   tops, chopped

3 medium tomatoes, peeled
   and chopped

2 cans (3½ ounces each)
   pitted ripe olives, chopped

8 ounces Cheddar cheese,
   shredded

1. Spread bean dip in large shallow
   serving dish.
2. Mash avocados with lemon juice,
   salt, and pepper. Spread over
   bean dip.
3. Mix sour cream, mayonnaise, and
   taco seasoning. Spread over
   avocado layer.
4. Sprinkle with onions, tomatoes,
   and olives.
5. Cover with shredded cheese and
   refrigerate.
6. Serve chilled with round tortilla
   chips.

Zippy Spinach Dip

Yield: 3 cups

Even children find this appealing.

10 ounces frozen spinach
½ cup chopped green onions
½ cup chopped fresh parsley
2 cups mayonnaise
1 teaspoon salt
⅛ teaspoon freshly ground
    pepper

1. Thaw spinach; squeeze out liquid.
2. In blender or processor, mix all ingredients thoroughly.
3. Chill 24 hours.
4. Serve with crackers or raw vegetables.

Dream Of Dill Dip

Yield: 3 cups

Good taste comes from subtle spices.

1 cup sour cream
1 cup mayonnaise
1 teaspoon parsley flakes
1 teaspoon Beau Monde
    Seasoning®
1 teaspoon dried green onion
1 teaspoon garlic salt
½ teaspoon dill weed
2 drops hot pepper sauce

1. Blend all ingredients.
2. Refrigerate 6 hours.
3. Serve with raw vegetables.

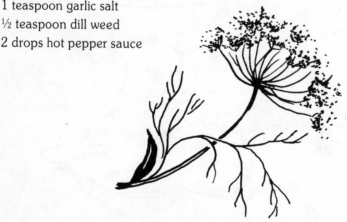

Artichoke Appetizer

Yield: 3 cups

2 cans (14 ounces each)
    artichoke hearts
1 cup (4 ounces) grated
    Parmesan cheese
1 cup mayonnaise
Dash garlic salt
Dash Worcestershire sauce
Dash hot sauce
Fresh parsley, optional

1. Drain and chop artichokes.
2. Mix all ingredients, except parsley. Spoon into lightly greased 1-quart baking dish.
3. Bake at 350° for 20 minutes.
4. Garnish with parsley; serve with Melba rounds.

Temperature: 350°
Time: 20 minutes

Benedictine

Yield: 2 cups

Classic and superlative.

2 packages (8 ounces each)
    cream cheese
1 small cucumber
½ small onion
2 teaspoons salad dressing
Green food coloring

1. Bring cream cheese to room temperature.
2. Place food strainer over bowl. Alternately grate cucumber and onion into strainer.
3. With wooden spoon, press as much juice as possible out of pulp into bowl. Put softened cream cheese into bowl; work in juice and salad dressing with fork.
4. Whip with mixer until creamy.
5. Add 1 to 2 drops green food coloring, and whip until color is uniform.
6. Refrigerate; serve with crackers or in sandwiches.

If You Love Beer Cheese Yield: 20 servings

You can keep this indefinitely, but you won't.

4 pounds Cheddar cheese
(sharp or mild)
1 teaspoon dry mustard
⅓ teaspoon red pepper
1 teaspoon hot pepper sauce
2 teaspoons onion juice
2 teaspoons garlic juice
¼ cup Worcestershire sauce
1½ to 2 cups beer

1. Bring cheese to room temperature. Grate into large bowl.
2. Add remaining ingredients. Beat with electric mixer until smooth.
3. Pack into crocks; cover tightly, and refrigerate.
4. Remove from refrigerator about ½ hour before serving.

Hot Chipped Beef Spread

Yield: 20 servings

Could become your new favorite.

5 or 6 ounces chipped beef,
finely chopped
2 packages (8 ounces each)
cream cheese
1 teaspoon chopped onion
1½ teaspoons Worcestershire
sauce
1½ cups sour cream
¼ teaspoon garlic salt
¼ teaspoon pepper
Sliced almonds for garnish

1. Soften cheese; blend with remaining ingredients, except almonds.
2. Spoon mixture into shallow ovenproof serving dish. Sprinkle with almonds.
3. Bake at 350° for 30 minutes. Serve hot with rye crackers or Melba rounds.

Temperature: 350°
Time: 30 minutes

Hint: Try sautéing almonds (or pecans) in butter before garnishing.

Caviar Rusticana

Yield: 3 cups

Delightful as a dip or spread.

1 package (1 tablespoon)
 unflavored gelatin
¼ cup cold water
1 medium onion, minced
6 hard-boiled eggs, minced
1 jar (3 ounces) caviar,
 drained on paper towels
1¼ cups mayonnaise
1 tablespoon Worcestershire
 sauce
Dash white pepper
½ cup heavy cream, softly
 whipped

1. Soften gelatin in cold water; then warm in pan over low heat. Cool.
2. Mix onion, eggs, caviar, mayonnaise, Worcestershire, and pepper. Add cooled gelatin.
3. Fold in whipped cream.
4. Pour into serving dish. Chill overnight.
5. Serve with crackers or Melba rounds.

Shrimp Mousse

Yield: 6 cups (30 servings)

For maximum effect, use a medium fish mold.

1½ tablespoons unflavored
 gelatin
½ cup cold water
8 ounces cream cheese
1 can (10¾ ounces) tomato
 soup
1 cup mayonnaise
1 cup cooked shrimp,
 chopped
¾ cup finely chopped onion
¾ cup finely chopped celery
Dash salt

1. Dissolve gelatin in cold water.
2. Melt cream cheese, soup, and mayonnaise over low heat.
3. Beat gelatin into warm mixture. Cool.
4. Stir in shrimp, vegetables, and salt.
5. Pour into greased 6-cup mold. Chill until firm.
6. Unmold and serve with crackers.

31

Salmon Log

Yield: 10-inch log

1 can (15½ ounces) red
  salmon
8 ounces cream cheese,
  softened
1 tablespoon lemon juice
2 teaspoons grated onion
¼ teaspoon salt
¼ teaspoon liquid smoke
¾ cup chopped pecans
3 tablespoons minced fresh
  parsley

1. Drain salmon; remove skin and bones.
2. Flake salmon with fork.
3. Add cream cheese, lemon juice, onion, salt, and liquid smoke.
4. Chill several hours or overnight.
5. Shape mixture into a log. Combine pecans and parsley; stir well. Roll salmon log in pecan mixture.
6. Chill several hours and serve with crackers.

Asparagus Twirls

Yield: 75 twirls

25 slices thin-sliced bread
1 can (20 ounces) asparagus
  spears
8 ounces cream cheese
4 ounces bleu cheese
1 egg
½ cup melted butter

1. Cut off crusts of bread. Roll bread slices flat with rolling pin.
2. Drain asparagus.
3. Cream together cheeses; mix in egg and beat well.
4. Spread cheese mixture on bread. Place an asparagus spear on each and roll up. Dip each in melted butter.
5. Place on cookie sheet seam side down. Freeze. Slice into 3 pieces.
6. Bake and serve warm.

Temperature: 375°
Time: 20 minutes

Hint: After frozen and sliced, place in plastic bag or container. Bake whenever needed.

Dilled Brussels Sprouts   Yield: 12 to 18 servings

Equally good for cocktails or as a salad.

1 box (10 ounces) frozen
  Brussels sprouts
1 box (10 ounces) frozen
  cauliflower
1 cup Italian dressing
2 teaspoons dill weed
2 tablespoons sliced green
  onions

1. Cook vegetables according to package directions. Drain.
2. Mix remaining ingredients, and pour over vegetables.
3. Cover and chill overnight.

Hint: You may halve or quarter Brussels sprouts to increase the flavor of the marinade. Florets of broccoli may also be used.

Chicken Liver Pâté   Yield: 20 servings

Serve with ease and elegance.

2 pints chicken livers
1 small onion, chopped,
  optional
1 tablespoon butter, optional
8 hard-boiled eggs, chopped
1 cup mayonnaise or schmaltz
  (rendered chicken fat)
Salt and pepper to taste

1. Spray skillet with Pam. Saute' livers 3 to 5 minutes (or you may broil them). Cool.
2. If using onion, saute' in butter until opaque.
3. Blend livers, onion, and eggs to paste consistency, using blender, food processor, or fine attachment on meat grinder.
4. Moisten with mayonnaise or schmaltz. Season to taste.
5. Refrigerate 3 to 4 hours.
6. Serve with crackers.

Hint: This can be a nice appetizer for 8, dipped with ice cream scoop and served on lettuce with a garnish of tomato wedges.

Potato Knishes

Yield: 60 knishes

People will love you forever for taking the time to make these.

Dough

5 cups unbleached flour

¼ cup sugar

Pinch of salt

¾ cup salad oil

3 eggs, beaten

1 cup lukewarm water

Melted butter or salad oil

Potato Filling

Mix together:

3 onions, chopped

¼ pound butter (or schmaltz)

2 cups mashed potatoes

1 egg

Salt and pepper to taste

1. To make dough, sift together dry ingredients. Make a well in center and add oil, eggs, and water. Mix well.
2. Dust bowl with flour, and turn over and pat to remove excess. Place dough in bowl and cover with towel. Let rest for 15 minutes.
3. Knead well on floured cloth.
4. Divide into 4 parts, and work with one part at a time.
5. Roll and stretch dough into a 20-inch circle. Brush with melted butter or oil.
6. Starting 1½ inches from edge nearest you, place a line of filling 1½ inches wide and 1 inch thick across width of dough. Take edge of dough nearest you and cover filling, then roll filled dough twice.
7. Cut this part away from the rest of dough. Repeat process with remaining sheets of dough. Brush tops of rolls with oil.
8. Slice the rolls every 1½ inches. Put each slice on greased baking sheet and press down with palm so that it is flattened and rounded. You may need to pinch ends together.
9. Repeat with other 3 pieces of dough.
10. Bake until lightly browned.

Temperature: 350°
Time: 1 hour (approximately)

Hint: The more filling in each knish, the better it tastes.

Swiss-Stuffed Mushrooms Yield: 3 dozen

½ cup shredded Swiss cheese

1 hard-boiled egg, finely grated

3 tablespoons fine dry bread crumbs

1 clove garlic, minced

2 tablespoons butter, softened

1 pound fresh mushrooms, each about 1 to 1½ inches in diameter

4 tablespoons butter, melted

1. In a mixing bowl combine cheese, egg, bread crumbs, garlic, and 2 tablespoons softened butter; blend thoroughly.
2. Remove stems from mushrooms. Place unfilled mushrooms, rounded side up, on baking sheet.
3. Brush tops with melted butter.
4. Broil 3 to 4 inches from heat for 2 to 3 minutes until lightly browned. Remove from broiler.
5. Turn mushrooms over; fill each with cheese mixture.
6. Return filled mushrooms to broiler. Broil 1 to 2 minutes more.

Hint: May be prepared early in day and broiled before serving.

Microwave Party Mix Yield: 9½ cups

Minimum effort, impressive result.

6 tablespoons butter

4 teaspoons Worcestershire sauce

1 teaspoon celery salt

1 teaspoon onion salt

2 teaspoons garlic salt

2 cups Corn Chex® cereal

2 cups Rice Chex® cereal

2 cups Cheerios® cereal

2 cups thin pretzels

1½ cups mixed nuts

1. Place butter, Worcestershire, and salts in 13 x 9 x 2-inch baking dish. Microwave 3 minutes on Medium High (until butter melts).
2. Add cereals, pretzels, and nuts. Stir to coat thoroughly. Microwave on High for 3 minutes.
3. Stir; microwave on High for 3 more minutes. Cool.

Hint: For additional bite, sprinkle with more garlic salt.

Easy Mushroom Crescent Squares

Yield: 24 squares

12 ounces fresh mushrooms, chopped

2 tablespoons butter or margarine

½ teaspoon garlic salt

2 tablespoons finely chopped onion or ½ teaspoon dried minced onion

1 teaspoon lemon juice

1 teaspoon Worcestershire sauce

1 can (8 ounces) refrigerator crescent or Italian dinner rolls

3 ounces cream cheese, softened

¼ cup grated Parmesan cheese

1. Brown mushrooms in butter. Stir in salt, onion, lemon juice, and Worcestershire; cook until liquid evaporates.
2. Separate dough into 2 rectangles and place on ungreased 13 x 9-inch pan. Press over bottom and ¼ inch up sides to form crust.
3. Spread cream cheese over dough. Sprinkle with mushroom mixture. Top with Parmesan cheese.
4. Bake 20-25 minutes at 350° until golden brown. Cool 5 minutes; cut into desired squares. Serve warm.

Temperature: 350°
Time: 20 to 25 minutes

Hint: May be made and refrigerated up to 2 hours before baking.

Elegant Marinated Mushrooms

Yield: 6 to 8 servings

Almost too good to be true.

1 pound fresh mushrooms
4 tablespoons olive oil
1 tablespoon lemon juice
1 large onion, sliced
1 clove garlic, minced
¼ teaspoon thyme
¼ teaspoon marjoram
¼ teaspoon oregano
1 bay leaf
1 cup peeled and chopped
   tomatoes
⅓ cup wine vinegar
Dash sugar
Salt, pepper, and hot pepper
   sauce to taste

1. Saute' mushrooms in 2 tablespoons olive oil until golden. Transfer to bowl and toss with lemon juice.
2. In remaining 2 tablespoons olive oil, saute' onions and garlic. Add remaining ingredients, including a little juice if canned tomatoes are used. Bring to a boil and simmer 15 minutes.
3. Pour marinade over mushrooms; cover tightly, and refrigerate overnight.

Hint: A fork is needed, whether this be served as appetizer or salad.

Petite Quiche

Yield: 6 dozen

Pastry

1½ cups butter, softened
9 ounces cream cheese,
   softened
3 cups flour

Filling

1 package Knorr Leek
   Soupmix
2 cups milk
1 cup cream
4 eggs
½ pound Swiss cheese, grated
1 teaspoon dry mustard
1 teaspoon salt
¼ teaspoon pepper

Hint: These freeze very well.

Pastry

1. Cream butter and cream cheese
   with hands.
2. Work flour into mixture.
3. Divide dough into fourths. Make
   eighteen balls out of each fourth.
4. Chill.
5. Press into petite cupcake pans.

Filling

1. Bring soup and milk to a boil over
   medium heat. Cool slightly. Stir in
   cream; cool.
2. Beat eggs with remaining
   ingredients and add to soup.
3. Fill pastry cups with soup
   mixture, and bake at 375° until
   brown (approximately 25
   minutes).

Temperature: 375°
Time: 25 minutes

Cheese Ball Surprise

Yield: 1 large ball

16 ounces cream cheese,
softened

½ pound sharp Cheddar
cheese, shredded

2 teaspoons grated onion

2 teaspoons Worcestershire
sauce

1 teaspoon dry mustard

1 teaspoon seasoned salt

¼ teaspoon salt

1 can (2¼ ounces) deviled
ham

¼ teaspoon paprika

1 teaspoon lemon juice

2 tablespoons red pimiento

2 tablespoons chopped
parsley

1 cup chopped nuts

1. Beat all ingredients except
pimiento, parsley, and nuts.
2. Add pimiento and parsley; chill
overnight.
3. Shape into one or two balls; roll in
nuts.
4. Chill again. Serve with crackers.

**Hint: May be prepared in food processor using steel knife. Blend
on then off for only a second or two. Must do ahead. May be
frozen.**

Raisin-Nut-Olive Ball
Yield: 1 large ball

8 ounces cream cheese,
  softened
¼ cup chopped pecans
¼ cup chopped olives
½ cup chopped raisins
3 tablespoons finely chopped
  pecans

1. Combine first four ingredients;
   mix well.
2. Shape into ball; roll in pecans.
   Refrigerate.
3. Serve with crackers.

Holiday Cheese Ball
Yield: 2 medium cheese balls

1 cup cottage cheese
⅓ cup finely grated sharp·
  Cheddar cheese
2 packages (8 ounces each)
  cream cheese, softened
1 ounce Roquefort cheese,
  crumbled
¼ cup finely grated onion
2 tablespoons Worcestershire
  sauce
Dash of seasoned salt
¾ cup chopped pecans
¾ cup chopped parsley

Hint: May be frozen.

1. Combine first seven ingredients;
   mix well.
2. Chill 1 to 2 hours; shape mixture
   into 2 balls.
3. Roll each ball in pecans and then
   in parsley. Chill thoroughly.
4. Serve with assorted crackers.

Marinated Shrimp

Yield: 6 to 8 servings

An eye-appealing taste treat.

2 pounds cooked shrimp

1 red onion, thinly sliced

1 lemon, thinly sliced

½ cup pitted black olives, drained

1 to 2 tablespoons chopped pimiento

¼ cup vegetable oil

½ cup lemon juice

1 tablespoon wine vinegar

1 tablespoon dry mustard

½ bay leaf, broken up

1 clove garlic, crushed

¼ teaspoon cayenne pepper

Freshly ground black pepper

Dash salt

1. Place cooked shrimp in serving bowl; add onion, lemon, olives, and pimiento. Toss.
2. In another bowl, combine remaining ingredients. Mix well.
3. Pour marinade over shrimp mixture.
4. Cover and chill at least 4 hours, stirring occasionally.

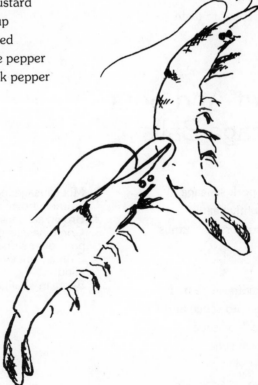

41

Clipper's Shrimp And Dill

A crowd pleaser!

1 pound bay shrimp (or
chopped large shrimp)

5 ounces Gruyère cheese,
diced finely

5 ounces Swiss cheese, diced
finely

¾ cup chopped green onions

1 cup mayonnaise

1 tablespoon white wine
vinegar

1 teaspoon dill seed

Salt and pepper to taste

1. Combine all ingredients and
   refrigerate.
2. Spread on small rounds of party
   rye bread. Put under broiler until
   cheese bubbles.
3. To use as a sandwich, mound the
   mixture on large slices of sour
   dough bread. Place in 450° oven
   until the cheese bubbles.

Temperature: 450°
Time: Until cheese bubbles

Sweet And Sour Sausage Balls

Yield: 48 balls

4 pounds pork sausage

4 eggs, slightly beaten

1½ cups soft bread crumbs

Sauce

3 cups tomato sauce or 1½
cups tomato sauce and 1½
cups cocktail sauce

¾ cup brown sugar

½ cup wine vinegar

½ cup soy sauce

1. Mix sausage, eggs, and bread
   crumbs. Form into balls.
2. Brown sausage balls and drain.
3. Combine all sauce ingredients and
   pour over sausage balls.
4. Simmer uncovered for 30
   minutes.
5. Serve in chafing dish.

Frozen Party Pizza

Yield: 20 servings

1 pound hot pork sausage
1 pound mild pork sausage
½ cup finely-chopped onion
Italian seasoning to taste
1 box (2 pounds) pasteurized
   process cheese spread
2 to 3 loaves party rye bread

1. Crumble sausage and fry with onion and seasonings.
2. Cut cheese into small pieces and add to sausage mixture. Stir and let melt.
3. Spread mixture rather thickly on rye bread, so it looks like pizza. Cheese will set quickly after spreading.
4. Put into serving portions and freeze.
5. To serve, bake directly from freezer.

Temperature: 400°
Time: 5 to 10 minutes

Oriental Chicken Wings

Yield: 12 servings

2½ pounds chicken wings
½ teaspoon salt
¼ cup soy sauce
¼ cup syrup from canned
   peaches
2 tablespoons sugar
½ teaspoon ginger
1 tablespoon lemon juice
5 drops hot pepper sauce
1 clove garlic, minced

1. Cut chicken wings at joints. Discard tips.
2. Place chicken wings on a foil-lined baking sheet and sprinkle with salt.
3. Mix other ingredients and brush on wings.
4. Roast at 350° for 1½ hours or more, turning wings once and basting frequently.

Temperature: 350°
Time: 1½ hours

Hint: Warm, wet finger cloths will be appreciated.

Guacamole

Yield: 12 servings

Uncommonly good.

4 fully ripe avocados
½ cup mayonnaise
¼ cup minced onion
1 tablespoon salt
2 teaspoons chili powder
1 teaspoon garlic powder
½ teaspoon hot pepper sauce
3 tablespoons lemon juice
2 medium tomatoes, peeled
   and chopped

1. Halve avocados lengthwise,
   twisting gently to separate halves.
   Pierce seeds with sharp knife, and
   twist to lift out.
2. Peel avocado halves, and mash
   (or mix a few seconds in blender).
3. Stir in mayonnaise, onion,
   seasonings, and lemon juice.
4. Chill thoroughly.
5. Garnish with tomatoes; serve with
   corn chips.

Broccoli Balls

Yield: 50 to 60 balls

Delicious and different!

2 packages (10 ounces each)
   frozen chopped broccoli
2 cups herb stuffing mix
1 cup grated Parmesan
   cheese
6 eggs, beaten
¾ cup butter or margarine,
   softened
Salt and pepper to taste

1. Cook frozen broccoli according
   to package directions; drain well.
2. Combine all ingredients, mixing
   well.
3. Roll mixture into small balls.
   Freeze, covered with foil.
4. To serve, place broccoli balls in
   oven until brown.

Temperature: 350°
Time: 20 minutes

**Hint: Substitute 2 packages (10 ounces each) frozen chopped
spinach for the broccoli. Even children like them!**

Soups & Sandwiches

Soups And Sandwiches

Mexican Cheese Soup

Yield: 4 servings

Delightful with cornbread.

5 medium potatoes, peeled
   and diced
1 medium onion, peeled and
   chopped
3 tablespoons butter
1 can (4 ounces) green chilies,
   chopped
1 large tomato, peeled,
   seeded and chopped
2½ cups milk or light cream
1 pound Monterey Jack
   cheese, cubed
Salt and pepper to taste
1 teaspoon parsley

1. Place potatoes and onions in saucepan, barely covering with salted water, and cook until tender. Do not drain.
2. Mash potatoes in saucepan.
3. Add butter, mix; add chilies, tomatoes, milk, and cheese. Stir over low heat until cheese is melted. Do not boil.
4. Season to taste. Garnish with parsley.

Garbanzo Bean Soup

Yield: 8 to 12 servings

An unusual and delicious soup.

1 package (16 ounces) dried
   garbanzo beans
10 cups water
1 cup chopped celery
1 cup chopped onion
1 large ham hock
Salt and pepper to taste
2 cups diced potatoes
½ pound pepperoni, sliced
½ pound Keilbasa and/or
   Italian sausage, sliced
3 cloves garlic, crushed

1. Soak beans in water overnight.
2. Bring beans to a boil, then turn off heat. Let stand 1 hour.
3. Add celery, onion, ham hock, salt, and pepper. Simmer, covered, 5 to 6 hours until beans are tender, but not mushy. Do not overcook.
4. Add potatoes, pepperoni, sausages, and garlic. Simmer 1 hour longer. Adjust seasonings to taste.

Ham And Lentil Soup

Yield: 5 servings

Hearty!

6 slices bacon, chopped

1 medium onion, sliced

2 or 3 fresh or canned
   tomatoes, chopped

¼ cup chopped parsley

6 cups chicken broth

½ cup tomato paste

½ teaspoon thyme

1 cup lentils

2½ cups diced, smoked ham

1 can (8 ounces) sliced
   mushrooms and juice

Salt and pepper to taste

1. Fry bacon until crisp.
2. Add onion and saute' until tender.
3. Add remaining ingredients. Stir well.
4. Simmer, covered, until lentils are tender. Do not overcook or lentils will become mushy.

Hint: Recipe easily doubled. Freezes well.

Spring Soup

Yield: 6 servings

A creamy, delicious, easy soup.

3 tablespoons butter

3 leeks, chopped

1 onion, chopped

2 potatoes, peeled and diced

1 carrot, sliced

2 quarts chicken stock

¼ cup rice

1 pound fresh spinach,
   chopped

Salt and pepper to taste

½ cup light cream

1. In large saucepan, melt butter and saute' leeks and onions.
2. Add potatoes, carrots, and stock and boil 15 minutes.
3. Stir in rice and cook 20 minutes longer.
4. Add chopped spinach and cook 10 to 15 minutes longer.
5. Salt and pepper to taste.
6. Gradually stir in light cream and heat to serving temperature.

Kentucky Burgoo

Yield: 1 gallon

A western Kentucky classic.

Stock - First day

1 hen, 4 to 5 pounds

1 pound beef stew meat

1 pound veal stew meat

1½ to 2 pounds beef or
   knuckle bones

1 stalk celery

1 carrot, peeled

1 small onion, peeled

5 to 6 sprigs parsley

1 can (10½ ounces) tomato
   puree

4 quarts water

1 red pepper pod

¼ cup salt

1 tablespoon lemon juice

1 tablespoon Worcestershire
   sauce

1 tablespoon sugar

1½ teaspoons black pepper

½ teaspoon cayenne pepper

1. Combine the 17 stock ingredients in large pot; bring to a boil. Cover and simmer 4 hours. Cool.
2. Strain meat mixture. Reserve meat and stock. Discard vegetables.
3. Remove skin, bone, and gristle from meat; then chop meat.
4. Return meat to stock and refrigerate overnight.
5. The next day, remove and discard fat layer from stock.
6. Add onions, tomatoes, turnip, peppers, beans, celery, cabbage, okra, corn, and lemon to the meat and stock.
7. Cover and simmer 1 hour.
8. Uncover and simmer 2 hours longer, stirring frequently to prevent sticking.
9. Burgoo is ready when it reaches the consistency of thick stew.

Second day

6 onions, finely chopped

8 to 10 tomatoes, peeled and
   chopped

1 turnip, peeled and finely
   chopped

2 green peppers, chopped

2 cups fresh butter beans

2 cups thinly-sliced celery

2 cups finely-chopped cabbage

2 cups sliced fresh okra

2 cups fresh corn

½ unpeeled lemon, seeded

Spicy Hoppin' John Soup Yield: 16 servings

Wonderful on a cold winter night.

1 pound dried black-eyed
  peas
8 cups water
1 can (16 ounces) tomatoes
8 ounces ham hock
1 cup chopped onion
1 cup chopped celery
1 tablespoon salt
2 teaspoons chili powder
¼ teaspoon dried crushed
  basil leaves
1 bay leaf
1 cup uncooked rice

1. Soak peas in water overnight or bring peas and water to a boil; cover, reduce heat, and simmer 3 minutes. Let stand for 1 hour and do not drain.
2. Drain tomatoes, reserve liquid, then chop tomatoes. Add tomatoes and liquid to peas.
3. Add remaining ingredients, except rice. Cover and simmer 1 to 1½ hours until peas are tender.
4. Remove ham hock and debone. Dice meat and return to peas.
5. Add rice; cover and simmer 20 minutes or until rice is tender. Remove bay leaf. Serve hot.

Sausage Bean Chowder Yield: 6 servings

A nice blend of flavors.

1 pound pork sausage
1 can (16 ounces) kidney
  beans
1 can (16 ounces) chili beans
3 cups canned tomatoes
2 cups water
2 small onions, chopped
2 bay leaves
1½ teaspoons salt
½ teaspoon garlic salt
½ teaspoon thyme
¼ teaspoon pepper
1 cup cooked, diced potatoes
½ green pepper, chopped

1. Cook sausage in skillet until brown. Pour off fat.
2. In large kettle, combine beans, tomatoes, water, onions, bay leaves, salt, garlic salt, thyme, and pepper. Mix well.
3. Add sausage. Simmer, covered, 1 hour.
4. Add potatoes and green pepper. Cook covered 15 minutes or until potatoes are tender. Do not overcook.
5. Remove bay leaves and serve.

Broccoli Cream Soup

Yield: 6 to 8 servings

Nice for lunch.

2 packages (10 ounces each) frozen chopped broccoli, thawed

¼ cup chopped onion

2 cups chicken broth

2 tablespoons butter

1 tablespoon flour

2 teaspoons salt

⅛ teaspoon mace

2 cups light cream

Pepper to taste

6 lemon twists

1 teaspoon paprika

1. Combine broccoli, onion, and chicken broth. Bring to a boil and simmer 10 minutes. Allow to cool. Put through blender until smooth.
2. Melt butter in saucepan; add flour and seasonings. Stir until very smooth.
3. Slowly add cream, then add broccoli mixture. Heat thoroughly.
4. Adjust seasoning with pepper.
5. Garnish each serving with lemon twist and paprika.

Tomato-Celery Soup

Yield: 3 to 4 servings

Quick and good!

½ cup finely-chopped celery

1 small onion, chopped

2 tablespoons butter

1 can (10½ ounces) tomato soup

10½ ounces water

1 teaspoon minced parsley

⅛ teaspoon pepper

1 tablespoon lemon juice

1 teaspoon sugar

¼ teaspoon salt

4 teaspoons unsweetened whipping cream

1 teaspoon chopped parsley

1. Saute' celery and onion in butter. Do not brown.
2. Add remaining ingredients except cream and chopped parsley. Simmer 5 minutes. Celery will remain crisp.
3. Garnish each serving with whipping cream and parsley.

Chili At Its Best

Yield: 5 quarts

Get out your largest pot.

½ pound dried pinto beans

5 cups canned tomatoes

4 medium green peppers, chopped

1½ tablespoons oil

4½ cups chopped onions

2 cloves garlic, crushed

½ cup minced parsley

½ cup butter

2½ pounds ground chuck

1 pound ground lean pork

⅓ cup chili powder

2 tablespoons salt

1½ teaspoons pepper

1½ teaspoons cumin seed

1. Wash beans; place in bowl with enough water to cover plus 2 inches. Soak overnight.
2. Pour beans and soaking water into large kettle; cover. Simmer 1 to 2 hours until tender.
3. Add tomatoes; simmer 5 minutes longer.
4. While beans are cooking, saute' green peppers in oil for 5 minutes in large skillet. Add onions; cook until tender. Add garlic and parsley; stir frequently.
5. In another large skillet, melt butter and saute' chuck and pork about 15 minutes or until brown. Add meat mixture to onion mixture, stir in chili powder, and simmer 10 minutes.
6. Add meat mixture to beans; season with salt, pepper, and cumin. Simmer, covered, for 1 hour. Simmer, uncovered, 30 minutes longer, stirring occasionally. Add more water if necessary.
7. Skim off fat. Serve in deep bowls.

Hint: Freezes beautifully.

Venison Soup

Yield: 12 servings

A hearty hunter's soup.

2 pounds venison, cubed
½ cup minced parsley
1 cup minced onion
2 cups diced celery
1 cup diced turnips
1 can (16 ounces) mixed
  vegetables
3 quarts beef stock
1 can (12 ounces) tomato
  paste
4 tablespoons sugar
½ teaspoon thyme
3 bay leaves
Salt and pepper to taste

1. Combine all ingredients in large kettle.
2. Cook over low heat 2 to 2½ hours.

Mushroom Chowder

Yield: 6 to 8 servings

Easy, rich, and tasty, but not too creamy.

½ cup chopped onion

½ cup butter, melted

1 pound fresh mushrooms,
　sliced

1 cup diced potatoes

1 cup finely chopped celery

½ cup diced carrots

1 teaspoon salt

¼ teaspoon pepper

1 tablespoon flour

2 tablespoons water

3 cups chicken stock

1 cup milk

¼ cup grated Parmesan
　cheese

1. In Dutch oven, saute' onion in butter until tender.
2. Add vegetables, salt, and pepper. Cover and simmer 15 to 20 minutes (until vegetables are tender).
3. Mix flour and water until smooth, and stir into vegetable mixture.
4. Add chicken stock and simmer 10 minutes.
5. Stir in milk and Parmesan cheese. Cover and heat (do not boil).
6. Garnish each serving with additional Parmesan cheese, if desired.

Hint: May be made ahead and then reheated.

Rich French Onion Soup

Yield: 12 servings

Delicious!

4 tablespoons butter

2 tablespoons olive oil

3 pounds yellow onions, thinly
   sliced

1 teaspoon salt

3 tablespoons flour

8 cans (10¾ ounces each)
   chicken broth (about 84
   ounces)

1 cup water

2 beef bouillon cubes

Topping

12 thin slices French bread

2 tablespoons olive oil

1 or 2 cloves garlic, split

1½ cups Swiss and Parmesan
   cheeses, mixed

1. Melt butter with oil in heavy 4 to
   5-quart saucepan over moderate
   heat.
2. Add onions; sprinkle with salt.
   Mix well. Cook uncovered over
   low heat, stirring occasionally,
   until onions are golden brown
   (approximately 2 hours.)
3. Sprinkle with flour; stir and cook
   another 2 to 3 minutes.
4. Add hot broth, water, and
   bouillon cubes. Bring to a boil,
   reduce heat, simmer, partially
   covered, 30 to 40 minutes.
5. Skim off fat occasionally. Taste
   for seasoning.
6. Rub garlic on each side of bread,
   then brush with olive oil. Lightly
   toast bread.
7. Pour soup into individual crock
   pots. Float bread slices on top of
   soup, and cover with desired
   amount of cheese. Place in oven;
   bake 20 minutes until cheese is
   melted and soup bubbly.

Hint: Amounts of both liquid and onions may be varied to taste.

Potato Soup

Yield: 6 to 8 servings

A great dish for cool weather.

2 stalks celery, sliced

1 medium onion, chopped

2 tablespoons margarine, melted

3 cups hot water

6 medium potatoes, peeled and cubed

2 carrots, peeled and sliced

5 chicken-flavored bouillon cubes

¾ teaspoon salt

½ teaspoon dried whole thyme

½ teaspoon rosemary, crushed

Dash of garlic powder

Dash of pepper

2 cups milk

1 cup shredded Cheddar cheese

1. Saute' celery and onion in margarine in large pot until tender.
2. Add water, potatoes, carrots, bouillon cubes, salt, thyme, rosemary, garlic, and pepper.
3. Cover and simmer about 20 minutes or until vegetables are tender.
4. Remove from heat, and mash vegetables with a potato masher. (This is optional. If you prefer, leave vegetables in chunks.)
5. Add milk and cheese; cook, stirring constantly until cheese is melted.

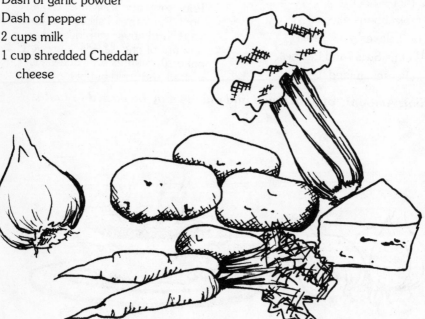

Chicken Gumbo

Yield: 6 to 8 servings

Serve with crusty rolls for a hearty meal.

1 chicken, 2 pounds
2 tablespoons butter
2 tablespoons flour
2 cups chicken broth
1 large onion, chopped
¼ cup chopped green pepper
⅛ teaspoon thyme
¼ teaspoon hot pepper sauce
1 bay leaf
2 tablespoons oil
1 can (16 ounces) whole
　　tomatoes and juice
2 cups drained, canned okra
1 tablespoon file' powder
Hot cooked rice (2 or 3 cups)

1. Boil chicken until tender. Cool.
2. Remove chicken from bones and chop into small pieces. Set aside.
3. Melt butter, stir in flour and allow to bubble 2 or 3 minutes, then stir in chicken broth.
4. Heat to boiling, stirring occasionally.
5. Place chopped chicken and sauce in heavy pan. Set aside.
6. Saute' onion, green pepper, thyme, hot pepper sauce, and bay leaf in vegetable oil until tender.
7. Add vegetables to chicken.
8. Cut tomatoes in half and add tomatoes and juice to chicken.
9. Bring chicken mixture to a boil. Reduce heat and simmer 15 minutes, stirring occasionally.
10. Stir in okra and simmer 15 minutes more.
11. Season with file' powder.
12. Stir in rice as desired.

Hearty Chicken Soup

Yield: 6 servings

Easy is the key!

1 can (16 ounces) tomatoes,
   cut up
1 cup uncooked noodles
½ cup sliced celery
1 teaspoon Worcestershire
   sauce
¼ teaspoon basil
2 cans (14½ ounces each)
   chicken broth
2 cups cubed cooked chicken

1. In a heavy pan, combine tomatoes, noodles, celery, Worcestershire, basil, and chicken broth.
2. Bring to a boil, then reduce heat.
3. Add chicken and simmer 15 minutes. Season to taste.

Bean Soup

Yield: 8 servings

Rich and satisfying.

1 pound dried navy beans
¾ cup chopped celery
½ cup chopped carrots
½ cup chopped onion
1 can (8 ounces) tomato
   sauce
1 teaspoon salt
1 teaspoon pepper

1. Place beans in large pan and cover with water.
2. Cook on high temperature until beans are tender (about 1½ hours). Check water level frequently.
3. Add remaining ingredients.
4. Simmer 30 to 40 minutes.

Captain Jeff's Fish Chowder

Yield: 6 to 8 servings

Northern Pike fillets or any
fish fillets (enough to equal
1½ to 2 cups boiled fish
chunks)
Water to cover fish
½ cup diced celery
½ cup chopped onion
3 tablespoons butter
1 cup frozen corn
2 cups finely-chopped
potatoes
½ cup finely-chopped carrots
½ cup finely-chopped
mushrooms
¼ cup crisply-cooked bacon
bits
1 teaspoon salt
Pepper and garlic salt to taste
2 tablespoons minced parsley
1 tablespoon lemon juice
1½ cups fish broth
1 can (10¾ ounces) chicken
broth
2 hard-boiled eggs, finely
chopped
1 cup light cream
Paprika

Hint: Leftover fish can be substituted.

1. Place fish in Dutch oven with water. Bring to a boil. Turn heat to low and simmer for 20 to 30 minutes or until fish is done.
2. Remove fish from broth and break into chunks, saving broth.
3. In Dutch oven, saute' celery and onion in butter.
4. Add remaining ingredients except the fish, cream, and paprika.
5. Mix and then bring to a boil. Reduce heat and simmer, covered, for 1 hour.
6. Test the vegetables. If tender, add fish and bring to a boil. Reduce to simmer for 15 minutes.
7. Stir in cream and heat until warmed through, about 10 minutes.
8. Serve in soup bowls and sprinkle with paprika.

Oyster Stew

Yield: 2 to 4 servings

Foolishly simple, but oh, so good!

4 tablespoons butter

1 pint oysters with liquor

1½ cups milk

½ cup cream

½ teaspoon salt

⅛ teaspoon pepper or paprika

2 tablespoons chopped
    parsley

1. Combine all ingredients except parsley, in top of double boiler and place over boiling water.
2. Simmer until butter is melted, milk hot and oysters float.
3. Garnish with chopped parsley and serve immediately.

Conch Chowder

Yield: 8 to 10 servings

2 onions, chopped

½ cup vegetable oil

Salt and pepper

1½ cups "bruised" conch

2 cans (28 ounces each)
    tomatoes, broken up

3 lemons, juiced

4 carrots

4 potatoes

4 stalks celery

2 cups water

¼ teaspoon hot pepper sauce

2 cups sliced okra

2 bay leaves

½ teaspoon parsley

1. Sauté onions in oil until slightly transparent. Salt and pepper and place in large pot.
2. Bruise conch by pounding with meat mallet or running through grinder.
3. Add conch, tomatoes, and lemon juice and heat.
4. Slice carrots and celery into 1½-inch pieces and potatoes into hearty chunks. Then add along with water, hot pepper sauce, okra, bay leaves, and parsley to conch mixture.
5. Bring to a boil, then simmer for 3 hours.

Hot Cheddar Cheese Sandwiches

Yield: 8 sandwiches

Nice to serve with Tomato-Celery Soup.

2 cups (8 ounces) shredded sharp Cheddar cheese

½ cup butter, softened

2 eggs

⅛ to ¼ teaspoon garlic powder

⅛ to ¼ teaspoon onion powder

16 slices white or rye sandwich bread

Paprika

1. Combine first 5 ingredients; beat at medium speed of mixer until smooth.
2. Spread about 1 tablespoon cheese mixture on each of 8 bread slices.
3. Top with remaining bread slices. Spread remaining cheese mixture on top of sandwiches.
4. Sprinkle with paprika.
5. Bake.

Temperature: 400°
Time: 10 to 12 minutes

Hint: Sandwiches may be frozen. Wrap unbaked sandwiches individually and freeze. Thaw just before baking.

Italian Beef

Yield: 8 to 10 servings

Great to have on hand.

2 tablespoons fat

1 beef roast, 7 pounds, or 2 beef roasts, 3½ pounds each

Salt and pepper to taste

4 cups water

5 green peppers, sliced and chopped

1 teaspoon garlic salt

10 sandwich buns

1. Heat fat in large Dutch oven.
2. Season roast with salt and pepper and brown in hot fat. Add water and simmer 1 hour 30 minutes.
3. Remove roast and cool.
4. Slice thinly.
5. Return meat to liquid and add green peppers and garlic salt.
6. Simmer 4 hours. Serve on sandwich buns.

Sloppy Joes

Yield: 16 to 18 servings

A teenager's favorite.

3 pounds ground beef
Salt and pepper to taste
1 medium onion, chopped
⅓ cup lemon juice
1 bottle (16 ounces) catsup
3 tablespoons Worcestershire
  sauce
4 tablespoons brown sugar
1 teaspoon dry mustard
2 cups sliced celery

Hint: Freezes well.

1. Brown ground beef and drain excess fat.
2. Add remaining ingredients and simmer at least 1 to 2 hours.

Pimiento Cheese

Yield: 8 to 10 servings

An old favorite.

2 boxes (8 ounces each)
  pasteurized process cheese
  spread
1 egg
5 tablespoons sugar
¼ cup vinegar
1 tablespoon butter
1 jar (2 ounces) pimientos

1. Soften and mash cheese. Set aside.
2. Combine egg and sugar in saucepan.
3. Add vinegar and butter. Cook over medium heat until mixture boils and thickens.
4. Pour over cheese, add drained pimientos, and mash it all together until smooth.
5. Spread on sandwich bread or celery sticks.

Sausage-Broccoli Sandwich Loaves

Yield: 8 to 10 servings

A delightfully different and hearty sandwich.

2 loaves (1 pound each) unbaked frozen bread dough

1 pound mild or hot pork sausage

2 cloves garlic, crushed, optional

½ teaspoon oregano

1 teaspoon parsley

2 boxes (10 ounces each) frozen chopped broccoli

16 ounces mozzarella cheese, grated

1 egg yolk

1. Let bread rise according to package instructions.
2. Punch down and divide each loaf in half.
3. Saute' sausage with garlic, oregano, and parsley. Drain.
4. Cook broccoli until tender and drain. Combine sausage mixture and broccoli.
5. Roll each piece of dough into a strip 12 inches long and 5 inches wide. Place two strips per 15x10x1-inch pan.
6. Spread ¼ of broccoli-sausage mixture down center of each strip. Sprinkle with ¼ of cheese. Bring sides together and seal with a little water. Seal ends also.
7. Brush loaves with egg yolk. Let rise 30 minutes then bake until golden brown.

Temperature: 350°
Time: 35 to 45 minutes

Hint: These freeze well after baking.

Kenai Clam Sandwich
Yield: 2 servings

Light and delicious.

1 English muffin, split

3 strips bacon, cut into pieces

1 small onion, chopped

¼ cup chopped green pepper

1 can (6½ ounces) clams in
  juice

Parmesan cheese

1. Toast ½ English muffin for each
   serving and place on salad plate.
2. Fry bacon pieces.
3. Add onion and green pepper and
   cook until tender.
4. Place clams in pan and heat.
5. With slotted spoon, place clams
   on top of toasted English muffin.
6. Spoon bacon mixture over clams.
7. Sprinkle heavily with Parmesan
   cheese and broil.

Coney Island Quail (Hot Dogs)
Yield: 6 servings

A favorite with children.

6 hot dogs

6 tablespoons mustard

½ cup chopped onions

2 potatoes, cooked and
  mashed

1 cup grated Cheddar cheese

1. Slit hot dogs lengthwise half way.
2. Spread with mustard.
3. Add chopped onions to mashed
   potatoes. Fill hot dogs with
   potatoes.
4. Cover with grated cheese.
5. Bake.

Temperature: 375°
Time: 15 minutes

Turkey, Ham, And Cheese Sandwiches

Yield: 8 servings

16 slices of bread (crust trimmed)

8 slices of turkey

8 slices of ham

8 slices of Cheddar or Swiss cheese

6 eggs, beaten

3 cups milk

½ teaspoon onion salt

½ teaspoon dry mustard

Topping

2 cups crushed corn flakes

½ cup margarine, melted

1. Make single layer of 8 slices of bread, in greased baking dish.
2. Top each slice with turkey, ham, and cheese.
3. Cover with remaining 8 slices of bread.
4. Make custard by combining eggs, milk, salt, and mustard.
5. Pour custard over sandwiches. Refrigerate overnight.
6. Mix corn flakes and melted margarine and sprinkle on sandwiches.
7. Bake.

Temperature: 350°
Time: 1¼ hours

Hint: Assemble the night before for an easy luncheon dish.

Famous Hot Brown

Yield: 4 servings

More than special - a Kentucky tradition.

⅓ cup plus 1 tablespoon
   butter, divided

1 medium onion, chopped

⅓ cup flour

3 cups milk, heated

1 teaspoon salt

½ teaspoon crushed red
   pepper

4 to 6 ounces American
   Cheese

2 eggs, well beaten

1 tablespoon butter
   (additional)

8 strips bacon

8 slices wheat bread, toasted

2 chicken breasts, cooked
   and sliced

Parmesan cheese

Paprika

1. Melt ⅓ cup butter in saucepan and add onion. Cook until transparent.
2. Add flour and blend until smooth.
3. Add milk, salt, and red pepper.
4. Stir and cook until mixture is thick and smooth.
5. Stir in cheese, eggs, and 1 tablespoon butter. Continue to cook, stirring until mixture almost reaches boiling.
6. Remove sauce from heat.
7. Fry bacon slices until crisp.

To assemble hot browns:
1. Toast 8 slices of wheat bread.
2. Cut 4 in half diagonally.
3. On 4 oven proof plates, place cut toast with points turned outward, with one whole slice in the middle. Then layer chicken, sauce, and bacon.
4. Sprinkle generously with Parmesan and paprika.
5. Broil 2 to 3 minutes.

Hint: Turkey may be substituted for chicken.

Salads

Salads And Salad Dressings

Shrimp Vegetable Mold
Yield: 12 servings

1 can (11 ounces) tomato
  soup, undiluted
8 ounces cream cheese
1½ tablespoons unflavored
  gelatin
½ cup cold water
½ cup mayonnaise
1 cup minced celery
½ cup minced onion
2 cups chopped shrimp
1 tablespoon hot pepper sauce
½ cup chopped green pepper
1 tablespoon horseradish

1. Bring undiluted tomato soup to
   boil. Remove from heat. Add
   cream cheese that has been
   broken up. Stir until creamy.
2. Dissolve gelatin in cold water; add
   to soup mixture. Let mixture cool;
   add other ingredients.
3. Turn into wet mold, or mold
   greased with mayonnaise. Chill
   until set.

Hint: Hot pepper sauce gives this salad a hot, spicy flavor.

Hot Chicken Salad
Yield: 8 servings

4 cups cooked, diced chicken,
  salted
4 cups thinly-sliced celery
4 tablespoons grated onion
2 cups mayonnaise
1 cup sliced almonds
1 cup grated Cheddar cheese
2 cups crushed potato chips

1. Lightly toss together chicken,
   celery, onion, mayonnaise, and
   almonds. Pour into 9 x 12-inch
   casserole dish.
2. Sprinkle Cheddar cheese and
   crushed chips on top.
3. Bake.

Temperature: 450°
Time: 10 to 15 minutes

Polynesian Chicken Salad

Yield: 12 servings

Dressing

1 cup mayonnaise
1 cup sour cream
½ teaspoon curry powder
4 tablespoons Major Grey's
    chutney

Dressing

1. Combine dressing ingredients and shake.

Salad

5 cups cooked, diced chicken
    breasts
½ cup chopped celery
1 cup chopped water
    chestnuts
¼ cup chopped green onions
    and tops
2 cups pineapple tidbits,
    drained
2½ cups Chow Mein noodles

Salad

1. Mix chicken, celery, water chestnuts, onions, and pineapple.
2. Toss chicken mixture with dressing.
3. Chow Mein noodles may be mixed in before serving or sprinkled on each portion.

Hint: Dressing may be mixed earlier and refrigerated.

Spinach And Mushroom Salad With Sweet And Sour Dressing

Dressing

1 cup sugar

½ cup white vinegar

1 cup vegetable oil

1 teaspoon celery seed

¼ teaspoon dill seed

¼ teaspoon mustard seed

¼ teaspoon paprika

¾ teaspoon salt

Salad

1 pound spinach

¾ pound fresh mushrooms

2 hard-boiled eggs, sliced

12 ounces bean sprouts,
    chilled and drained

Dressing

1. Combine sugar and vinegar in saucepan. Bring to a boil. Remove from heat and add remaining ingredients, mixing well.
2. Pour into jar and chill overnight.

Salad

1. Wash, drain, and tear spinach into bite-size pieces.
2. Wash and slice fresh mushrooms.
3. Combine spinach, mushrooms, eggs, and sprouts in large bowl.
4. Serve with sweet and sour dressing.

Romaine-Orange-Almond Salad

Yield: 6 servings

Dressing

½ cup oil
2 tablespoons sugar
2 tablespoons parsley
1 teaspoon salt
4 tablespoons vinegar
Dash of pepper

Salad

¼ cup sliced almonds
1½ tablespoons sugar
½ head leaf lettuce, torn
½ head Romaine lettuce, torn
½ cup chopped celery
4 green onions, sliced
1 can (11 ounces) Mandarin
   oranges, drained

Dressing

1. Combine dressing ingredients and shake. Chill at least one hour.

Salad

1. Cook and stir almonds and sugar in skillet over low heat until sugar is melted and nuts coated and browned. Cool and set aside.
2. Combine both lettuces, celery, and onions. Refrigerate covered.
3. When ready to serve, pour dressing over lettuce mixture and add oranges. Sprinkle nuts over top just before serving.

Sunshine Onion Salad   Yield: 8 servings

A delicious treat with seafood!

1 large sweet onion
3 oranges
1½ to 2 pounds spinach
6 slices bacon, cooked and
   crumbled
2 tablespoons cider vinegar
1 tablespoon sugar
¼ teaspoon salt
¼ teaspoon dry mustard
⅓ cup salad oil

1. Peel and thinly slice onion. Separate into rings.
2. Peel and slice oranges. Cut slices in half.
3. Wash and trim spinach; break into bite-size pieces.
4. In salad bowl, combine onion rings, oranges, and spinach; sprinkle with bacon.
5. Combine vinegar, sugar, salt, mustard, and oil; mix well. Toss with salad to coat thoroughly.

Easy Broccoli Salad   Yield: 8 servings

1 large bunch of broccoli,
   broken into florets
⅔ cup chopped ripe olives
½ pound fresh mushrooms,
   chopped
1 egg
2 tablespoons Parmesan
   cheese
1 clove garlic, crushed
¾ teaspoon Dijon mustard
Freshly ground pepper
Salt to taste
⅓ cup lemon or lime juice
½ cup oil
4 hard-boiled eggs, chopped

1. Toss broccoli, olives, and mushrooms in large container.
2. Put egg, cheese, garlic, mustard, pepper, and salt into blender. Add lemon juice and oil, alternately, and blend.
3. Pour dressing over salad 1 hour before serving.
4. Garnish with chopped eggs.

Oriental Salad

Yield: 10 to 12 servings

Colorful!

1 can (17 ounces) tiny peas,
   drained
1 can (16 ounces) bean
   sprouts, drained
1 can (12 ounces) whole
   kernel white corn, drained
2 cans (5 ounces each) water
   chestnuts, drained and
   sliced
1 can (4 ounces) sliced
   mushrooms, drained
1 jar (4 ounces) pimiento,
   drained and sliced
1 large green pepper, thinly
   sliced
1 large onion, thinly sliced
1 cup celery, sliced
1 cup salad oil
1 cup water
1 cup sugar
½ cup vinegar
Seasoned salt and pepper to
   taste

1. Combine first nine ingredients in large bowl, stirring gently.
2. Combine remaining ingredients and pour over vegetables. Cover and chill 24 hours. Drain before serving.

Greek Village Salad

Yield: 2 to 4 servings

A meal in itself.

3 tomatoes, cut into wedges

1 cucumber, sliced

1 red onion, sliced into rings

2 green peppers, cut into
    rings

6 tablespoons olive oil

2 tablespoons wine vinegar

Salt and pepper

⅓ pound feta cheese,
    crumbled or sliced

2 dozen ripe olives

Dried oregano, crumbled

1. Place tomatoes, cucumber, onion, and pepper in large salad bowl.
2. In small bottle or jar, shake together oil, vinegar, salt and pepper. Pour over salad.
3. Arrange sliced feta cheese and olives on top of salad. Sprinkle with oregano.

Hint: Serve with thick slices of Greek or Italian bread.

Elegant Spinach Mold

Yield: 12 to 16 servings

A molded salad with substance.

2 envelopes unflavored gelatin

¼ cup cold water

1 can (10½ ounces) beef
    broth, divided

½ teaspoon salt

2 tablespoons lemon juice

1 cup salad dressing

1 medium onion, quartered

1 package (10 ounces) frozen
    chopped spinach

4 hard-boiled eggs

½ pound bacon, fried and
    crumbled

1. Sprinkle gelatin over cold water and ¼ cup beef broth.
2. Heat remaining beef broth to boiling and blend with gelatin mixture.
3. Pour into blender, cover and process at low speed until gelatin dissolves.
4. Add salt, lemon juice, and salad dressing, and blend well. Add onion and process at high speed.
5. Add spinach and eggs. Process at high speed until eggs are coarsely chopped. Stir in bacon.
6. Pour into 9-inch ring mold (6 cups). Refrigerate until set.

Kentucky Wilted Lettuce Salad

Yield: 6 servings

A summertime favorite.

Large bunch leafy green
  lettuce, torn

½ cup chopped green onion

1 egg, well-beaten

4 tablespoons sugar

½ cup wine vinegar

½ cup water

10 slices bacon

1. Toss lettuce and onions slightly.
2. Mix egg, sugar, vinegar, and water.
3. Fry bacon until crisp. Crumble and set aside.
4. Pour off half bacon grease. To remainder, add egg mixture, and cook until thickened.
5. When ready to serve, pour hot dressing over lettuce and add crumbled bacon.
6. Serve immediately.

Hint: Good served with croutons. Cube bread and melt enough butter to coat. Toss together and place on baking sheet. Sprinkle with garlic salt and bake at 250° for several hours.

Forever Slaw

Yield: 10 to 12 servings

This salad keeps "forever."

1 large head cabbage, diced

2 large Bermuda onions,
  diced

1 green pepper, diced

1½ cups sugar

1. Mix onions and peppers.
2. Layer cabbage, onion, and pepper mixture until filled to top of tightly-sealed shallow container. Do not mix.
3. Pour sugar on top of salad mixture.

Dressing

4 teaspoons sugar

1 cup vinegar

¾ cup vegetable oil

1 teaspoon dry mustard

1 teaspoon celery seed

1 tablespoon salt

Dressing

1. Bring combined dressing ingredients to boil, and pour over slaw mixture while still hot. Do not stir.
2. Refrigerate while hot. Let set at least 4 hours before serving.

Mexican Salad

Yield: 8 servings

2 cups shredded lettuce
1 can (15 ounces) kidney
   beans, drained
2 medium tomatoes, chopped
   and drained
1 tablespoon chopped green
   chilies
½ cup sliced ripe olives
1 large avocado, mashed
½ cup sour cream
2 tablespoons Italian salad
   dressing
1 teaspoon minced onion
¼ teaspoon salt
¾ teaspoon chili powder
½ cup shredded Cheddar
   cheese
½ cup coarsely crushed corn
   chips

1. Combine lettuce, beans,
   tomatoes, chilies, and olives in
   salad bowl.
2. Blend avocado and sour cream;
   add Italian dressing, onion, salt,
   and chili powder. Mix well and
   chill.
3. Toss salad with avocado mixture.
   Top with cheese and corn chips.
   Garnish with ripe olives.

Orange-Cream Fruit Salad

Yield: 10 servings

1 can (20 ounces) pineapple
tidbits, drained
1 can (16 ounces) peach
slices, drained
1 can (11 ounces) Mandarin
orange sections, drained
3 medium bananas, sliced
2 medium apples, cored and
sliced
1 package (3½ ounces) instant
vanilla pudding mix
1½ cups milk
⅓ cup frozen orange juice
concentrate, thawed
¾ cup sour cream
Lettuce cups

1. In large bowl, combine fruits; set
aside.
2. In small bowl, combine dry
pudding mix, milk, and orange
juice concentrate. Beat with
rotary beater until blended; beat
in sour cream. Fold into fruit
mixture. Cover and chill.
3. Serve in lettuce cups. Garnish
with additional Mandarin orange
sections, if desired.

Strawberry Fruit Freeze

Yield: 10 to 12 servings

1 cup mayonnaise
1 tablespoon lemon juice
2 cups chopped fruit
(peaches, pineapple, pears,
or grapes)
2 bananas, chopped
1 package (10 ounces) frozen
strawberries
½ pint whipping cream
¾ cup sugar

1. Mix mayonnaise and lemon juice
with chopped fruit, bananas, and
strawberries.
2. Whip cream. Fold sugar into
whipped cream.
3. Fold whipped cream into fruit
mixture. Put into 9 x 12-inch glass
dish and freeze.
4. Cut into squares and serve on crisp
lettuce. Garnish with cherries or
strawberries.

Holiday Pineapple Salad

Yield: 6 servings

1 tablespoon flour
1 cup sugar
1 cup milk
2 eggs
2 tablespoons butter
½ cup vinegar
2 cans (20 ounces each)
pineapple chunks, drained
1 cup pecans
1 pound mild Cheddar
cheese, grated

1. Mix together flour and sugar. Add
milk, eggs, and butter. Cook until
thick, stirring constantly. Cool.
Add vinegar, and blend well.
2. Mix pineapple, pecans, and
cheese.
3. Pour dressing over pineapple
mixture and chill overnight.

Apple Salad With Curry Dressing

Yield: 6 servings

Salad

3 cups cored and diced
   Golden Delicious apples
1 teaspoon lemon juice
½ cup sliced celery
½ cup raisins
¼ cup chopped green pepper
½ cup salted peanuts

Dressing

⅓ cup mayonnaise
⅓ cup orange-flavored yogurt
½ to 1 teaspoon curry powder

Salad

1. Drizzle lemon juice over apples. Add celery, raisins, and peppers; chill.
2. Just before serving, stir in peanuts and toss with curry dressing. Serve on individual plates.

Dressing

1. Combine all ingredients and chill.

Banana-Orange Slush

Yield: 12 servings

Delightful for a summer brunch.

1 cup sugar
2 cups boiling water
1 can (6 ounces) frozen
   orange juice concentrate,
   undiluted
1 can (15¼ ounces) crushed
   pineapple, undrained
1 jar (10 ounces) maraschino
   cherries, drained
3 bananas, peeled and sliced

1. Combine all ingredients and mix well. Refrigerate for 24 hours, stirring occasionally.
2. Freeze overnight or until firm. Remove from freezer 45 minutes before serving. (Mixture should be slushy.) Serve in sherbet glasses.

French Dressing

Yield: 2½ cups

Makes any salad a treat.

1 cup catsup
1 cup salad oil
½ cup sugar
¼ teaspoon paprika
Juice of 1 lemon
¼ cup vinegar
1 small onion, finely chopped

Hint: Add garlic salt if desired.

1. Mix all ingredients except onion in blender or with wire whisk.
2. Add onion and serve.

Bleu Cheese Dressing

Yield: 6 cups

Gets better as it ages.

1 meduim onion, chopped
1 to 2 cloves garlic
Juice of ½ lemon
6 to 8 ounces bleu cheese
½ teaspoon salt
Ground pepper
⅓ quart salad dressing
1 quart mayonnaise
Optional for color:
1 to 2 tablespoons catsup

1. Blend onion, garlic, and lemon juice in blender. Add mixture to crumbled bleu cheese, salt, pepper, salad dressing, mayonnaise, and catsup.
2. Store and age in refrigerator for 3 days before using.

Seedy Dressing

Yield: 1½ cups

Excellent for fruit salad.

½ cup sugar
1 teaspoon dry mustard
1 teaspoon salt
¼ cup grated onion
⅓ cup vinegar (white or
  tarragon)
1 cup salad oil
1 tablespoon celery or poppy
  seed
⅓ cup honey, optional

1. Place all ingredients in blender in order listed. Thoroughly blend on high speed until thickened and smooth.

Hint: This dressing keeps well in the refrigerator for a long time.

Tropical Fruit Fluff

Yield: 1¾ cups

1 cup sour cream
¼ cup flaked coconut
2 tablespoons chopped
  walnuts
2 tablespoons apricot
  preserves
Milk

1. In small mixing bowl, combine sour cream, coconut, walnuts, and preserves. Add enough milk to make mixture of dipping consistency. Chill.
2. Serve over fruit such as apples, melons, pineapple, strawberries, peaches, bananas, and Mandarin oranges.

Fluffy Citrus Dressing

Yield: 1½ cups

Try this over melon or warm gingerbread.

1 egg
½ cup sugar
1 tablespoon grated orange
  peel
2 teaspoons grated lemon
  peel
2 tablespoons lemon juice
1 cup whipping cream,
  whipped

1. In saucepan, beat egg. Add sugar, fruit peels, and lemon juice. Cook over low heat, stirring constantly until thickened (about 5 minutes). Cool.
2. Fold in whipped cream. Chill.
3. Serve over fresh fruit salad.

Tarragon Dressing

Yield: ¾ cup

Great on Bibb lettuce and with spinach salad.

½ cup salad oil
1½ tablespoons white wine
  vinegar
1½ tablespoons tarragon
  vinegar
2 teaspoons Dijon mustard
1 teaspoon salt
1 teaspoon sugar
Freshly ground pepper
1 tablespoon grated onion

1. Combine first 7 ingredients in jar and shake well to blend. Add onions before serving.

Sylvia's Mayonnaise

Yield: 1 cup

Great for tuna and chicken salads.

1 egg yolk
1 tablespoon vinegar
1 tablespoon Dijon mustard
½ tablespoon sugar
Salt and pepper
1 cup vegetable oil
Salt and pepper to taste
½ teaspoon lemon juice

1. Put egg yolk, vinegar, mustard, sugar, salt, and pepper into mixing bowl. Beat with wire whisk.
2. Gradually add oil, beating vigorously. If desired, add additional salt and vinegar for taste.
3. Add lemon juice. When thickened and smooth, pour into jar with screw-on top.

Vinegar And Oil Dressing

Yield: 2 cups

Creamy and delicious!

½ cup sugar
⅓ cup plus 1 tablespoon white wine vinegar
1 tablespoon prepared mustard
1 cup oil
1 teaspoon pepper
1 tablespoon onion flakes or instant minced onion
1 teaspoon salt
⅛ teaspoon garlic powder
1 teaspoon celery seed

1. Combine all ingredients in blender container.
2. Blend about one minute.

Eggs, Cheese, Pasta & Grain

Eggs, Cheese, Pasta And Grain

Eggs Creole

Yield: 8 servings

2 onions, thinly sliced

2 green peppers, finely chopped

2 cups celery, finely chopped

2 tablespoons butter

1 can (4 ounces) mushrooms, drained

1 can (28 ounces) tomatoes, drained

2 tablespoons flour

8 eggs, hard-boiled and sliced

1. Saute' onions, green peppers, and celery in butter. Add mushrooms and tomatoes. Add flour, and stir until thickened.
2. Arrange mixture alternately with sliced hard-boiled eggs in a baking dish. Set aside.

White Sauce

4 tablespoons flour

2 cups milk, divided

4 tablespoons butter

1 cup grated sharp Cheddar cheese

White Sauce

1. In a jar, mix flour and ½ cup milk.
2. In saucepan, heat butter and remaining milk until butter is melted. Stir in flour mixture, and cook over medium heat until thickened.
3. Pour white sauce over top of eggs and sprinkle with Cheddar cheese.
4. Bake as directed.

Temperature: 350°
Time: 30 minutes

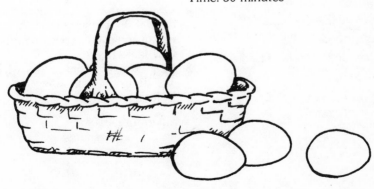

Nice 'n' Cheesy Casserole

Yield: 8 to 10 servings

Delightful for brunch!

6 slices bread, crusts removed
and cubed

1½ cups cubed pasteurized
process cheese spread

1½ cups cubed sharp
Cheddar cheese

1 can (4 ounces)
mushrooms, drained

½ cup butter, melted

6 eggs, well beaten

1 pint light cream

1. Grease 2-quart casserole.
2. Layer bread, half of pasteurized
process cheese spread, half of
Cheddar cheese, mushrooms,
and remainder of cheeses.
3. Melt butter; add eggs and light
cream. Pour over layered
ingredients.
4. Cover and refrigerate overnight.
5. Bake at 350°, uncovered, for 1
hour in a pan of water.

Temperature: 350°
Time: 1 hour

Hint: For a cheesier dish, use 2 cups of each cheese.

Eggs a la Barkley

Yield: 8 servings

6 slices white bread

1 pound hot sausage

1 pound mild sausage

1 can (8 ounces) chopped
mushrooms

1 pound Cheddar cheese,
grated

6 eggs

1 pint light cream

1. Tear bread into bite-size pieces,
and place in 9 x 13-inch casserole
dish.
2. Crumble sausages; cook and
drain. Spread over bread. Add
mushrooms and top with grated
Cheddar cheese.
3. Beat eggs; add light cream. Mix
well. Pour over casserole.
4. Bake uncovered.

Temperature: 350°
Time: 30 to 45 minutes

Bacon-Mushroom Quiche

Yield: 4 to 6 servings

1 unbaked pie shell (8-inch)
8 ounces cream cheese
½ cup heavy cream
3 egg yolks
1 egg
¼ teaspoon salt
¼ teaspoon pepper
6 slices bacon
1 can (4 ounces) mushrooms,
   chopped

1. Beat cream cheese with the next five ingredients until smooth.
2. Cut bacon into 1-inch pieces, and cook until almost brown. Drain.
3. Arrange bacon and mushrooms in pastry shell. Pour cheese mixture over bacon.
4. Bake at 400° for 20 minutes. Reduce heat to 350° and bake for 10 minutes, or until firm in center.

Temperature: 400°
Time: 20 minutes
Temperature: 350°
Time: 10 minutes

Two-Step Quiche

Yield: 4 to 6 servings

4 eggs
½ cup biscuit mix
½ cup oil
½ cup grated Parmesan
   cheese
¼ teaspoon salt
⅛ teaspoon pepper
3 cups zucchini or broccoli
Onions, optional
Mushrooms, optional
Ham, optional
1 teaspoon parsley flakes

1. Mix eggs, biscuit mix, oil, cheese, salt, and pepper thoroughly. Set aside.
2. Cut zucchini or broccoli into bite-size pieces, and put in quiche dish or small casserole dish. Add any amount of onions, mushrooms, and ham to the zucchini or broccoli.
3. Pour first mixture over ingredients in the quiche dish, making surface level. Sprinkle parsley flakes on top.
4. Bake.

Temperature: 350°
Time: 30 minutes

Alaskan Crab Quiche

Yield: 6 servings

An exquisitely unique quiche!

1 package (6 ounces) king
  crab meat
½ pound fresh mushrooms,
  sliced
2 tablespoons butter
4 eggs
1 cup sour cream
1 cup small curd cottage
  cheese
1 cup grated Parmesan cheese
¼ cup flour
1 teaspoon onion powder
¼ teaspoon salt
4 drops hot pepper sauce
2 cups shredded Monterey
  Jack cheese

1. Thaw and drain crab meat.
2. In medium-size skillet, sauté
   mushrooms in butter until tender.
   Drain. Set aside.
3. In blender, mix next eight
   ingredients.
4. Fold in mushrooms, Jack cheese,
   and crab meat. Pour into 10-inch
   quiche dish.
5. Bake at 350° for 45 minutes until
   golden brown, or until a knife
   inserted in center comes out
   clean. Let stand 5 minutes before
   cutting.

Temperature: 350°
Time: 45 minutes

Scrambled Egg Casserole

Yield: 8 to 10 servings

1 cup cubed or ground country ham

¼ cup chopped green onion

7 tablespoons melted butter, divided

12 eggs, beaten

1 can (4 ounces) sliced mushrooms, drained

2¼ cups soft bread crumbs

⅛ teaspoon paprika

1. In large skillet, saute' ham and green onion in 3 tablespoons melted butter until onion is tender. Add eggs, and cook over medium-high heat, stirring to form large, soft curds.
2. When eggs are set, stir in mushrooms and cheese sauce. Spoon egg mixture into greased 9 x 13-inch baking dish.
3. Combine 4 tablespoons melted butter and bread crumbs, mixing well. Spread evenly over egg mixture. Sprinkle with paprika. Cover and chill overnight.
4. Bake uncovered at 350° for 30 minutes or until thoroughly heated.

Temperature: 350°
Time: 30 minutes

Cheese Sauce

2 tablespoons butter

2½ tablespoons flour

2 cups milk

½ teaspoon salt

⅛ teaspoon pepper

4 ounces Cheddar cheese, shredded

Cheese Sauce

1. Melt butter in heavy skillet over low heat. Blend in flour and cook 1 minute. Gradually add milk; cook over medium heat until thickened, stirring constantly.
2. Add salt, pepper, and cheese, stirring until cheese melts and mixture is smooth.

Cheese Souffle'

Yield: 6 servings

2 tablespoons butter
3 tablespoons flour
1 cup milk
1 teaspoon salt
¼ teaspoon mustard
1 cup grated American cheese
3 eggs, separated

1. Melt butter over low heat; add flour and milk. Cook over low heat, stirring until thickened and smooth.
2. Add salt, mustard, and cheese, stirring until cheese is melted. Cool.
3. Fold in 3 egg yolks beaten until light in color.
4. Fold in stiffly-beaten egg whites.
5. Pour into ungreased casserole or soufflé dish.
6. Set in pan of hot water and bake 50 minutes, or until top is firm and browned.

Temperature: 325°
Time: 50 minutes

Almond Rice

Yield: 12 servings

A meal in itself.

2 pounds sausage
2 stalks celery, cut diagonally
2 medium onions, chopped
1 green pepper, chopped
¼ cup butter or margarine
2 cups raw rice
8 cups water
3 envelopes Lipton Cream of Chicken Flavor Cup-a-Soup
1 can (4 ounces) mushrooms
4 ounces sliced almonds

1. Brown and drain sausage.
2. Sauté celery, onions, and pepper in butter. Add to sausage.
3. Place raw rice on the bottom of a 9 x 13-inch casserole dish. Add water.
4. Sprinkle soup over rice. Add meat mixture.
5. Cover with drained mushrooms and almonds. Bake.

Temperature: 350°
Time: 45 to 55 minutes

Jalapeño Rice

Yield: 6 servings

Great addition to Mexican dinners.

2½ cups cooked and cooled
  rice
8 ounces sour cream
1 can (4 ounces) green chilies
8 ounces Monterey Jack
  cheese, grated

1. Mix rice with sour cream and green chilies.
2. In a 1½ to 2-quart casserole dish, layer half of rice mixture and half of cheese. Repeat, ending with cheese.
3. Bake 30 minutes covered; then remove lid and bake for an additional 10 minutes.

Temperature: 350°
Time: 30 minutes, covered
      10 minutes, uncovered

Wild Rice Casserole

Yield: 10 to 12 servings

Delicious!

1½ cups wild rice (or combine
  it with brown or long grain
  rice)
4 cans (10½ ounces each)
  bouillon, undiluted
1 cup onion, chopped
1 cup green pepper, chopped
1 cup sliced mushrooms
¼ cup butter, softened
1 cup heavy cream
Salt
Pepper

1. Soak wild rice overnight according to package directions; drain.
2. Cook rice with bouillon until liquid is absorbed and rice has opened.
3. Sauté vegetables in butter. Add cream.
4. Stir in rice.
5. Pour into a greased 9 x 13-inch baking dish. Bake.

Temperature: 350°
Time: 20 minutes

Tasty Fried Rice

Yield: 4 to 6 servings

Great with any oriental dish!

2 onions, chopped
2 tablespoons vegetable oil
2 cups cooked rice
2 eggs
1 tablespoon soy sauce

1. Saute' onions in oil until limp and transparent. Add the rice.
2. Stir together eggs and soy sauce. Add to rice.
3. Saute' entire mixture until eggs are done.

Main dish, optional

1 to 2 cups chopped, cooked meat (pork, chicken, beef or shrimp)
1 tablespoon soy sauce

Main dish, optional

1. Marinate chopped meat in soy sauce for at least 30 minutes.
2. Add to rice mixture.
3. Cook as above.

Green Rice And Broccoli Casserole

Yield: 6 servings

Children love this!

1 package (10 ounces) frozen chopped broccoli
1 cup raw rice
¼ cup butter
¼ cup celery, chopped
⅛ cup onion, chopped
1 jar (14 ounces) pasteurized process cheese spread
½ can (½ of 11 ounces) cream of chicken soup

1. Thaw broccoli.
2. Cook rice according to package directions.
3. Sauté celery and onion in butter.
4. Combine broccoli, rice, celery, onion, pasteurized process cheese spread, and soup. Pour into 2-quart casserole.
5. Bake until bubbly.

Temperature: 350°
Time: 20 to 30 minutes

Hint: Recipe doubles well, but do not double pasteurized process cheese spread. Use only an extra 7 ounces.

Auntie's Cheese Grits   Yield: 8 to 10 servings

Wonderful for brunch!

1 cup grits or 2 cups quick
  grits

1 teaspoon salt

2¼ cups water

2¼ cups milk

½ cup margarine

1 roll (6 ounces) sharp or
  nippy cheese

1 roll (6 ounces) garlic cheese

2 eggs, well-beaten

1. Cook grits, salt, water, and milk in a two-quart saucepan until thick. Stir occasionally.
2. To thickened grits, add margarine and cubed cheese.
3. Beat eggs and stir a portion of the hot grits into the eggs to keep them from cooking. Add to remaining grits mixture.
4. Stir until cheese melts and no white grits show.
5. Pour into a large casserole and bake uncovered.

Temperature: 350°
Time: 35 to 40 minutes

Hint: May be prepared ahead of time and cooked when needed. Also good warmed-up.

Noodle Kuegel (Noodle Pudding)   Yield: 8 generous servings

Sweet and rich!

1 package (6 ounces) of
  noodles (½ inch wide)

½ cup butter or margarine,
  softened

1 cup sugar

1 cup sour cream

4 eggs, beaten

1 cup sweet cream

½ teaspoon salt

¾ cup raisins, plumped

1. Cook noodles according to directions on package.
2. Cream butter and sugar.
3. Add remaining ingredients and stir into drained noodles.
4. Pour into buttered 3-quart glass dish and bake uncovered.

Temperature: 375°
Time: 45 minutes

Fettucine Alfredo With Broccoli

Yield: 4 to 6 servings

Colorful and rich!

8 tablespoons olive oil

1 package (8 ounces) broccoli florets, cooked

2 large onions, minced

1 clove garlic, minced

⅔ cup whipping cream

1 pound fettucine, cooked

¾ cup grated Parmesan cheese

Salt

Pepper

1. Heat oil in non-aluminum skillet over medium high heat. Add broccoli and sauté.
2. Remove broccoli with slotted spoon and set aside.
3. Add onions to oil and sauté until golden.
4. Add garlic and cook one additional minute.
5. Stir in cream. Increase heat and boil until sauce is reduced by one-third.
6. Add cooked fettucine, broccoli, one-half cup Parmesan cheese, salt, and pepper. Toss thoroughly.
7. Sprinkle remaining Parmesan on top. Serve immediately.

Easy Fettucine

Yield: 4 servings

A yummy, delicious dish!

¼ cup butter or margarine
    (room temperature)
2 tablespoons dried parsley
1 teaspoon dried basil
8 ounces cream cheese
Freshly ground pepper
⅔ cup boiling water
¼ cup butter or margarine
1 clove garlic, minced
8 ounces fettucine (cooked al
    dente and drained)
¾ cup grated Romano cheese

1. Combine ¼ cup butter, parsley, and basil in a medium bowl.
2. Blend in cream cheese; season with pepper.
3. Mix in water; blend thoroughly.
4. Set bowl in large pan of hot water to keep warm.
5. Melt remaining butter in large skillet over low heat.
6. Add garlic and cook 1 to 2 minutes being careful not to burn.
7. Add pasta and toss gently. Sprinkle with one-half cup cheese and toss again.
8. Transfer to serving platter and spoon sauce over top. Sprinkle with remaining cheese and serve immediately.

Baked Macaroni And Cheese

Yield: 6 servings

Onion makes the difference.

2 tablespoons butter
2 tablespoons flour
½ teaspoon salt
Dash of pepper
1 cup hot milk
1 cup cream
1 small onion, diced
1 cup diced Cheddar cheese
1 cup grated Parmesan cheese
2 cups elbow macaroni or 7-
 ounce package (cooked
 and drained)
¾ cup bread crumbs

1. Put butter, flour, salt, pepper, milk, and cream in blender for 35 seconds.
2. Add onion and cheeses.
3. Mix above ingredients with cooked macaroni in 2-quart casserole.
4. Top with bread crumbs and bake.

Temperature: 350°
Time: 20 to 30 minutes

Baked Rice

Yield: 8 servings

Good and easy!

2 cups long grain rice
1 small onion, chopped
1 can (10½ ounces) beef
 bouillon
1 can (10½ ounces) beef
 consommé
1 can (4 ounces) mushroom
 stems and pieces
¼ cup butter

1. Mix together all ingredients. Place in a medium-size baking dish.
2. Bake uncovered, stirring twice.

Temperature: 300°
Time: 1 to 1½ hours

Vegetables & Fruits

Vegetables And Fruits

Parslied Artichokes

1 artichoke per person
1 small clove garlic per
artichoke, chopped
1 teaspoon chopped parsley
per artichoke
Dash salt per artichoke
Dash pepper per artichoke
2 teaspoons olive oil per
artichoke
½ teaspoon salt
1 clove garlic, chopped
1 teaspoon chopped parsley

1. Cut ¼ inch off top of each
   artichoke. Tap upside down on
   hard surface to open. Dig inside
   with spoon to pull out prickly
   leaves, being careful not to touch
   heart. Cut off stalk completely,
   then peel it and place inside
   artichoke. Pull off small leaves at
   bottom and discard.
2. Place small clove of garlic and
   parsley in center of artichoke. Add
   peeled stalk.
3. Sprinkle inside center with salt,
   pepper, and olive oil. Also sprinkle
   olive oil around top leaves.
4. Fill saucepan with about 1 inch of
   water and sprinkle ½ teaspoon
   salt, garlic, and 1 teaspoon parsley
   into it. Place artichokes in water
   and bring to boil. Watch carefully.
5. Cook standing about 30 minutes.
   Turn on sides until all sides are
   done. To test for doneness, sample
   leaf.

*Hint: Try to prepare the day they will be eaten as they lose part of
their flavor when refrigerated.*

101

Asparagus And Cheese Casserole

Yield: 10 servings

Water chestnuts add a surprising crunch.

¾ cup butter, melted and
   divided
1½ cups butter-flavored
   cracker crumbs
2 cans (16 ounces each) long
   asparagus spears
1 can (8 ounces) water
   chestnuts, sliced
3 tablespoons flour
1½ cups milk
1 jar (5 ounces) sharp
   pasteurized process cheese
   spread
½ cup grated Cheddar
   cheese
Salt
Pepper

1. Mix ½ cup butter and cracker
   crumbs. Set aside.
2. Drain asparagus and water
   chestnuts. Set aside.
3. Melt ¼ cup butter over low heat.
   Stir in flour until smooth. Slowly
   stir in milk.
4. Add cheeses and seasonings.
   Cook over medium heat until
   cheese is melted.
5. Layer one half of crumb mixture,
   asparagus, water chestnuts, and
   cheese sauce in 2-quart casserole
   dish. Repeat.
6. Bake.

Temperature: 350°
Time: 40 minutes

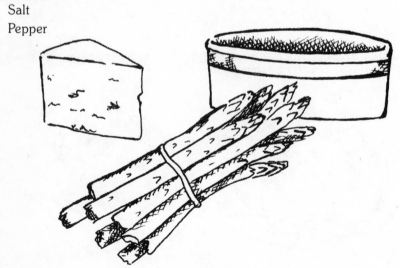

Asparagus-Almond Casserole

Yield: 4 to 6 servings

6 tablespoons butter, divided
2 tablespoons flour
1 cup milk
½ teaspoon salt
Dash pepper
8 ounces American cheese, grated
1 can (16 ounces) asparagus, drained
3 hard-boiled eggs, sliced
1½ cups cracker crumbs
½ cup sliced almonds

1. Melt 2 tablespoons butter over low heat. Stir in flour one tablespoon at a time.
2. Add 1 cup milk all at one time. Stir until thickened. Add salt and pepper.
3. Add cheese and stir until melted.
4. In a 2-quart casserole dish, layer one half of asparagus, one half of cheese sauce, and one half of hard-boiled eggs. Repeat.
5. Melt 4 tablespoons butter. Add crackers and almonds. Spread over casserole.
6. Bake until cracker mixture is brown.

Temperature: 350°
Time: 15 to 20 minutes

Hint: This dish may be prepared ahead and kept in the refrigerator until ready to bake.

Savory Beets

Yield: 4 servings

An attractive, easily prepared dish.

1 can (16 ounces) beets or 2 cups fresh beets
1 small onion, thinly sliced
1 tablespoon plus 1 teaspoon butter
1 tablespoon lemon juice
1 teaspoon chopped parsley
¼ teaspoon salt

1. If using fresh beets, parboil until tender and skin.
2. Saute' onion in butter until soft but not brown.
3. Drain beets and add to onion and butter.
4. Add lemon juice and parsley.
5. Toss beets and add salt.
6. Simmer until hot, then serve.

Fresh Green Bean Casserole

Yield: 6 servings

4 cups fresh green beans, cut into 2-inch pieces (or 2 cans, 16 ounces each)

3 to 6 slices bacon

½ cup chopped onion

4 large tomatoes, peeled and chopped

2 large whole pimientoes, chopped (or 2-ounce jar)

¼ teaspoon salt

⅛ teaspoon pepper

½ to ¾ cup shredded American cheese

1. Cook beans, uncovered, in boiling salted water for 2 to 3 minutes. Cover and cook 20 to 30 minutes more. Drain and set aside. (If using canned beans, just drain; do not cook.)
2. Fry bacon until crisp. Remove from pan and crumble.
3. Sauté onion in bacon drippings until tender.
4. Combine everything except cheese, tossing gently. Spoon into greased 2-quart casserole dish.
5. Sprinkle with cheese.
6. Bake until cheese is slightly browned.

Temperature: 350°
Time: 15 to 20 minutes

Cream Cheese Limas

Yield: 6 servings

A nice dish to compliment a meal.

2 cups fresh or frozen lima beans

1 onion, finely chopped

1 clove garlic, minced

2 tablespoons butter, melted

1 can (8 ounces) tomato sauce

1 teaspoon salt

½ teaspoon pepper

3 ounces cream cheese, cut into pieces

1. Cook lima beans in small amount of boiling salted water until tender (about 20 minutes). Drain, reserving ¼ cup cooking liquid.
2. Sauté onion and garlic in butter until tender.
3. Add tomato sauce, salt, and pepper. Simmer 5 minutes.
4. Add cream cheese and reserved bean liquid, stirring until smooth.
5. Stir in limas and heat thoroughly.

Broccoli Casserole Delight

Yield: 10 to 12 servings

A deliciously different dish.

2 boxes (10 ounces each)
chopped broccoli, thawed
1 cup mayonnaise
1 can (10¾ ounces) cream of
mushroom soup
2 eggs, well beaten
Salt
Pepper
6 tablespoons butter, melted
1 medium onion, chopped and
sautéed
1 pound fresh mushrooms,
sliced
1 cup plain bread crumbs
8 ounces grated sharp
Cheddar cheese

1. Combine broccoli, mayonnaise,
   soup, eggs, salt, and pepper (to
   taste), butter, sautéed onion, one-
   half mushrooms, and one-half
   bread crumbs in a 9 x 13-inch pan.
   Mix well.
2. Place remaining mushrooms on
   top. Sprinkle with remainder of
   bread crumbs and top with cheese.
3. Bake.

Temperature: 350°
Time: 40 to 45 minutes

Clarified Butter Sauce

Yield: 1¼ cups

Add sparkle to any fresh vegetable.

1 cup butter (unsalted)
4 tablespoons fresh lemon
juice
1 teaspoon grated lemon peel
¼ teaspoon salt
4 grinds white pepper

1. Melt butter over medium heat; let
   stand 20 to 30 minutes.
2. With a spoon remove foamy crust
   from the top; discard. Spoon the
   deep yellow liquid butter into a
   bowl, leaving the whey on the
   bottom of the pan. Discard the
   whey.
3. Add remaining ingredients to
   liquid yellow butter and reheat as
   needed.
4. Pour over cooked vegetable.

Fresh Cabbage And Cheese Casserole

Yield: 12 to 16 servings

This recipe generates excitement over cabbage!

1 large head of cabbage
½ cup butter
¼ cup flour
1½ cups milk
½ to ¾ pound sharp cheese, grated
Browned bread crumbs
Butter

1. Coarsely shred cabbage (slicing disk of food processor works well).
2. Steam or boil in small amount of water for 10 minutes. Drain well.
3. Make white sauce. Melt butter in saucepan. Add flour and cook 3 minutes. Gradually stir in milk. Cook until thick, stirring constantly.
4. Grease 3-quart casserole and layer cabbage, white sauce, and cheese until all is used.
5. Cover with bread crumbs and dot with butter. Bake.

Temperature: 350°
Time: 35 minutes

Cauliflower Parmesan

Yield: 6 to 8 servings

Delightful!

1 head cauliflower
½ cup bread crumbs
½ cup grated Parmesan cheese
1 egg
1 tablespoon milk
2 tablespoons melted butter

1. Wash and separate cauliflower into 12 pieces.
2. Cook cauliflower for 7 minutes in salted water. Drain.
3. Mix bread crumbs with cheese.
4. Beat egg with milk.
5. Dip cauliflower in egg mixture then in bread crumbs.
6. Arrange in buttered casserole and pour melted butter over cauliflower.
7. Cover and bake.

Temperature: 350°
Time: 20 to 30 minutes

Kentucky Corn Pudding   Yield: 6 servings

Appealing and so easy to prepare.

2 tablespoons flour
2 tablespoons sugar
2 eggs, beaten
1 can (16 ounces) white
   whole-kernel corn,
   undrained
½ cup milk
2 tablespoons margarine,
   melted

1. Mix together flour and sugar. Add
   to beaten eggs.
2. Add corn, milk, and melted
   margarine.
3. Mix well and pour into 8 x 8-inch
   baking dish.
4. Bake until golden brown.

Temperature: 350°
Time: 1 hour

Corn Souffle'   Yield: 6 servings

A light and fluffy vegetable dish.

2 cups fresh corn or 1
   package (10 ounces) frozen
   corn, thawed
2 tablespoons flour
2 tablespoons sugar
½ teaspoon salt
⅛ teaspoon pepper
1 cup milk
2 eggs, separated
Butter

1. Mix together corn, flour, sugar,
   salt, pepper, and milk.
2. Add egg yolks to mixture.
3. Beat egg whites until stiff and fold
   into corn mixture.
4. Pour into a 1-quart casserole and
   dot with butter.
5. Bake.

Temperature: 350°
Time: 45 to 50 minutes

Southern Fried Corn

Yield: 4 servings

A *taste of summer*.

3 to 4 strips of bacon
1 onion, chopped
1 green pepper, cut into strips
4 ears of corn, kernels cut off
    cob, or 1 can (16 ounces)
    whole-kernel corn, drained,
    or 1 package (10 ounces)
    frozen corn, thawed

1. Fry bacon and remove from skillet.
2. Add onion and green pepper to bacon drippings and sauté until onion is clear.
3. Stir in corn. Cover and simmer 5 minutes. Garnish with crumbled bacon.

Eggplant Patties

Yield: 6 servings

1 medium eggplant
20 butter-flavored crackers, finely crushed
1¼ cups shredded American cheese
2 eggs, slightly beaten
2 tablespoons chopped parsley
2 tablespoons minced onion
¾ teaspoon garlic salt
½ teaspoon pepper

1. Pare, cube, and cook eggplant until tender. Drain well. Mash or whirl in food processor.
2. Add remaining ingredients. Drop by tablespoon (forming patties) into ¼ inch oil in skillet. Fry until well-browned, turning once.
3. Keep warm on paper towel on cookie sheet in oven while frying remaining patties. Serve warm.

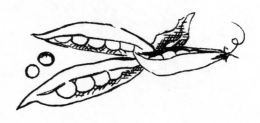

Mushroom Florentine

Yield: 6 servings

2 packages (10 ounces each)
  frozen chopped spinach
½ teaspoon salt
¼ cup chopped onion
6 tablespoons butter or
  margarine, melted and
  divided
1 cup grated Cheddar cheese,
  divided
1 pound fresh mushrooms
¼ teaspoon garlic powder

1. Cook spinach according to
   directions. Drain and squeeze dry.
   Spoon into shallow casserole.
2. Sprinkle spinach with salt, onion, 2
   tablespoons butter, and ½ cup
   grated cheese.
3. Rinse and dry mushrooms. Sauté
   in 4 tablespoons of butter or
   margarine.
4. Spoon mushrooms over cheese
   layer. Sprinkle with garlic powder
   and top with ½ cup Cheddar
   cheese. Bake.

Temperature: 350°
Time: 20 to 25 minutes

Hint: Broccoli may be substituted for the spinach.

Escalloped Mushrooms

Yield: 8 servings

A tasty alternative to traditional stuffing.

1½ pounds fresh mushrooms
1 medium onion, minced
½ cup butter or margarine
Salt and pepper to taste
1 cup milk
1 can (10¾ ounces) cream of
  mushroom soup
1 package (8 ounces) herb-
  seasoned stuffing mix

1. Sauté mushrooms and onion in
   butter. Season with salt and
   pepper.
2. Blend milk with mushroom soup.
3. In 2-quart dish make alternate
   layers of mushrooms, stuffing, and
   soup mixture, ending with stuffing
   layer on top.
4. Dot with butter. Bake.

Temperature: 350°
Time: 40 minutes

Hint: Try this as a side dish with game.

Hot Mushroom Cabbage

Yield: 6 to 8 servings

6 slices bacon
2 tablespoons butter
1 pound fresh mushrooms,
  sliced, or 16-ounce can,
  drained
¼ cup minced onion
4 cups thinly-sliced cabbage
½ cup water
3 tablespoons vinegar
1 tablespoon brown sugar
1 teaspoon salt
1 teaspoon dillweed
¼ teaspoon pepper

1. Saute' bacon in skillet. Crumble and set aside. Drain all but 2 tablespoons bacon fat from skillet.
2. Add butter to skillet and melt. Saute' mushrooms and onion for 5 minutes. Add remaining ingredients and bring to boiling point.
3. Reduce heat. Cover and simmer for 7 minutes or until cabbage is crisp tender.
4. Serve with crumbled bacon.

Green Pea Casserole

Yield: 10 servings

Mmmmm!

1 medium onion, chopped
½ green pepper, chopped
½ cup margarine
2 packages (10 ounces each)
  frozen peas, cooked and
  drained
1 can (10¾ ounces) cream of
  mushroom soup
1 can (8 ounces) water
  chestnuts, drained and
  sliced
1 jar (2 ounces) pimiento,
  chopped, optional

1. Saute' onion and green pepper in margarine.
2. Mix with remaining ingredients. Cover and bake.

Temperature: 350°
Time: 25 minutes

Savory Stuffed Onions

Yield: 6 servings

6 large white onions
6 slices of bacon
1 can (10¾ ounces) cream of mushroom soup
1 package (10 ounces) frozen chopped spinach, cooked and drained
1 tablespoon brown sugar
1 tablespoon vinegar

1. Cut off tops of onions. Scoop out, leaving last two rings intact. Chop onion centers.
2. Fry bacon until crisp; crumble.
3. Using one-half of the chopped onion, sauté in a little of the bacon drippings until tender.
4. Add soup, spinach, brown sugar, vinegar, and bacon to sautéed onions. Blend well.
5. Fill onion shells with spinach mixture. Place filled onion shells on baking sheet and cover with foil.
6. Bake until tender.

Temperature: 375°
Time: 30 to 45 minutes

Hint: When doubling recipe, do not double soup.

Buck's Taters

Yield: 6 servings

Great for cookouts.

6 baking potatoes
4 onions, thinly sliced
Seasoned salt
Pepper to taste
6 tablespoons butter

1. Peel potatoes. Make crosswise slices in potatoes about ¼ inch apart, being careful not to cut all the way through.
2. About every second slice in potato, insert slice of onion.
3. Sprinkle with seasoned salt and pepper. Place 1 tablespoon of butter on top and wrap each potato in foil.
4. Bake.

Temperature: 400°
Time: 1 hour

Potato Latkes (Pancakes)

Yield: 4 to 6 servings

Crispy and delicious.

2 cups grated raw potatoes

2 eggs, beaten

1 teaspoon salt

1 heaping tablespoon flour or
   matzo meal

Pinch of baking soda

1 small onion, grated

1. Grate raw potatoes into ice water. Squeeze out all water and measure. Mix with other ingredients.
2. Drop mixture by tablespoons into skillet with about ¼ inch of very hot oil. Flatten with spoon. Fry until brown and crisp on both sides.
3. Serve piping hot with sour cream or applesauce.

Hint: Great as a vegetable or at breakfast.

Springtime Potatoes

Yield: 4 servings

Colorful as spring!

1½ pounds small, new
   potatoes

½ cup sour cream

⅓ cup chopped, seeded
   cucumber

2 tablespoons chopped green
   onion

2 tablespoons chopped green
   pepper

2 tablespoons sliced radishes

1 tablespoon milk

½ teaspoon salt

Dash of pepper

1. Cook potatoes in boiling, salted water 15 to 25 minutes until tender. Drain.
2. Combine remaining ingredients in small saucepan. Cook over low heat, stirring often. Do not boil.
3. Pour sour cream mixture over hot potatoes and serve immediately.

Golden Potatoes

Yield: 8 servings

4 baking potatoes (about 4
  inches long)
¼ cup butter
½ teaspoon salt
¼ teaspoon garlic powder
Milk
3 ounces cream cheese, cut
  into small cubes
2 tablespoons minced onion
2 tablespoons minced parsley
1 cup shredded Cheddar
  cheese
Paprika

1. Bake potatoes at 400° for 1 hour
   or until done. Cut in half
   lengthwise.
2. Scoop out potatoes with spoon
   and combine with butter, salt, and
   garlic powder. Mash with potato
   masher, adding enough milk to
   make them fluffy. Fold in cream
   cheese, onion, and parsley.
3. Spoon potato mixture lightly into
   potato shells. Place on baking
   sheet. Sprinkle with Cheddar
   cheese; dust with paprika. Cover
   with plastic wrap and refrigerate
   overnight.
4. Heat potatoes at 450° for 25
   minutes or until cheese melts.

Temperature: 400°
Time: 1 hour

Temperature: 450°
Time: 25 minutes

Sweet Potato Casserole

Yield: 6 to 8 servings

3 medium sweet potatoes
6 tablespoons butter
1½ cups sugar
1 teaspoon vanilla
2 eggs
1 cup evaporated milk

Topping

6 tablespoons butter
¾ cup light brown sugar
1 cup crushed cornflakes
½ cup chopped pecans

1. Cook potatoes until tender. Peel and mash.
2. Cream butter and sugar together. Add to potatoes and mix well.
3. Add remaining ingredients to potato mixture and heat until thick, beating with hand mixer. Pour into 1½-quart casserole.
4. Bake at 350° for 10 minutes.

Topping

1. Melt butter; add remaining ingredients.
2. Spread on top of potato mixture. Bake 5 to 7 minutes or until browned.

Temperature: 350°
Time: 10 minutes
Time: 5 to 7 minutes

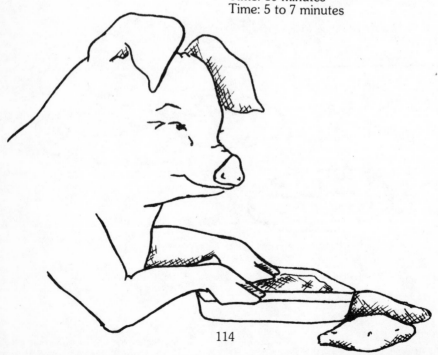

Cranberry Yams

Yield: 6 to 8 servings

This will become a family tradition.

½ cup packed brown sugar
½ cup flour
½ cup oats
1 teaspoon cinnamon
1 tablespoon margarine
2 cups fresh cranberries
2 cans (17 ounces each) yams
Marshmallows

1. Blend together sugar, flour, oats, cinnamon, and margarine.
2. Mix one cup of this mixture with cranberries and yams (including liquid from yams).
3. Put into casserole dish and sprinkle remaining mixture on top.
4. Bake at 350° for 35 minutes. After baking, top with marshmallows and return to oven until brown.

Temperature: 350°
Time: 35 minutes

Spinach And Artichoke Casserole

Yield: 6 to 8 servings

Very tasty and different!

3 boxes (10 ounces each) frozen chopped spinach
1 can (10¾ ounces) cream of celery soup
2 slices white bread soaked in milk
1 egg, beaten
1 can (14 ounces) artichoke hearts, drained and squeezed
Salt
Pepper
Garlic
Parmesan cheese
Butter

1. Cook and drain spinach.
2. Add soup, bread, and egg; season the mixture with salt, pepper, and garlic to taste.
3. Grease large casserole dish, and line bottom with artichoke hearts.
4. Place a large layer of spinach mixture on top; then sprinkle with a thick layer of Parmesan cheese.
5. Continue to alternate spinach and cheese layers.
6. Sprinkle top with cheese, and dot with butter. Bake.

Temperature: 350°
Time: 30 to 45 minutes

Fresh Spinach Quiche

Yield: 6 servings

The aroma will win the hardest to please.

1 unbaked pie shell (9-inch)
½ pound freshly-torn spinach
1 tablespoon butter or
   margarine
1 medium onion, chopped
6 slices cooked and crumbled
   bacon
1 cup (4 ounces) shredded
   Swiss cheese
4 eggs
2 cups light cream
½ teaspoon salt
½ teaspoon pepper

1. Prick pie shell and bake at 400°
   for 8 minutes.
2. Cook spinach 8 to 10 minutes in
   salted water. Drain and squeeze
   off excess water.
3. Melt butter in skillet, add onion,
   and saute' until tender.
4. Sprinkle bacon and cheese in the
   pastry shell; top with spinach.
5. Beat eggs until foamy; add cream,
   salt, pepper, and sautéed onion.
   Mix well and pour into pastry
   shell.
6. Bake for 1 hour at 350° until knife
   inserted into center comes out
   clean.
7. Remove from oven. Allow to cool
   10 minutes before serving.

Temperature: 400°
Time: 8 minutes

Temperature: 350°
Time: 1 hour

Hint: Freezes well.

Yellow Squash Casserole

Yield: 8 servings

5 or 6 small squash, sliced
1 medium onion, chopped
8 ounces cream cheese
3 tablespoons sugar
Salt
½ cup butter or margarine
2 stacks crushed butter-
   flavored crackers

1. Cook squash and onion until
   tender. Drain off excess water.
2. Mix in cream cheese, sugar, and
   salt. Place in buttered 1½-quart
   casserole.
3. Melt butter or margarine. Add
   cracker crumbs. Sprinkle on top of
   casserole. Bake.

Temperature: 325°
Time: 45 minutes

Stuffed Acorn Squash

Yield: 4 servings

2 acorn squash
½ cup bread crumbs
¼ cup chopped onion
¼ cup chopped green pepper
4 ounces grated sharp
   Cheddar cheese
2 tablespoons melted butter
Salt and pepper to taste
Paprika

1. Cut squash in half and scrape out seeds.
2. Place in greased baking dish with skin side up and bake at 350° until tender (about 30 minutes).
3. Scrape pulp into bowl, being careful to keep shell intact. Mix pulp with bread crumbs, onion, green pepper, Cheddar cheese, and butter. Season with salt and pepper.
4. Stuff shells with mixture and sprinkle with paprika.
5. Heat in 350° oven until hot.

Temperature: 350°
Time: 30 minutes

Italian Zucchini

Yield: 6 to 8 servings

Rich and delicious.

4 small zucchini
1 large onion
1 small green pepper
¼ cup cooking oil
1¼ teaspoons salt
¼ teaspoon garlic salt
¼ teaspoon pepper
¼ teaspoon oregano
1 can (16 ounces) tomatoes
¼ cup grated Parmesan
   cheese

1. Wash zucchini and remove ends. Do not peel; cut into ½-inch slices. Cut onion and pepper into rings.
2. Heat oil in 12-inch skillet; place zucchini in skillet and lightly brown on both sides. Add onion and green pepper.
3. Sprinkle in salt, garlic salt, pepper, and oregano. Top with tomatoes. Cover; bring to a boil and simmer 15 minutes.
4. Uncover; sprinkle cheese over vegetables and simmer 15 minutes, or until zucchini is tender and a fairly thick sauce is formed.

Hint: Try adding 1½ cups cooked meat to the recipe for a complete meal.

117

Stuffed Zucchini

Yield: 10 servings

6 medium zucchini

3 cups bread crumbs

½ cup grated Parmesan
  cheese

1 small onion, minced

3 tablespoons minced parsley

1 teaspoon salt

½ teaspoon pepper

2 beaten eggs

4 tablespoons butter

1. Parboil the zucchini
   approximately 30 minutes. Cut
   zucchini in half lengthwise.
2. Scoop out pulp carefully, leaving
   shells intact. Mix pulp with
   remaining ingredients. Stuff shells
   with mixture. Place on baking
   sheet and bake.

Temperature: 350°
Time: 30 minutes

Tomato-Green Bean Casserole

Yield: 8 servings

Interesting combination of two favorites.

4 strips bacon

2 cups stewed tomatoes

1 quart canned green beans

1 teaspoon Worcestershire
  sauce

½ teaspoon salt

Dash pepper

Dash cayenne pepper

2 tablespoons mayonnaise

1 cup buttered bread crumbs

1. Fry bacon until crisp; crumble and
   set aside.
2. Pour off bacon drippings; add
   tomatoes to skillet and simmer a
   few minutes.
3. Add bacon, beans, seasonings,
   and mayonnaise. Heat thoroughly.
4. Place in greased 1½-quart baking
   dish.
5. Cover with buttered crumbs and
   bake.

Temperature: 350°
Time: 15 minutes

Hint: May be made ahead and baked at the last minute.

Spinach-Stuffed Tomatoes

Yield: 8 servings

Add special elegance to any meal.

8 medium tomatoes

Salt to taste

2 packages (10 ounces each)
   frozen chopped spinach

1 cup bread crumbs

1 cup grated Parmesan cheese

3 green onions, chopped

2 eggs

3 tablespoons melted butter

½ teaspoon thyme

½ teaspoon monosodium
   glutamate

¼ teaspoon garlic salt

Dash of hot sauce

Salt and pepper to taste

1. Cut off tops of tomatoes and remove pulp, leaving shells intact.
2. Sprinkle inside of shells with salt; invert to drain.
3. Cook spinach according to package directions; drain well.
4. Combine spinach with remaining ingredients. Spoon into tomatoes.
5. Place tomatoes in flat baking dish and bake.

Temperature: 325°
Time: 30 minutes

Turnip Souffle'

Yield: 8 servings

Presto! A royal dish from the lowly turnip.

4 cups mashed turnips

½ cup butter

1 rounded teaspoon salt

2 tablespoons sugar

2 cups bread cubes

4 eggs, well beaten

1. Cook turnips in boiling water. Drain and mash while hot.
2. Add butter to hot turnips, stir until melted.
3. Mix in salt, sugar, and bread cubes.
4. Add eggs and pour into buttered 1½-quart baking dish.
5. Bake.

Temperature: 350°
Time: 45 minutes

Bill's "Stuff"

Yield: 4 to 6 servings

A wonderful dish for gardeners.

4 medium potatoes
5 medium carrots
2 medium zucchini squash
4 medium yellow squash
1 pound small fresh
   mushrooms
2 medium onions
1 head broccoli (separated
   into small bunches)
5 tablespoons oil
¼ teaspoon salt
2 ounces honey
5 slices American cheese

1. Slice potatoes, carrots, squash, mushrooms, and onions.
2. Heat oil at medium temperature in a large skillet. Put in potatoes and carrots. Cook until tender. Add other vegetables and sprinkle with salt.
3. Cook about 5 minutes, stirring often.
4. Turn heat down and pour honey over vegetables; arrange cheese on top.
5. Allow cheese to melt and stir.

Cheese-Topped Tomatoes

Yield: 4 servings

Great on the grill!

2 tomatoes
¾ cup soft bread crumbs
½ cup (2 ounces) shredded
   sharp cheese
2 tablespoons butter, melted
2 tablespoons parsley
Salt and pepper

1. Slice each tomato in half.
2. Sprinkle cut surfaces with salt and pepper.
3. Combine bread crumbs, cheese, and butter. Sprinkle mixture over tomatoes.
4. Garnish with parsley and wrap each tomato half loosely with a square of heavy foil.
5. Grill over medium-hot coals until heated through.

Temperature: Medium hot coals
Time: 15 to 20 minutes

Savory Lemon Vegetables

Yield: 8 servings

A spectacular buffet item.

2 pounds carrots

1 medium head cauliflower or
    2 packages (10 ounces
    each) frozen cauliflower

½ pound bacon

1 cup chopped onion

½ cup lemon juice

½ cup water

4 teaspoons sugar

1 teaspoon salt

1 teaspoon thyme

1. Cut carrots into thin slices and cook in boiling water until tender; drain.
2. Break apart cauliflower and cook in boiling water until tender; drain.
3. Cook bacon, reserving drippings. Crumble and set aside.
4. In bacon drippings, saute' onions until translucent. Add remaining ingredients and bring to a boil.
5. Arrange cauliflower in center of round bowl. Encircle the mound with carrots.
6. Pour on hot mixture. Sprinkle with crumbled bacon.

Hint: Leftovers may be refrigerated and reheated in oven. For additional color, you might add broccoli.

Carrots Lyonnaise

Yield: 6 to 8 servings

A beautiful dish!

4 tablespoons butter or
    margarine, divided

1 large onion, thinly sliced

2 pounds carrots, pared and
    cut into 2-inch sticks

¼ teaspoon salt

2 tablespoons lemon juice

2 tablespoons parsley

Fresh ground pepper to taste

1. Melt 3 tablespoons butter in skillet. Sauté onion until tender and golden. Remove from skillet with slotted spoon.
2. Add remaining tablespoon butter to skillet. Toss carrots in skillet over medium heat to coat with butter. Cover and lower heat. Cook 15 minutes until carrots are tender.
3. Uncover; continue to cook until liquid evaporates. Season with lemon juice, parsley, salt, and pepper.
4. Return onions; toss with carrots and serve.

Hot Curried Fruit

Yield: 10 to 12 servings

1 can (29 ounces) pear halves
1 can (20 ounces) pineapple
  chunks
1 can (29 ounces) peach
  halves
1 can (29 ounces) apricot
  halves
½ cup butter
1 cup brown sugar
1 tablespoon cornstarch
1½ teaspoons curry powder

1. Drain fruit well. Place in 9 x 13-inch casserole dish.
2. Make a paste from remaining ingredients; spoon over fruit.
3. Bake at 325° for 1 hour, basting occasionally.

Temperature: 325°
Time: 1 hour

Hint: May be made ahead and baked just before serving.

Hot Cranberry Casserole

Yield: 8 to 10 servings

Serve as a side dish or over vanilla ice cream.

3 cups chopped apples
2 cups whole raw cranberries
1 teaspoon lemon juice
1½ cups sugar
1⅓ cups uncooked, quick-cooking oatmeal
1 cup chopped walnuts
⅓ cup packed brown sugar
½ cup margarine, melted

1. Spray 2-quart casserole dish with oil.
2. Place chopped apples and raw cranberries in dish. Sprinkle with lemon juice. Cover with sugar.
3. In medium mixing bowl, blend, just to moisten oatmeal, walnuts, brown sugar, and melted margarine. Pour over fruit.
4. Bake uncovered.

Temperature: 325°
Time: 1¼ hours

Escalloped Pineapple

Yield: 6 to 8 servings

A side dish or dessert. It's delicious hot or cold.

2 cups sugar
½ cup butter, melted
2 eggs
½ cup cream
1 can (20 ounces) chunk
   pineapple
1 quart fresh bread cubes (10
   slices)

1. Mix sugar and butter. Add eggs, stirring well.
2. Stir in cream and pineapple with juice.
3. Fold in bread cubes and pour into greased 9 x 12-inch glass baking dish.
4. Bake.

Temperature: 325°
Time: 40 minutes

Southern Fried Apples

Yield: 8 servings

A comforting addition to breakfast.

8 ounces sliced bacon
10 large cooking apples (2
   quarts sliced)
½ cup sugar
½ cup brown sugar

1. Cut bacon into 1-inch pieces. Fry until crisp. Drain, leaving 4 tablespoons of drippings in skillet. Set bacon aside.
2. Wash apples. Cut unpeeled apples into fourths and remove core. Slice into ¼-inch slices.
3. Lightly brown sliced apples in skillet. Sprinkle with sugars.
4. Cover and cook over low heat until tender.
5. Remove cover and let simmer, stirring frequently and gently, until liquid disappears.
6. Serve with bacon pieces on top.

Hot Fruit Compote
Yield: 10 to 12 servings

A most comforting dish - just good fruit flavor.

1 can (16 ounces) sliced peaches, drained

1 can (16 ounces) pear halves, drained and coarsely chopped

1 can (16 ounces) whole purple plums, drained and pitted

1 can (20 ounces) pineapple chunks, drained

1 jar (6 ounces) maraschino cherries, drained

2 bananas, sliced

¾ cup packed brown sugar

⅓ cup butter

1 can (16 ounces) applesauce

3 tablespoons brown sugar

½ cup chopped pecans

1. Combine first six ingredients in 9 x 13 x 2-inch baking dish. Set aside.
2. Combine ¾ cup brown sugar, butter, and applesauce in a saucepan. Heat thoroughly, stirring occasionally.
3. Spoon applesauce mixture over fruit. Sprinkle with 3 tablespoons brown sugar and pecans. Bake; serve hot.

Temperature: 300°
Time: 1 hour

Hint: Compote may be prepared ahead. Cover baking dish with plastic wrap and freeze. To serve, let thaw overnight in refrigerator; bake according to directions.

Broiled Grapefruit

Grapefruit
Sugar and cinnamon mixture
Whole maraschino cherries

1. Halve grapefruit and loosen sections.
2. Sprinkle liberally with sugar mixture and place cherry in center.
3. Broil until hot and bubbly.

Meats

Meats

Beef Roulades

Yield: 12 servings

Prepare ahead and enjoy your guests.

1¾ pounds ground pork
1 teaspoon poultry seasoning
¾ teaspoon salt
½ clove garlic, crushed
2 tablespoons chopped onion
¼ cup bread crumbs
3 pounds sirloin tip, sliced
   thickness of bacon
Bacon
¼ cup melted shortening
1 pound white onions, thickly
   sliced
⅓ cup flour
1 can (10½ ounces) beef
   bouillon
2½ cups red Burgundy wine
1½ pounds fresh mushrooms,
   sliced
1 bay leaf
1 tablespoon chopped parsley

Hint: Freezes well.

1. Combine ground pork, poultry seasoning, salt, garlic, chopped onion, and bread crumbs.
2. Form pork mixture into 2-inch balls and place each on slice of beef. Roll up from short side. Wrap with ½ slice bacon and tie with twine.
3. Melt shortening in Dutch oven and brown roulades and onion slices.
4. Remove roulades from Dutch oven. Stir flour into meat drippings and onions; gradually stir in bouillon and wine. Bring to boil, stirring constantly.
5. Return roulades to Dutch oven with mushrooms and bay leaf. Cover and bake.
6. Discard bay leaf and twine from roulades.
7. Sprinkle with parsley and serve.

Temperature: 350°
Time: 2 hours or until tender

Flank Steak Bordelaise

Yield: 4 servings

Low cost, pretty, and delicious!

⅓ cup wine vinegar

⅓ cup vegetable oil

¼ cup chopped onion

1 tablespoon Worcestershire
   sauce

½ teaspoon salt

2 cloves garlic, minced

¼ teaspoon dry mustard

1 pound beef flank steak

1. In plastic bag combine vinegar, oil, onion, Worcestershire, salt, garlic, and dry mustard. Add steak.
2. Tie bag and place in bowl. Refrigerate 6 to 12 hours, turning bag occasionally to distribute marinade.
3. Prepare sauce.
4. Prepare vegetables.
5. Remove steak from marinade and pat dry. Place on unheated rack or broiler pan. Discard marinade.
6. Broil steak 4 inches from heat for 12 to 14 minutes (rare), turning halfway through cooking time.
7. Slice steak thinly across grain.
8. To serve, arrange zucchini and carrot mixture on serving platter. Place meat slices on top. Spoon some sauce over meat. Garnish with carrot curls.
9. Serve remaining sauce as an accompaniment.

Sauce

3 green onions, chopped

2 tablespoons butter or
   margarine

1 tablespoon flour

½ teaspoon dried thyme,
   crushed

1 can (10½ ounces)
   condensed beef broth

½ cup dry red wine

Sauce

1. In saucepan, cook green onions in butter or margarine until tender.
2. Blend in flour and thyme.
3. Add broth and wine. Bring to boil.
4. Simmer uncovered for 15 minutes or until reduced to 1 cup.
5. Keep sauce warm.

Flank Steak Bordelaise, continued

Vegetables

4 cups coarsely-shredded
   zucchini
1 cup coarsely-shredded
   carrots
1 clove garlic, minced
2 tablespoons butter or
   margarine
⅓ cup chopped walnuts,
   optional
Salt
Pepper
Carrot curls, optional

Vegetables

1. Combine zucchini, carrots, and garlic.
2. Place in steamer basket over boiling water and steam for 5 minutes (until tender).
3. Stir in butter or margarine.
4. Add walnuts, if desired.
5. Season with salt and pepper. Keep warm.

Hint: Beef tenderloin may be substituted.

Beef Roast On The Grill   Yield: 6 servings

Tender and juicy with a different taste!

1 cup soy sauce
6 tablespoons sugar
3 cloves garlic, minced, or 1
   teaspoon garlic powder
1 teaspoon ginger
3 tablespoons lemon juice
1 lean roast, 3 to 4 pounds

1. Mix soy sauce, sugar, garlic, ginger, and lemon juice.
2. Cover roast with mixture; marinate in refrigerator for 24 hours, occasionally turning roast.
3. Cook roast on grill for approximately 20 minutes on each side, or until done.

T.C.'s Wellington

Yield: 8 servings

8 filet mignon steaks
Salt
Pepper
8 canned artichoke hearts
8 large mushroom caps
1 can (8 ounces) refrigerator
  crescent rolls
2 egg whites, slightly beaten

1. Broil filets until almost done.
   Bottom of filet should be lightly
   seared to seal in juices.
2. Season filets with salt and pepper
   and set aside to cool.
3. Place one mushroom cap over
   artichoke heart and arrange on
   each filet.
4. Using crescent dough, completely
   cover each filet, sealing carefully.
5. Brush egg whites on uncooked
   dough to form glaze.
6. Brown lightly in oven.

Temperature: 350°
Time: Until lightly browned

Sauce
1 can (10¾ ounces) cream of
  mushroom soup
8 ounces sour cream
Paprika

Sauce
1. Mix soup and sour cream and
   heat.
2. Serve over Wellington and
   sprinkle with paprika.

Peppercorn Steak With Sauce

Yield: 4 servings

4 tenderloin, rib-eye, or strip
   steaks
2 tablespoons vegetable oil,
   divided
2 tablespoons cracked pepper
2 tablespoons butter
Parsley

1. Dry steaks thoroughly on paper towels; rub with tablespoon of oil.
2. Press pepper into each side of steaks with heel of hand.
3. Let steaks stand for an hour or two, allowing flavor to penetrate the meat.
4. Saute' steaks on each side in 1 tablespoon of hot oil and butter. They are cooked medium rare when they feel slightly resistant to finger and when faint pearling of red juices appears at surface.
5. Remove steak to hot serving platter.
6. Prepare sauce and pour over steaks. Garnish with parsley.

Sauce

1 teaspoon cornstarch
¼ cup beef bouillon
2 tablespoons minced green
   onions or shallots
½ cup dry white vermouth
2 tablespoons butter

Sauce

1. Spoon out excess fat from skillet.
2. Combine cornstarch and beef bouillon.
3. Combine bouillon mixture, minced onions, and vermouth in skillet.
4. Simmer, scraping up meat drippings with wooden spoon, until sauce has thickened.
5. Remove from heat. Swirl in butter and pour sauce over steak.

Pepper Steak

Yield: 4 servings

1½ pounds round or sirloin
   steak, ½-inch thick
¼ cup salad oil
1 cup beef bouillon
1 onion, cut into ¼-inch slices
1 clove garlic, minced
2 green peppers, cut into ¾-
   inch strips
1 tablespoon cornstarch
1 tablespoons soy sauce
Hot cooked rice

1. Trim fat from meat and cut into 1-inch strips.
2. Heat oil in large skillet. Brown meat in oil, turning frequently while cooking.
3. Stir in bouillon, onion, and garlic. Heat to boiling.
4. Reduce heat; cover and simmer 12 to 15 minutes for round steak, 4 to 8 minutes for sirloin.
5. Add green peppers during last 5 minutes of simmering.
6. Blend cornstarch and soy sauce. Stir into meat mixture.
7. Cook, stirring constantly, until mixture thickens and boils. Boil one minute, stirring constantly.
8. Serve over hot rice.

Doc's Stuffed Steak

Yield: 4 servings

Everyone will love these!

4 beef tenderloin steaks, 1¼ to
   1½-inches thick
Soy sauce
1 box (6 ounces) Uncle Ben's®
   Original Long Grain and
   Wild Rice
1 egg, beaten
Pepper to taste
Garlic salt to taste

1. Marinate steaks in soy sauce for 2 to 3 hours at room temperature, turning at least once.
2. Cook wild rice mix according to package directions. Let cool and add beaten egg, mixing well.
3. Cut pocket in each steak lengthwise; stuff with rice. Secure with toothpicks.
4. Charcoal broil to desired doneness. Serve any remaining rice with steaks.

Pan-Barbecued Steak

Yield: 6 servings

Very tasty and so easy!

1 round steak, about 2
  pounds
½ teaspoon salt (or garlic salt)
½ teaspoon pepper
3 tablespoons shortening
1 onion, chopped
1 tablespoon celery seed
1 clove garlic, chopped
4 tablespoons brown sugar
4 tablespoons prepared
  mustard
3 tablespoons Worcestershire
  sauce
2 tablespoons lemon juice
1 can (10¾ ounces) tomato
  soup

1. Sprinkle steak with salt and
   pepper.
2. Melt shortening in heavy skillet;
   brown steak with onion, celery
   seed, and garlic.
3. Add remaining ingredients;
   simmer, covered, for 1½ hours.
   Check after 45 minutes; add a
   little water, if necessary, and stir.

Marinated Beef
Shish Kabobs

Yield: 6 to 8 servings

2 pounds sirloin, 1½-inches
  thick
⅔ cup vegetable oil
¼ cup soy sauce
3 tablespoons honey
2 tablespoons vinegar
1½ teaspoons ginger
1 clove garlic, crushed
8 ounces fresh mushrooms

1. Cut steaks into 1½-inch cubes.
2. Combine next 6 ingredients and
   pour over meat. Let stand 1 to 3
   hours.
3. Place meat cubes and mushrooms
   on skewers, alternately.
4. Cook on grill, turning once.
   (Cooking time varies with steak
   preference.)

Marinated Eye Of Round

Yield: 8 servings

Excellent main course, easily prepared, and a real man-pleaser!

½ cup butter
Garlic salt
Pepper
Juice of 2 lemons
8 ounces Kentucky bourbon
2½ pounds eye of round roast

1. Combine butter, garlic salt, pepper, lemon juice, and bourbon in saucepan; boil about two minutes.
2. Pour marinade over roast; marinate four hours, or overnight, turning occasionally.
3. Cook on grill for 30 to 40 minutes (rare), basting with marinade intermittently.
4. Serve immediately, using remaining marinade as an accompaniment.

One Meal Brisket

Yield: 8 servings

A whole meal and so good!

7 pounds brisket
2 cans (12 ounces each) beer
2 bottles (12 ounces each) chili sauce
3 tablespoons A.1.® Steak Sauce from Del Monte
3 tablespoons Heinz 57® Sauce
1 bottle (14 ounces) catsup
Dash Worcestershire sauce
Dash hot pepper sauce
4 onions, cut into pieces
7 carrots, sliced
6 potatoes, cut into pieces
3 celery stalks, sliced

1. Preheat oven to 250°.
2. Place beef brisket in large baking dish or roaster.
3. Mix next seven ingredients and pour over brisket. Place in oven and bake for 2 hours.
4. Add vegetables to pan and continue baking for 2 additional hours until done.

Temperature: 250°
Time: 4 hours

Hint: Leftovers make delicious sandwiches!

Zucchini-Beef Casserole

Yield: 6 to 8 servings

Shortening
2 pounds zucchini squash
2½ teaspoons salt, divided
1½ pounds ground round beef
1 can (15½ ounces) tomato
    sauce
½ teaspoon pepper
1 cup mozzarella cheese,
    shredded

1. Grease 13 x 9-inch baking dish.
2. Wash and peel squash. Slice lengthwise (about ¼-inch thick) and place overlapping layers in dish, using half of squash. Sprinkle with 1 teaspoon salt.
3. Brown meat; drain well.
4. Add tomato sauce, ½ teaspoon salt, and pepper to meat; simmer for 2 minutes. Spread this mixture over squash.
5. Sprinkle with 1 cup mozzarella cheese.
6. Place another layer of squash over meat and cheese.
7. Sprinkle squash with remaining 1 teaspoon salt.
8. Prepare cream sauce and pour over squash.
9. Bake at 350° for 1 hour or until squash tests tender with fork and top is lightly browned.

Sauce
2 tablespoons margarine
2 tablespoons flour
1¼ cups milk
1 cup mozzarella cheese,
    shredded

Sauce
1. Melt margarine; stir in flour.
2. Remove from heat and slowly add milk.
3. Return to heat and bring to boil, stirring until thick.
4. Add cheese.
5. When mixture is smooth and creamy, spread evenly over top of squash.

Temperature: 350°
Time: 1 hour

Hint: This casserole may be baked for ½ hour, cooled to room temperature, and frozen.

Beef Casserole Delight
Yield: 12 servings

Water chestnuts add a nice texture!

2 pounds ground beef
1 cup chopped celery
¼ cup chopped green pepper
¾ cup chopped onion
½ cup margarine
1 can (29 ounces) tomatoes
1 can (16 ounces) tomatoes
1 can (8 ounces) mushroom
   pieces, drained
1 can (8 ounces) water
   chestnuts, drained and
   sliced
1 cup cubed American cheese
½ cup chopped green olives
½ cup chopped black olives
½ teaspoon salt
¼ teaspoon pepper
6 ounces egg noodles,
   uncooked
2 cups shredded Cheddar
   cheese

1. Brown ground beef; drain.
2. Saute' celery, green pepper, and onion in margarine.
3. Add tomatoes and their juices.
4. Add all remaining ingredients, except Cheddar cheese, and simmer 20 minutes. Pour into 13 x 9-inch pan.
5. Sprinkle Cheddar cheese on top and bake.

Temperature: 350°
Time: 40 minutes

Wok Supper (or Stir-Fry Supper)

Yield: 6 servings

Eye and palate pleasing!

1 pound round steak
¼ cup soy sauce
1 tablespoon sherry
⅓ cup plus 2 tablespoons
 peanut oil, divided
1 teaspoon ginger
1 clove garlic, crushed
2 cups fresh broccoli florets
1 onion, sliced
1 large tomato, coarsely
 chopped
1 cup sugar snap peas
1 cup fresh mushrooms, sliced
 in halves
1 tablespoon cornstarch
¼ cup water

1. Slice steak into very thin diagonal pieces.
2. Mix together soy sauce, sherry, ⅓ cup oil, ginger, and garlic; pour mixture over steak. Marinate in refrigerator 3 to 12 hours.
3. Heat wok until very hot. Cook steak and marinade, stirring constantly. Remove steak mixture; set aside.
4. Add 2 tablespoons oil to wok. Stir-fry broccoli and onion for two minutes.
5. Add tomatoes, peas, mushrooms, and half of steak marinade to broccoli mixture. Cover and steam for five minutes.
6. Combine cornstarch with ¼ cup water; add to vegetables, along with meat and remaining marinade. Stir until thickened.
7. Serve with rice.

137

Deep-Dish Taco Squares

Yield: 4 to 6 servings

½ pound ground beef
1 envelope (1¼ ounces) taco
  seasoning
½ cup sour cream
⅓ cup mayonnaise
¾ cup shredded Cheddar
  cheese
1 tablespoon chopped onion
1 cup biscuit mix
¼ cup cold water
1 to 2 medium tomatoes,
  thinly sliced
½ cup chopped green pepper
Paprika

1. Brown ground beef in skillet;
   drain. Stir in taco seasoning.
2. Mix sour cream, mayonnaise,
   cheese, and onion. Reserve.
3. Combine biscuit mix and ¼ cup
   cold water to form soft dough. Pat
   dough into 8 x 8 x 2-inch greased
   baking dish, pressing dough ½
   inch up sides of dish.
4. Layer beef, tomatoes, and green
   pepper over dough. Spoon sour
   cream mixture over top; sprinkle
   with paprika.
5. Bake until edges of dough are
   light brown.

Temperature: 375°
Time: 40 to 50 minutes

Swiss Liver

Yield: 4 servings

Liver can be beautiful!

¾ pounds calves liver
Seasoned flour
4 tablespoons butter
1 clove garlic or 2 teaspoons
  grated onion, optional
1 teaspoon lemon juice
1 or 2 tablespoons dry white
  wine

1. Cut liver into 2½ x ½-inch strips.
2. Roll strips in seasoned flour, one
   at a time. Place on rack to dry.
3. Melt butter (with garlic or onion, if
   desired) over medium heat.
4. Add liver, stirring to prevent
   sticking. Brown lightly; turn.
5. Add lemon juice and wine.
6. Serve hot.

Beef Enchiladas

Yield: 8 to 10 servings

Serve this with Jalapeño Rice.

1½ pounds ground beef
3 cups shredded Monterey
    Jack cheese, divided
¾ cup diced green onions
¾ cup sour cream
3 tablespoons fresh parsley
1½ teaspoons salt
¼ teaspoon pepper
12 to 16 flour tortillas
¼ cup chopped black olives,
    optional

1. Brown beef; drain, and remove from heat.
2. Stir in 2 cups cheese, green onions, sour cream, parsley, salt, and pepper. Cover and set aside.
3. Prepare sauce.
4. Cook tortillas, one at a time, on greased hot griddle until golden brown, turning once.
5. Spoon about ¼ cup beef filling into each tortilla; roll tortilla around filling and arrange in 2 ungreased 12 x 7 x 2-inch baking dishes.
6. Pour sauce over enchiladas and sprinkle with remaining cheese.
7. Bake uncovered at 350° for 20 to 30 minutes (until bubbly).
8. Garnish with olives, if desired.

Sauce

½ cup diced green pepper
4 tablespoons seeded and
    chopped hot green chilies
1 tablespoon chili powder
3 cans (8 ounces each)
    tomato sauce
¼ teaspoon ground cumin

Sauce
1. Combine all ingredients in saucepan.
2. Bring to boil; reduce heat and simmer uncovered for 5 minutes.

Temperature: 350°
Time: 20 to 30 minutes

Hint: May make enchiladas and sauce ahead. Pour sauce over enchiladas and sprinkle with cheese before cooking.

Spaghetti Pie

Yield: 6 servings

Attractive and tasty!

6 ounces spaghetti

2 tablespoons butter or margarine

⅓ cup grated Parmesan cheese

2 eggs, well beaten

1 pound ground beef or Italian sausage (may use ½ pound of each)

1 medium onion, chopped

1 can (8 ounces) tomatoes, chopped

1 can (6 ounces) tomato paste

1 teaspoon sugar

1 teaspoon dried oregano, crushed

½ teaspoon garlic salt

1 cup cottage or ricotta cheese

1 cup shredded mozzarella cheese

1. Cook spaghetti according to package directions; drain.
2. Stir butter or margarine into hot spaghetti.
3. Add in Parmesan cheese and eggs.
4. Form spaghetti mixture into a crust in buttered 9-inch pie plate. Set aside.
5. In skillet, brown meat and onion. Drain excess fat.
6. Stir in undrained tomatoes, tomato paste, sugar, oregano, and garlic salt. Heat thoroughly.
7. Spread cottage or ricotta cheese over bottom of spaghetti crust.
8. Fill pie with meat and tomato mixture.
9. Bake uncovered for 20 minutes.
10. Sprinkle mozzarella cheese on top. Bake 5 minutes longer or until cheese melts.

Temperature: 350°
Time: 20 minutes
      5 minutes (with cheese)

Beef Parmigiana

Yield: 4 servings

1½ to 2 pounds sirloin steak

½ cup grated Parmesan
  cheese

½ cup fine, dry bread crumbs

1 egg, beaten

⅓ cup oil

1 medium onion, minced

1 teaspoon salt

½ teaspoon sugar

½ teaspoon marjoram

1 can (6 ounces) tomato paste

2 cups hot water

½ pound mozzarella cheese,
  sliced

1. Pound meat to ¼-inch thickness. Trim fat and cut into approximately 8 pieces.
2. Combine Parmesan cheese and bread crumbs.
3. Dip meat in egg; roll in crumb mixture.
4. Heat oil in skillet and brown steak on both sides over medium heat until golden brown.
5. Place browned meat in shallow baking dish.
6. In same skillet, cook onion until tender. Stir in seasonings and tomato paste. Add hot water and stir well.
7. Pour most of sauce over meat. Top with cheese slices and remaining sauce. Bake.

Temperature: 325°
Time: 35 to 45 minutes

Hints: 1. For spicier sauce, add one or two cloves of minced garlic and ½ teaspoon oregano.
2. Double sauce recipe if serving with spaghetti.
3. May be assembled a day ahead and refrigerated. Let come to room temperature before baking to ensure proper baking time.

Lasagna With Meat Sauce

Yield: 8 servings

½ cup chopped onion
1 clove garlic, minced
2 tablespoons oil
½ pound ground round or ground chuck beef
2 Italian sausages, chopped
1 can (2 pounds 3 ounces) tomatoes, chopped
1 can (6 ounces) tomato paste
2 teaspoons crumbled leaf basil
2 teaspoons crumbled leaf oregano
2 teaspoons salt
¼ teaspoon pepper
8 ounces lasagna noodles
1 pound ricotta cheese
16 ounces mozzarella cheese, sliced
1 box (3 ounces) grated Parmesan cheese

1. In large skillet, saute' onion and garlic in oil until translucent. Add beef and sausage; brown. Drain all but 2 tablespoons fat from skillet.
2. Stir in tomatoes, tomato paste, basil, oregano, salt, and pepper. Simmer, uncovered, stirring frequently for 45 minutes or until sauce thickens.
3. While sauce simmers, cook lasagna noodles, following package directions. Drain and place in bowl of cold water to prevent sticking.
4. To assemble, drain noodles and spoon a little sauce on bottom of 13 x 9 x 2-inch baking dish. Arrange 3 strips of noodles over sauce; spoon on ⅓ of Ricotta cheese, ⅓ of mozzarella cheese slices, and ⅓ of Parmesan cheese. Spoon more sauce.
5. Continue layering until all ingredients have been used. Top with mozzarella cheese.
6. Bake.

Temperature: 350°
Time: 45 minutes

Burtoni's Marinara Sauce

Yield: 4 to 6 servings

1 clove garlic, minced
Oregano
Basil
Thyme
3 tablespoons olive oil
1 can (16 ounces) stewed
    tomatoes, well drained and
    mashed
1 can (16 ounces) tomato
    sauce
1 can (6 ounces) tomato paste
1 to 2 tablespoons sugar
1 pound thin spaghetti
Parmesan cheese, fresh
    grated

1. Saute' garlic and spices in olive oil for 2 or 3 minutes.
2. Add stewed tomatoes, tomato sauce, and tomato paste; stir.
3. Add sugar; stir well.
4. Simmer 30 minutes.
5. While sauce is simmering, bring 4 quarts of salted water to boil; add spaghetti and cook until firm. Drain.
6. Serve spaghetti with sauce on top; sprinkle with cheese.

Hints: 1. A pound of browned ground chuck or Italian sausage (or ½ pound of each) may be added to sauce before simmering. May need to add 1 to 1½ cups of water to thin sauce.
2. Sauce freezes well.

Meatloaf Supreme

Yield: 8 servings

A *flavorful treat!*

6 slices bacon
3 eggs
2 teaspoons salt
¼ teaspoon pepper
¼ teaspoon thyme
Pinch of ground cloves
¼ cup milk
¼ cup sour cream
1 cup bread crumbs
1½ pounds ground beef
½ pound pork sausage
2 tablespoons finely chopped onion
2 tablespoons chopped parsley

1. Partially cook bacon; drain.
2. Beat eggs with spices. Stir in milk, sour cream, and bread crumbs. Let stand 5 minutes.
3. Add ground beef, pork sausage, onion, and parsley; blend well.
4. Form into loaf and place in shallow pan. Arrange bacon on top.
5. Bake 45 minutes at 350°.

Sauce

½ cup chili sauce
2 tablespoons light brown sugar
¼ teaspoon dry mustard

Sauce

1. Combine ingredients for sauce.
2. Spread sauce over meatloaf, and return to oven for 15 minutes longer.

Temperature: 350°
Time: 45 minutes
      15 minutes (with sauce)

Spicy Meatloaf

Yield: 6 servings

Prepare this in the morning and bake it in the evening.

3 slices soft bread, cubed

1 cup milk

1 egg

1½ pounds ground beef

¼ cup minced onion

1¼ teaspoons salt

¼ teaspoon pepper

¼ teaspoon dry mustard

¼ teaspoon sage

¼ teaspoon celery salt

¼ teaspoon garlic salt

1 tablespoon Worcestershire
   sauce

1. Combine bread, milk, and egg in mixing bowl.
2. Add beef, onion, and seasonings; mix well.
3. Form into loaf and place in shallow baking pan.
4. Bake in preheated oven for 1 hour.

Temperature: 350°
Time: 1 hour

Hint: May be decorated with bacon strips and frosted with catsup before baking.

Homemade Salami

Yield: 2 rolls

What an intriguing recipe! Delicious!

2 pounds ground beef or 1½
   pounds ground beef plus ½
   pound pork sausage

1½ teaspoons fresh ground
   black pepper

1½ teaspoons mustard seeds

1½ teaspoons garlic powder

1¼ teaspoons liquid smoke

2½ tablespoons tender quick
   salt

1 bottle capers, optional

1. Mix all ingredients and form into two rolls.
2. Wrap each roll tightly in foil, being careful to make it water-proof.
3. Refrigerate for 24 hours.
4. After 24 hours, place salami rolls in pan, cover with water, and boil slowly for one hour.
5. Pour off water and stick holes in bottom of foil to drain and cool salami rolls.
6. Refrigerate again for 24 hours; slice thinly.

Veal Forrestier

Yield: 4 to 6 servngs

A real taste treat.

1½ pounds veal cutlets
1 clove garlic
½ cup unsifted flour
¼ cup butter
½ pound fresh mushrooms
Juice of ½ lemon
1 can (10¾ ounces) chicken
   broth
½ teaspoon salt
Pepper to taste

1. Pound cutlets to ¼ inch.
2. Cut garlic in half and rub on both sides of meat.
3. Cut meat into 2-inch pieces.
4. Lightly coat veal with flour.
5. Heat butter in heavy skillet and saute' veal until brown.
6. Slice mushrooms and heap them on meat.
7. Squeeze lemon into measuring cup and add enough broth to make ⅓ cup.
8. Sprinkle meat and mushrooms with salt and pepper.
9. Add chicken broth to veal and simmer covered for 20 minutes or until tender. If liquid starts to evaporate, add more chicken broth.

Veal Cordon Bleu With Mushroom Sauce

Yield: 4 servings

8 thin slices prosciutto ham or
    country ham
8 veal cutlets, thinly sliced
2 tablespoons grated Romano
    cheese
½ cup flour
1 egg, beaten
¾ cup bread crumbs
1 tablespoon Parmesan
    cheese
¼ teaspoon paprika
6 tablespoons butter
¼ cup chopped shallots
¼ cup chopped green pepper
1 clove garlic, minced
1 cup sliced fresh mushrooms
¼ teaspoon black pepper
½ cup condensed cream of
    mushroom soup
¼ cup milk
2 tablespoons Marsala wine

1. Place 2 slices of ham on 1 slice of veal. Sprinkle with Romano cheese. Top with another slice of veal. Press edges together.
2. Dredge veal in flour, dip in egg, and roll in mixture of bread crumbs, Parmesan cheese, and paprika.
3. Melt butter in skillet. Saute' veal until golden, turning once. Remove veal from skillet.
4. Add shallots, green pepper, and garlic; saute' until tender.
5. Return veal to skillet and add mushrooms and pepper. Simmer for 2 minutes.
6. Warm mushroom soup and milk in saucepan. Add wine to mixture. Stir and pour over veal.
7. Simmer until veal is tender or until desired consistency.

Veal Scallopine Marsala Yield: 4 to 6 servings

Tasty and elegant.

8 veal cutlets, thinly sliced
½ cup flour
Salt and pepper to taste
¼ cup olive oil or cooking oil
½ cup butter, divided
1 clove fresh garlic, minced
1 cup fresh mushrooms,
   sliced
¼ cup dry Marsala or Rose'
   wine
2 tablespoons flour, optional

1. Pound veal cutlets flat.
2. Dredge in flour with salt and pepper.
3. Heat oil and ¼ cup butter. Saute' garlic and brown veal in skillet. Set aside.
4. Add mushrooms and remaining ¼ cup butter to skillet. Cook over low heat.
5. Gradually add wine, stirring until consistency of medium thickened gravy. Add more flour if needed.
6. Add veal to mixture and simmer covered for 7 minutes.

Saltimbocca

Yield: 4 servings

Impress your guests.

4 veal cutlets, thinly sliced
Dash of salt
½ cup flour
¼ cup butter
¼ cup Marsala wine
½ cup chicken stock
4 slices prosciutto ham, thinly
   sliced
4 slices mozzarella cheese
Poultry seasoning to taste
Fresh parsley, chopped

1. Saute' salted and floured cutlets in butter until lightly browned.
2. Add wine and simmer 2 to 3 minutes.
3. Add chicken stock and stir until thickened.
4. Cover each cutlet with 1 slice of ham and cheese. Sprinkle with poultry seasoning.
5. Place under broiler until cheese melts. Baste veal with sauce and return to broiler for about one more minute.
6. Top with parsley and serve at once.

Veal Parmigiana

Yield: 6 to 8 servings

A very spicy dish.

¼ cup olive oil or vegetable oil

1 medium onion, chopped

2 cloves garlic, crushed

3 tablespoons chopped green
pepper

¼ pound fresh mushrooms

4 cups tomato sauce

1 bay leaf

2 eggs, well beaten

¼ cup milk

½ teaspoon salt

⅛ teaspoon pepper

1 cup fine bread crumbs

½ cup fresh grated Parmesan
cheese

⅓ cup clarified butter

2 pounds veal steaks (3 x
3-inch)

6 ounces mozzarella cheese,
shredded

1. Heat oil in large skillet. Saute'
   onion, garlic, green pepper, and
   mushrooms until tender.
2. Add tomato sauce and bay leaf.
   Cover and simmer for 20 to 25
   minutes. Discard bay leaf.
3. Beat together eggs, milk, salt, and
   pepper.
4. Combine bread crumbs and
   Parmesan cheese.
5. Dip veal in egg mixture, then coat
   with bread crumbs and Parmesan
   cheese.
6. Brown in clarified butter until
   golden.
7. Arrange veal in shallow baking
   dish, cover with tomato sauce
   mixture, and bake at 400° for 20
   minutes.
8. Sprinkle mozzarella cheese on
   top and bake 5 to 10 minutes
   longer at 350°.

Temperature: 400°
Time: 20 minutes

Temperature: 350°
Time: 5 to 10 minutes

Rio Grande Pork

Yield: 6 servings

4 to 5 pound boneless pork loin
½ teaspoon salt
1 teaspoon chili powder, divided
½ teaspoon garlic salt
½ cup apple-mint jelly
½ cup tomato catsup
1 tablespoon vinegar
1 cup crushed corn chips

1. Place roast, fat side up, on rack in shallow roaster.
2. Combine salt, ½ teaspoon chili powder, and garlic salt. Rub into roast.
3. Roast until meat thermometer reaches 165° (about 2 to 2½ hours).
4. In small saucepan combine jelly, catsup, vinegar, and ½ teaspoon chili powder; bring to boil. Reduce heat and simmer for 2 minutes, uncovered.
5. Brush roast with glaze. Sprinkle top with corn chips.
6. Continue roasting 10 to 15 minutes.
7. Remove from oven and let stand 10 minutes.
8. Measure pan drippings, including corn chips. Add water to make one cup. Heat to boiling and serve with meat.

Temperature: 325°
Time: 2 to 2½ hours
10 to 15 minutes

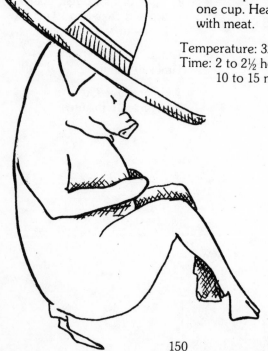

Tenderloin Of Pork
Yield: 8 to 10 servings

6 to 8 pounds boneless pork
  tenderloin
4 to 5 bay leaves
¾ to 1 teaspoon basil
Salt to taste
6 to 8 peppercorns
1½ cups white wine

1. Place meat in baking dish.
2. Add bay leaves, basil, and salt.
3. Stick 3 to 4 peppercorns into
   meat and sprinkle remainder
   around meat.
4. Pour wine around meat.
5. Bake, covered, until done.

Temperature: 325°
Time: 2½ to 3 hours

Barbecued Ribs
Yield: 2 servings

Pass the napkins!

½ box (8 ounces) dark brown
  sugar
3½ cups catsup
2 tablespoons Worcestershire
  sauce
⅓ cup vinegar
1 tablespoon dry mustard
1 tablespoon ginger
Garlic powder to taste
2½ pounds pork ribs

1. Mix first seven ingredients to
   make sauce.
2. Spoon mixture onto both sides of
   ribs.
3. Bake, turning and basting every
   45 minutes, until ribs are
   well-done.

Temperature: 325°
Time: 2½ hours

Hint: For chicken, bake about 1½ hours. Baste and turn every 15
*   minutes.*

Country-Style Ribs

Yield: 4 servings

4 pounds country-style pork ribs

1. Simmer ribs in salted water until tender (approximately 45 minutes).
2. Drain, cover, and set aside until ready to grill.
3. Charcoal ribs 30 to 45 minutes, turning and basting occasionally with sauce.

Sauce

1 cup catsup

¼ cup olive oil

¼ cup tarragon vinegar

2 tablespoons wine vinegar

2 tablespoons Worcestershire sauce

2 drops liquid smoke, optional

2 tablespoons minced onion

1 clove garlic, minced

1 tablespoon brown sugar

1 tablespoon whole mustard seed

2 teaspoons paprika

1 teaspoon crushed oregano

1 teaspoon chili powder

½ teaspoon salt

½ teaspoon ground cloves

1 bay leaf

Sauce

1. Combine all ingredients; stir well.
2. Heat to boiling; reduce heat and simmer 25 minutes, stirring occasionally. Remove bay leaf.

Hint: For more smoked flavor add dampened hickory chips to coals.

Marinated Pork Chops Yield: 8 to 10 servings

A real man-pleaser!

½ cup oil

½ cup soy sauce

¼ cup lemon juice

⅓ cup Worcestershire sauce

1 teaspoon pepper

1 teaspoon dry mustard

¾ teaspoon garlic salt

8 to 10 1-inch loin cut pork
  chops

1. Mix all ingredients except chops.
2. Marinate pork chops 12 hours,
   turning once.
3. Cook on grill, basting pork chops
   with marinade.

*Hint: This marinade is also great with beef, expecially shish
    kabobs.*

Orange Pork Chops Yield: 6 servings

Delicious served with fried rice.

6 thick pork chops

1 can (11 ounces) Mandarin
  oranges

4 tablespoons brown sugar

½ teaspoon cinnamon

3 whole cloves

½ teaspoon salt

1 teaspoon prepared mustard

¼ cup catsup

1 tablespoon vinegar

1. Brown chops on both sides in
   large skillet.
2. Add drained oranges to skillet,
   reserving juice.
3. Combine ½ to ¾ cup of reserved
   liquid with remaining ingredients.
   Pour over pork chops.
4. Cover and simmer gently until
   chops are done (about 45
   minutes).

Pork Chops Supreme

Yield: 6 servings

6 pork chops
¾ teaspoon sage
½ teaspoon seasoned salt
2 tablespoons shortening
1 beef bouillon cube
¼ cup water
2 medium onions, sliced
½ cup sour cream
1 tablespoon flour
2 tablespoons parsley flakes

1. Rub chops with sage and salt.
2. Brown in hot shortening. Drain.
3. Dissolve bouillon cube in water. Add bouillon and onions to pork chops. Cover and simmer 30 minutes.
4. Place pork chops on serving platter.
5. Combine sour cream, flour, and parsley flakes in separate bowl. Slowly add meat drippings.
6. Return this mixture to skillet. Cook and stir until desired consistency. Serve over chops.

Pork Jambalaya

Yield: 4 servings

4 to 6 pork chops
Salt
Pepper
2 stalks celery, chopped
5 green onions, chopped
½ cup chopped green pepper
⅔ cup raw rice
1⅓ cups chicken broth
½ teaspoon garlic salt
Dash red pepper

1. Salt and pepper pork chops. Brown in lightly greased skillet. Remove.
2. Saute' celery, onion, and green pepper until tender.
3. Add rice, broth, garlic salt, and red pepper. Bring to boil.
4. Return chops to pan. Cover and simmer until tender (30 to 40 minutes).

Hint: Instead of chicken broth, use 2 chicken bouillon cubes in 1⅓ cups of water.

Ham and Cheese Pie   Yield: 4 to 6 servings

A wonderful breakfast treat.

1 can (8 ounces) refrigerator crescent dinner rolls

2 cups (8 ounces) Monterey Jack cheese, cut into ½-inch cubes

⅛ teaspoon salt

⅛ teaspoon pepper

1 tablespoon grated Parmesan cheese

2 eggs, slightly beaten

12 ounces ham, cut into ½-inch cubes

1. Unroll crescent rolls and separate into eight triangles. Place five triangles in 9-inch pie pan. Press pieces together to form crust. Reserve three triangles for top crust.
2. Combine remaining ingredients in large mixing bowl. Pour into crust.
3. Roll out each remaining triangle until longest side is 8 inches.
4. Cut into ½-inch strips. Criss-cross strips over filling to form lattice top. Flute edge.
5. Bake until knife inserted 2 inches from edge comes out clean. Do not overbake.

Temperature: 325°
Time: 40 to 50 minutes

Old-Fashioned Country Ham

Frequent basting is the key to this Kentucky specialty!

1 country ham
Vinegar
1 cup black molasses
1 cup vinegar
Garlic
Cloves
Port wine

1. Cover ham with cold water, adding 1 cup vinegar for each gallon of water. Soak ham 12 hours, changing vinegar water after 6 hours.
2. Rinse ham in cold water; place in large roaster on top of stove. Pour over ham 1 gallon water, 1 cup black molasses, and 1 cup vinegar. Cover and bring to rolling boil. Simmer about 2 hours.
3. Remove ham from solution. Remove skin; puncture at intervals with ice pick and insert very small slivers of garlic. Score and dot with whole cloves. Bake at 300° for remainder of cooking time, basting every 20 minutes with port wine. Add water in bottom of pan as needed.

Temperature: 300°
Time: 25 minutes per pound for
    10 to 12-pound ham
    20 minutes per pound for
    larger ham

Moussaka

Yield: 6 servings

1 onion, chopped
1 clove garlic, minced
1 pound ground lamb or 2 cups
  leftover lamb
1 tablespoon butter
¾ teaspoon oregano
¾ teaspoon basil
¾ teaspoon cinnamon
¾ teaspoon salt
1 can (10¾ ounces) tomato
  puree
1 eggplant, unpeeled
¼ cup melted butter
¼ cup freshly-grated Parmesan
  cheese
¼ cup grated Swiss cheese

Sauce
1 tablespoon butter
1 tablespoon flour
1 cup milk
1 egg

1. Saute' onion, garlic, and lamb in 1
   tablespoon butter until meat is
   brown. Drain excess grease.
2. Add oregano, basil, cinnamon,
   salt, and tomato puree. Simmer ½
   hour, uncovered.
3. Cut unpeeled eggplant into ½-inch
   slices. Quickly dip slices into ¼
   cup melted butter. Broil eggplant
   4 minutes on each side.

Sauce
1. Melt butter in saucepan and stir in
   flour.
2. Add milk gradually and bring to
   boil, stirring until thick. Remove
   from heat.
3. Beat small amount of sauce into
   egg. Blend egg mixture into
   remaining sauce. Mix well.

To assemble
1. Arrange half of eggplant slices
   (overlap if necessary) in baking
   dish.
2. Sprinkle ⅓ of cheeses over the
   eggplant.
3. Spread meat sauce over eggplant.
4. Sprinkle ⅓ of cheese over meat
   sauce.
5. Layer remaining eggplant over
   top.
6. Pour sauce over all.
7. Sprinkle with remaining cheeses.
8. Bake uncovered.

Temperature: 350°
Time: 40 minutes

Pork-Stuffed Leg Of Lamb

Yield: 10 servings

A sensational party dish!

1 tablespoon dry mustard

1 tablespoon lemon juice

2 teaspoons salt

½ teaspoon crushed dried
 thyme leaves

½ teaspoon crushed dried
 rosemary leaves

½ teaspoon crushed dried
 marjoram leaves

¼ teaspoon pepper

1 clove garlic

1 leg of lamb, 6 to 8 pounds,
 boned (not tied)

1 pork tenderloin, about one
 pound

¼ cup water

2 tablespoons flour

1. Mix mustard, lemon juice, salt,
 thyme, rosemary, marjoram,
 pepper, and garlic. Brush mixture
 inside leg of lamb.
2. Place tenderloin inside lamb.
 Wrap lamb around tenderloin and
 tie securely.
3. Insert meat thermometer so tip is
 in center of pork tenderloin.
4. Place meat on rack in open
 shallow roasting pan. Do not
 cover.
5. Roast at 325° until thermometer
 registers 170 degrees (2½ to 3½
 hours).
6. Remove roast from oven; let
 stand while preparing gravy.
7. Skim off fat. Add enough water to
 meat juices to measure 1¾ cups.
 Shake an additional ¼ cup water
 and 2 tablespoons flour until
 smooth. Stir into drippings. Heat
 to boiling, stirring constantly. Boil
 one minute.

Temperature: 325°
Time: 2½ to 3½ hours

Savory Shish Kabobs

Juice of 2 large lemons or
    limes
4 tablespoons olive oil
2 tablespoons grated onion
2 tablespoons ground chili
    peppers
1 tablespoon powdered ginger
1 clove garlic, crushed
2 teaspoons curry powder
3 teaspoons salt
2 pounds tender lamb, cut
    into 1½-inch cubes
Cherry tomatoes
Small potatoes, canned or
    fresh
Green pepper
Apple slices
Mushroom caps
Smoked sausage, cubed
Bacon squares
Butter for basting while
    cooking

1. Combine first eight ingredients.
   Pour over meat and marinate at
   least 2 hours, preferably
   overnight.
2. Thread on skewers, alternating
   meat and vegetables/fruit.
3. Cook kabobs under broiler or grill
   outside approximately 20 minutes.
   Baste with butter while cooking.

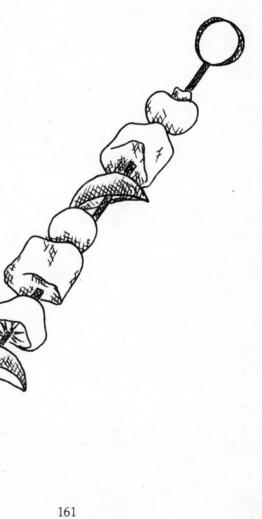

Daviess County Barbecued Mutton

Building the Pit

A concrete block pit can be constructed 4 to 6 feet deep, 4 feet wide and 6 to 100 feet long depending on the amount of meat to be cooked.

The pit should contain logs of hardwood. Oak, hickory or sassafras may be used. The logs should burn for a couple of hours until a good bed of hot coals remains. More wood may be added for heat and water may be sprayed to cool the fire. Proper temperature for cooking is necessary. Do not cook too quickly. A fire that is too hot will dry the outside of the meat and leave the middle uncooked.

1 butchered sheep

1. Parboil sheep for 4 hours in large vats or kettles.
2. Remove sheep sections and place meat on a metal wire rack on pit.
3. Baste sheep generously and frequently with barbeque sauce. Continue to baste each time the meat is turned.

Barbecue Sauce

1 gallon Worcestershire sauce
1 gallon vinegar
1 dozen lemons, sliced
4 pounds lard
4 pounds margarine
¼ pound pickling spice
12 ounces hot sauce
4 ounces black pepper
1 cup salt
6 ounces garlic powder
6 ounces onion powder
2 quarts catsup

1. Mix all ingredients in a large container.
2. Bring to low boil. Reduce heat and simmer for 1 hour or until lemons are cooked.
3. Baste sheep generously while smoking for 6 to 8 hours.

Hint: A cotton mop makes a good basting tool. The long handle protects your hands from the heat.

Game

The day
of the long rifle
has passed, but
Kentuckians
continue to answer
the call of the wild.
The modern hunter
has become a sportsman
rather than a provider. Accordingly game cooking, no longer
a necessity, has become an art. If this is your introductory
course in wild game appreciation, you may feel secure. We have created
this section with particular pride.

Game

General Hints for Game Preparation

Consider the fact that **game** has no additives or chemicals and is therefore a healthy natural food.

Cooking time for **game** can be either low and slow or hot and fast.

To marinate **game**, use a good dry wine (never a sweet wine) or seasoned water with vinegar added.

Duck should be washed well in salted water with vinegar added, then thoroughly rinsed with cool clear water.

To baste a roasting **bird**, use fruit juices. This adds a delicious flavor.

Trim all fat from **venison** before cooking to minimize the strong gamey taste.

Tenderize **venison** by soaking overnight in milk or in vinegar water.

Herbs and spices may be used liberally with **game**. Lemon Pepper Marinade is an especially good seasoning for **venison, elk,** and **antelope**.

Always marinate **bear** meat for at least 24 hours before cooking, either in a mixture of oil and vinegar or in dry wine.

Bear, like pork, should always be well-done.

The meat of a young **squirrel**, light-red or almost pink in color, is less gamey in flavor than most other wild meat.

Roast Duck

Yield: 2 servings

Duck
Butter
Garlic
Salt
Pepper
½ onion
1 apple, halved
1 orange, halved
Chopped celery and garlic
¾ cup sherry
½ cup orange juice

1. Wash duck thoroughly and dry with a paper towel.
2. Rub inside and out with butter, garlic, salt, and pepper. Put ½ onion, ½ apple, ½ orange, chopped celery, and garlic into duck cavity.
3. Place in roaster with 1½ inches of water in the bottom. Place ½ apple and ½ orange in water. Bake covered at 400° for 1 hour.
4. After first hour pour ¾ cup sherry and ½ cup orange juice over duck. Reduce heat to 300° and uncover duck.
5. Roast for 1 hour, basting every 10 minutes. (Note: More water, sherry, and orange juice may have to be added.)
6. Remove stuffing and discard before serving duck.

Temperature: 400°
Time: 1 hour
Temperature: 300°
Time: 1 hour

Hint: All game birds are delicious when cooked with fruit—pineapple, cherries, oranges, grapes, or plums.

Wine selection: Cabernet Sauvignon.

Sauerkraut Duck

Yield: 4 servings

Delightfully different!

2 ducks

¼ cup vinegar

Salt

Pepper

1 quart sauerkraut

1 apple, chopped

4 bay leaves

Tarragon

Apple butter

Cinnamon

½ cup dry white wine

1. Cover and soak two ducks in water and vinegar for 6 to 10 hours.
2. Drain ducks and pat dry.
3. Salt and pepper cavity and stuff with half of sauerkraut mixed with chopped apple.
4. Place ducks in pan and arrange remaining kraut and bay leaves around them.
5. Sprinkle tarragon on duck breasts and spread apple butter generously on breasts and legs.
6. Sprinkle with cinnamon and pour wine over sauerkraut.
7. Cover and cook until tender. Remove cover last 10 minutes to brown ducks.

Temperature: 325° to 350°
Time: 3 to 4 hours

Hint: Water chestnuts may be added to kraut. Flambe' with Cognac or Grand Marnier if desired.

Wine-Spiced Wild Duck Breasts

Yield: 4 servings

1 cup white wine or broth
1 clove garlic, crushed
1 teaspoon thyme
1 teaspoon oregano
1 teaspoon seasoned salt
1 teaspoon pepper
¼ cup olive oil or melted
   butter
2 duck breasts
Bacon strips

1. Combine first seven ingredients; pour over duck breasts. Refrigerate for 2 to 3 days.
2. Place marinade and duck breasts in saucepan. Cover. Simmer for 2 hours or until tender, adding water if necessary.
3. Place breasts on broiler rack; top with bacon strips. Broil 3 to 5 minutes.

Baked Doves With Fruit Juices

Yield: 4 to 8 servings

6 to 12 doves or quail
Olive oil
Dry mustard
Curry powder
Celery salt
Garlic salt
Salt
Pepper
¾ cup white wine
3 teaspoons Worcestershire
   sauce
Juice of 2 oranges
Juice of 1 lemon

1. Grease doves or quail well with olive oil. Sprinkle dry mustard, curry powder, celery salt, garlic salt, salt, and pepper on birds and place in a Dutch oven. Add white wine and a little water to Dutch oven.
2. Bake at 250° for 2½ to 3 hours.
3. Add Worcestershire sauce, orange juice, and lemon juice. Cook for 15 minutes or longer until birds are tender.

Temperature: 250°
Time: 2½ to 3 hours
Time: 15 minutes or until birds are
   tender

Wine Selection: Semi-sweet German Riesling.

Baked Dove Breasts

Yield: 6 to 12 servings

12 to 24 dove breasts
Salt and pepper
Flour
½ cup butter or margarine
¼ pound fresh mushrooms,
  sliced
1 medium onion, sliced
1 can (10¾ ounces) cream of
  chicken soup
Prepared brown rice

1. Salt and pepper dove breasts and lightly flour. Brown in skillet with butter.
2. Arrange in glass baking dish and add pan drippings on top. Place sliced mushrooms and onions on top of breasts. Top with cream of chicken soup. Cover baking dish with aluminum foil.
3. Bake at 350° for 25 minutes. Uncover and continue baking for 15 minutes longer.
4. Serve in baking dish with brown rice.

Temperature: 350°
Time: 25 minutes
        15 minutes

Potted Doves

Yield: 6 servings

Men will enjoy preparing this tasty dish.

6 doves
6 slices bacon
1 small onion, sliced
Salt
Pepper
2 tablespoons Worcestershire
  sauce
1 tablespoon butter
Red pepper
Hot pepper sauce
1 cup catsup

1. Place birds in Dutch oven with a little water. Simmer for 20 minutes on top of stove.
2. Remove birds from pan and wrap each with one slice of bacon. Secure with a toothpick. Return birds to pan and add remaining ingredients.
3. Cook covered for 1½ hours or until very tender. Remove cover and brown in oven.

Wine Selection: Beaujolais or a rose' wine.

Antelope Steak With Gravy Supreme

Yield: 4 to 6 servings

A tasty way to serve game.

3 antelope or venison round
  steaks, ½ to ¾-inch thick
1 bay leaf
¼ cup vinegar
1 clove garlic, minced
2 teaspoons salt
Dash of pepper
Dash of garlic salt
Flour
3 to 6 tablespoons oil
2 cans (10¾ ounces each)
  cream of chicken or
  mushroom soup
1 can water

1. Place antelope steaks in shallow pan; cover with water.
2. Add next four ingredients and soak overnight in the refrigerator.
3. Drain steaks and sprinkle with pepper and garlic salt. Dredge steaks in flour. Brown well on both sides in oil and cover. Cook over low heat for approximately 45 minutes or until tender, turning occasionally.
4. Add soup and water to steaks and simmer 15 to 20 minutes.
5. Serve gravy over rice or potatoes with steaks.

Elk Roast

Yield: 4 servings

1 elk roast or venison roast, 4
  to 6 pounds
8 to 10 small potatoes
8 to 10 carrots, sliced
8 small onions
Celery salt
Onion salt
½ cup wine vinegar

1. Place elk in roasting pan and surround with vegetables. Sprinkle with seasonings.
2. Bake in a 325° oven for 3 hours, or until tender, basting frequently with grape wine vinegar.

Temperature: 325°
Time: 3 hours

Wine Selection: Serve a good bottle of Cabernet Sauvignon with elk and venison.

Easy Venison Roast With Sauce

Yield: 6 to 8 servings

So easy and so delicious!

1 venison roast, 3 to 4 pounds
Flour
1 cooking bag to fit roast
2 to 3 celery stalks
4 to 6 slices bacon
1 can (15 ounces) tomato
   sauce
2 tablespoons vinegar
1 onion, finely chopped
3 to 5 tablespoons sugar
Worcestershire sauce to taste
Salt and pepper to taste

1. Rub roast with flour. Place celery stalks in bottom of cooking bag; place roast on celery and lay bacon strips over roast.
2. Combine tomato sauce, vinegar, onion, sugar, Worcestershire, salt, and pepper. Pour over roast.
3. Seal cooking bag per directions. Bake.

Temperature: 350°
Time: 2 hours

Venison Meat Loaf

Yield: 8 servings

2 pounds ground venison
2 pounds pork sausage
2 cups cracker crumbs
1 to 2 onions, chopped
½ cup evaporated milk
3 eggs, beaten
1 cup barbecue sauce
Salt and pepper to taste
1 can (8 ounces) tomato
   sauce
Catsup

1. Combine venison, sausage, cracker crumbs, and onions; mix well.
2. Add milk, eggs, barbecue sauce, salt, pepper, and half of tomato sauce to meat mixture. Combine well and form into loaf.
3. Bake in 350° oven for 30 minutes.
4. Top with remaining tomato sauce and catsup. Bake 1 hour or until done.

Temperature: 350°
Time: 30 minutes
      1 hour or until done

Hint: Antelope, elk, or moose may be substituted for venison.

Venison Roast

Yield: 12 servings

Great for a wild-game party!

1 venison roast, 5 to 6 pounds
2 tablespoons vinegar
1 tablespoon salt
Pepper
¼ cup venison sauce
1 onion, chopped

1. Soak venison in water, 2 tablespoons vinegar, and 1 tablespoon salt for 4 to 5 hours. Remove and wipe dry.
2. Sprinkle lightly with pepper and brush with venison sauce. Add onion and enough water to cover bottom of roaster.
3. Bake, covered, in 325° oven for 1 hour. Reduce heat to 275° and bake for 3 hours. Baste often with venison sauce and juices from roast.

Temperature: 325°
Time: 1 hour

Temperature: 275°
Time: 3 hours

Venison Sauce
1 tablespoon black pepper
1 tablespoon salt
1 box (1.5 ounces) dry mustard
¼ cup sugar
1¼ cups vinegar
¼ cup water
½ cup margarine or butter

Venison Sauce
1. Mix dry ingredients. Add vinegar and water; mix well.
2. Bring mixture to a full boil and add margarine or butter. Continue to cook until butter melts. Makes 1 pint.

Crock-Pot Venison

Yield: 6 servings

1 venison roast, 3 to 4 pounds
½ cup vinegar
2 tablespoons salt
4 garlic cloves, chopped
Salt
Flour
1 large onion, sliced
3 tablespoons brown sugar
1½ teaspoons dry mustard
3 tablespoons flour
3 tablespoons Worcestershire
   sauce
1 can (14 ounces) tomatoes
1 tablespoon Pickapeppa
   sauce
⅓ cup vinegar
3 garlic cloves, chopped

1. Put roast in dish. Make a marinade using next three ingredients. Pour marinade over roast, adding enough water to cover venison. Refrigerate overnight.
2. Remove venison from marinade. Salt, flour, and brown meat in a hot skillet or under a broiler.
3. Place roast in a crock-pot. Add all remaining ingredients. Cook on low for 8 to 10 hours.

Barbecued Venison Rib Steaks

Yield: 6 to 8 servings

Children love it!

6 to 8 venison rib steaks
Pepper to taste
½ cup onion slices
1 lemon, thinly sliced
1 cup catsup
1 cup water
1 teaspoon salt
1 teaspoon chili powder
Dash of hot pepper sauce
⅓ cup Worcestershire sauce
¼ cup vinegar

1. Place venison steaks in Dutch oven and season with pepper. Cover with onion and place lemon slices over onion.
2. Bake at 400° for 15 minutes.
3. Mix remaining ingredients in saucepan and bring to boil. Pour over the venison.
4. Reduce oven heat to 350° and bake for 1 hour, or until tender, basting with sauce often. Add water if sauce becomes dry.

Temperature: 400°
Time: 15 minutes

Temperature: 350°
Time: 1 hour or until tender

Venison Meatballs

Yield: 10 servings

Quick and easy appetizer.

2 pounds ground venison
2 to 3 slices bread, torn into pieces
1 egg
1 package (1.37 ounces) onion soup mix
Salt and pepper to taste
1 bottle (12 ounces) chili sauce
½ cup grape jelly

1. Combine venison, bread, egg, soup mix, salt, and pepper. Roll into balls about walnut-size and bake in oven at 375° for 10 minutes.
2. Heat chili sauce and grape jelly until dissolved. Pour sauce over meatballs and simmer in slow cooker for 2 hours.
3. Serve in chafing dish as an appetizer.

Temperature: 375°
Time: 10 minutes

Venison Stew

Yield: 6 servings

1¾ pounds venison, 1½-inches
   thick

⅓ cup flour

¼ teaspoon salt

Pepper

3 tablespoons shortening,
   melted

¼ cup diced onion

1 clove garlic, minced

2¾ cups boiling water

1½ cups canned tomatoes

½ teaspoon salt

½ teaspoon Worcestershire
   sauce

3 to 4 medium potatoes, cut
   into desired serving size

4 small white onions

4 carrots, cut into 1-inch
   pieces

Salt and pepper

1 cup frozen peas

1. Trim excess fat from meat; cut into
   1½-inch cubes.
2. Combine flour, salt, and pepper in a
   paper bag. Add meat and shake.
3. Add meat to melted shortening in
   Dutch oven; brown.
4. Add next six ingredients to meat.
   Cover and reduce heat. Simmer 2
   hours or until meat is tender, stirring
   occasionally.
5. Add potatoes, onions, and carrots.
   Season with salt and pepper.
6. Bring stew to a boil; reduce heat and
   simmer, covered, for 45 minutes or
   until vegetables are tender. Add peas
   and simmer an additional 15 minutes.

Rabbit Stew

Yield: 4 servings

A most tasty dish!

3½ pounds rabbit

1 cup red wine

1 cup red wine vinegar

1 cup sliced onions

½ teaspoon cloves

3 teaspoons salt

3 bay leaves

1 teaspoon hot pepper sauce

1 cup flour

½ cup shortening

¼ teaspoon thyme

1 cup water or stock marinade

3 teaspoons sugar

1. Cut rabbit into serving pieces.
2. Combine wine, vinegar, onions, cloves, 2 teaspoons salt, bay leaves, and hot pepper sauce; mix well. Add rabbit and refrigerate for 2 days.
3. Drain rabbit and strain reserved marinade.
4. Combine flour and remaining salt; coat rabbit pieces. Heat shortening in skillet and brown rabbit on all sides. Drain excess fat. Add reserved marinade, thyme, and water.
5. Cover and simmer 45 minutes or until tender, stirring occasionally. Add sugar and mix well before serving.

Hint: Rabbit and squirrel may be substituted for chicken in almost any recipe.

Wine Selection: Rhine or California Riesling.

Savory Rabbit In Crust

Yield: 4 servings

1 rabbit, cut into serving pieces

Salt

Pepper

1 bay leaf

Celery leaves

¼ teaspoon thyme

Beef bouillon cube

Slice of onion

Parsley sprigs

2 hard-boiled eggs, quartered

2 tablespoons butter

1 small onion, chopped

½ cup finely-chopped celery

½ cup sliced mushrooms

2 tablespoons flour

1½ cups rabbit stock

⅛ teaspoon thyme

Salt and pepper to taste

1. Place rabbit in Dutch oven and cover with water. Add next 8 ingredients. Bring to boil, then simmer until rabbit is tender.
2. Remove rabbit and strain. Reserve stock.
3. Strip the meat from the rabbit and cut into bite-size pieces.
4. Butter a 2½-quart deep dish casserole.
5. Arrange pieces of rabbit and egg quarters in casserole.
6. Melt butter and lightly brown onion, celery, and mushrooms in frying pan.
7. Stir in flour and slowly add stock, stirring until stock thickens into gravy.
8. Add thyme and a little salt and pepper.
9. Pour gravy over rabbit and cover casserole with pie crust.

Crust

1 cup flour

¾ teaspoon baking powder

½ teaspoon salt

⅓ cup shortening

3 tablespoons ice water

Crust

1. Combine dry ingredients; thoroughly cut in shortening.
2. Add ice water, and lightly stir.
3. Press dough into ball.
4. Turn dough out onto lightly-floured board. Roll to ¼-inch thickness or to ½ inch larger than casserole.
5. Cover casserole with crust; cut slits in crust for steam to escape.
6. Bake until the crust is golden brown and the contents bubbly.

Temperature: 425°
Time: 20 to 25 minutes

Hint: Chicken broth may be substituted for extra rabbit stock.

Squirrel Brunswick

Yield: 20 servings

Squirrels at one time were so popular that the famous Kentucky Squirrel Gun was developed especially for squirrel hunting.

10 squirrels, disjointed

2 cups corn

1 pound bacon, diced

5 pounds potatoes, diced

2 quarts tomatoes

3 pounds onions, diced

2 pounds lima beans

1 cup diced celery

Salt and pepper to taste

¼ cup Worcestershire sauce

Flour

1. Place the squirrels in large kettle; add water to half cover. Bring to boil. Cover and simmer until squirrels are tender. Cool.
2. Remove squirrels from stock and remove meat from bones.
3. Place squirrel meat back into stock and add next nine ingredients; cook for 2 hours.
4. Thicken stew with a small amount of flour mixed with water; simmer for 30 minutes longer.

Hint: Squirrel is more likely to become freezer-burned than many other game animals because of the small size.

Wine Selection: California Burgundy.

Mustard Bear Steaks

Yield: 6 servings

1 cup tarragon vinegar
2 bay leaves
1 cup red wine
1 cup water
6 bear steaks, 1-inch thick
Salt and pepper to taste
6 tablespoons dry mustard
Flour
Shortening
2 cups beef stock

1. Combine first four ingredients. Place the bear steaks in bowl and pour the vinegar and wine mixture over steaks. Marinate in refrigerator for 24 hours, turning steaks occasionally.
2. Pat steaks dry, season with salt and pepper and sprinkle with mustard.
3. Dredge steaks with flour and brown on both sides in small amount of hot shortening in Dutch oven. Add beef stock and reserved marinade; cover and simmer for 1 hour or until steaks are tender. Add water as needed.

Hint: Bear calls for marinades, powerful herbs, and sauces.

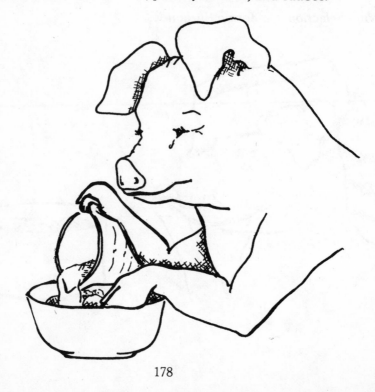

Savory Bear With Mushrooms

Yield: 6 servings

3 bay leaves

1 pint tarragon vinegar

1 stick cinnamon

2 peppercorns

2 onions, quartered

½ teaspoon thyme

½ teaspoon basil

1 cup minced celery

½ teaspoon rosemary

3 pounds bear meat, cut into
  cubes

Shortening

1 cup minced shallots

Salt and pepper to taste

Flour

1 pint water

½ cup butter

2 tablespoons Worcestershire
  sauce

1 can (8 ounces) sliced
  mushrooms

1. Combine first nine ingredients and pour over the bear meat in bowl. Marinate in refrigerator for 24 hours.
2. Drain bear meat; strain and reserve marinade.
3. Brown bear meat in Dutch oven in small amount of shortening. Sprinkle with shallots, salt, pepper, and small amount of flour.
4. Add water, butter, Worcestershire, mushrooms, and reserved marinade. Simmer 2 hours until tender, adding water as needed.

Hint: All fat should be removed from bear before cooking.

Wild Game Stroganoff

Yield: 6 servings

2 pounds elk
2 teaspoons salt
½ teaspoon pepper
3 tablespoons flour
2 teaspoons paprika
¼ teaspoon garlic salt
1 onion, chopped
3 tablespoons bacon drippings
  or oil
1 can (10¾ ounces) cream of
  mushroom soup
⅔ cup water
1 can (3.0 ounces) button
  mushrooms
1½ cups sour cream
Prepared rice

1. Cut elk into small cubes. Combine elk with next 5 ingredients in a bag and shake well.
2. Brown elk and onion in bacon drippings in a skillet. Combine mushroom soup and water; pour over meat. Simmer covered until elk is tender, about 2 hours.
3. Add mushrooms and sour cream. Stir and heat thoroughly. Serve over hot rice.

Baked Rattlesnake

Yield: 6 servings

The first trick is acquiring a rattlesnake!

1 rattlesnake
1 recipe of thin white sauce
¼ pound fresh mushrooms,
  sliced
2 limes, thinly sliced
1 teaspoon basil
1 teaspoon white pepper
1 teaspoon rosemary

1. Skin snake, dress, and wash in cold water. Cut in 3-inch sections.
2. Place snake meat in large baking dish. Cover with cream sauce; add sliced mushrooms and remaining ingredients. Cover tightly.
3. Bake.

Temperature: 300°
Time: 1 hour

Hint: Be sure to include as a SPECIAL dinner guest, the individual who "came to terms" with the rattlesnake!

Fish

Fish

Fish Preparation

Fish are at their peak of flavor when cooked fresh. Avoid freezing if possible.

When cleaning fish, remove bloodline (dark area on the side of fillets) from saltwater fish to improve flavor. Run a finger over fillets to locate any bones that need removing before cooking.

Freezing tips:

Freshwater fish should be frozen in water to protect them from freezer burn and drying out.

Saltwater fish should be rinsed in clean ocean water, if possible, before freezing. Freeze without water and use within two months for optimum flavor.

Cooking tips:

Always sprinkle fish fillets with lemon juice and allow to stand for at least 10 minutes. Lemon juice not only preserves whiteness, it also gives a milder flavor to the fish.

Poaching is a very tasty method of preparing fish and also makes an extremely low-calorie entree. A splash of white wine in the liquid adds a bit of extra zest to the fish. Slices of carrot, zucchini, and celery add much to the flavor of the poaching liquid and may be reserved and served as part of the meal. Crab Boil may be used to add a spicy flavor and interest to the water needed to poach fish and frog legs.

Frying fish should be carefully watched to avoid overcooking. The color of the browned fillets and flakiness when fork-tested should determine cooking time. The best temperature range for fish is between 385° and 400°. Butter added to the cooking oil will give fried fish a golden brown color and enhance flavor as well. Never overcrowd the frying pan.

Astrin Bay Sauce

Yield: 4 to 6 portions

A delightful blend of flavors.

1 medium onion
¼ cup oil
2 tablespoons butter
Salt
Pepper
2 or 3 stalks celery, cut
   diagonally into 1 or 2-inch
   pieces
28 ounces canned tomatoes
½ to 1 cup fresh mushrooms,
   sliced or quartered
½ teaspoon tarragon
¼ teaspoon thyme
¼ teaspoon sweet basil

1. Lightly sauté onion in oil and butter until transparent.
2. Add salt, pepper, and celery and sauté lightly.
3. Cut tomatoes into quarters and add with juice to celery and onion mixture.
4. Add mushrooms, tarragon, thyme, and basil. Simmer until mushrooms are desired tenderness.
5. Serve over poached or baked fish.

Hint: Baste roasting chicken or pork with this sauce or serve over rice.

Creamy Seafood Sauce

Yield: 1¼ cups

Especially good with cold shrimp.

1 cup mayonnaise
1 tablespoon capers
½ cup coarsely-cut sour
   pickles
½ teaspoon dry mustard
1 tablespoon dried parsley
1 teaspoon tarragon

1. Combine all ingredients in blender container.
2. Blend at high speed for 6 seconds.

Shrimp In Beer Batter

Fruit sauce is delicious dip for this recipe.

1 can (12 ounces) of beer
1¼ cups flour
1 tablespoon salt
1 teaspoon paprika
½ teaspoon baking powder
Jumbo shrimp

1. In a mixing bowl, pour beer and flour. Stir in salt, paprika, and baking powder. Let stand 1 to 2 hours at room temperature; batter will thicken as it stands.
2. Butterfly shrimp. Cut shrimp from underside; vein does not have to be removed.
3. Dip shrimp into flour, patting to remove excess, and then into batter. Fry shrimp in deep fat until brown, 2 to 3 minutes. Do not overcook.
4. Serve with fruit sauce.

Fruit Sauce

1 cup orange marmalade
1 tablespoon mustard
2 teaspoons ginger
1 lemon, grated and juiced
2 tablespoons prepared
   horseradish

Fruit Sauce

1. Mix all ingredients. Serve hot, if desired.

Shrimp Casserole

Yield: 6 servings

2 pounds fresh shrimp,
   cooked
1 can (3½ ounces)
   mushrooms
½ green pepper, chopped
½ cup chopped onion
½ cup chopped pimiento
1 cup chopped celery
1 cup mayonnaise
½ teaspoon salt
⅛ teaspoon pepper
1 cup cream
1 tablespoon Worcestershire
   sauce
½ cup raw rice, cooked
Bread crumbs

1. Preheat oven to 375°.
2. Mix all ingredients except bread crumbs and place in a 2-quart buttered casserole.
3. Sprinkle with bread crumbs and bake for 30 minutes.

Temperature: 375°
Time: 30 minutes

Hint: Serve in pastry shells for an elegant lunch or dinner.

Shrimp Creole

Yield: 2 to 4 servings

2 tablespoons bacon drippings
1 medium yellow onion,
   chopped
1 medium green pepper,
   chopped
1 bunch green onions,
   chopped
2 stalks celery, chopped
1 can (16 ounces) tomatoes,
   drained
1 can (8 ounces) tomato
   sauce
4 cloves garlic, chopped
1 teaspoon sweet basil
½ teaspoon thyme
1 bay leaf
Cayenne pepper to taste
2 pounds shrimp, boiled in
   Crab Boil
Rice

1. Heat bacon drippings in electric
   skillet to 250° to 300°. Saute'
   yellow onion and green pepper
   until translucent.
2. Add green onions and celery to
   electric skillet and saute' 3
   minutes.
3. Add tomatoes, tomato sauce,
   garlic, and seasonings. Cook for
   40 minutes.
4. About 15 minutes before this is
   ready, boil shrimp in Crab Boil as
   per directions on package.
5. Add shrimp to creole mixture and
   cook an additional 20 to 30
   minutes. Serve over steamed rice.

Kentucky "Backwoods" Trout

Yield: 4 servings

4 whole trout (leave skin on
    fish)
Lemon
Salt
Pepper
Pinch of garlic powder
Pinch of celery salt
Vegetable oil
Salt
Pepper

1. Build a "hot" coal bed of hickory and sassafras wood, or charcoal, in an outdoor grill.
2. Open the fish cavity and freely squeeze lemon. Add salt, pepper, garlic powder, and celery salt.
3. Lightly oil the outside of the fish and place on the grill.
4. Cook for approximately 10 minutes on each side, turning carefully with spatula. When done, the skin should remove easily.
5. Lightly salt and pepper the outside.
6. Enjoy immediately!

*Hint: **This type of cooking always requires timing and careful attention. Usually 10 minutes per inch of thickness is a good estimate.***

Salmon Broccoli Casserole

Yield: 6 servings

1 can (10¾ ounces) cream of
  mushroom soup
½ cup milk
2 tablespoons chopped
  pimiento
1 tablespoon lemon juice
1 can (16 ounces) salmon,
  drained
1 package (6 ounces) long
  grain and wild rice mix,
  prepared
1 package (10 ounces) frozen
  chopped broccoli,
  cooked and drained
2 tablespoons seasoned bread
  crumbs

1. Preheat oven to 375°.
2. In a mixing bowl, blend soup and
   milk. Stir in next five ingredients.
3. Put mixture into a greased deep
   1½-quart casserole. Sprinkle top
   with bread crumbs.
4. Bake uncovered 20 to 25 minutes.

Temperature: 375°
Time: 20 to 25 minutes

Hint: For special luncheon dish, bake in individual casseroles.

Baked Salmon Croquettes

Yield: 6 servings

1 can (15 ounces) pink salmon
Milk
¼ cup butter
2 tablespoons finely-chopped
    onion
⅓ cup flour
½ teaspoon salt
¼ teaspoon pepper
1 tablespoon lemon juice
1 cup crushed corn flakes,
    divided

1. Drain salmon, reserving liquid. Add enough milk to liquid to make one cup. Set aside.
2. Melt butter in heavy saucepan over low heat. Add onion and cook until tender.
3. Add flour to saucepan, stirring until smooth. Cook 1 minute, stirring constantly.
4. Gradually add milk mixture. Cook over medium heat, stirring constantly, until thick and bubbly. Stir in salt and pepper and set aside.
5. Remove skin and bones from salmon; flake salmon with a fork.
6. To the salmon add lemon juice, ½ cup cornflakes, and white sauce, stirring well. Refrigerate until chilled.
7. Shape salmon mixture into patties and then roll in remaining corn flakes.
8. Place salmon patties on lightly-greased baking sheet and bake.

Temperature: 400°
Time: 30 minutes

Crab Crêpes

Yield: 6 servings

12 Crêpes (See page 210.)

Step I

2 tablespoons butter

3 tablespoons minced shallots

1½ cups frozen crab meat,
    thawed and drained

Salt and pepper

¼ cup dry white vermouth

Step II

⅓ cup dry white vermouth

2 tablespoons cornstarch

2 tablespoons milk

1½ cups heavy cream

¼ teaspoon salt

White pepper

½ cup grated Swiss cheese

Step I

1. Heat butter to bubbling in skillet.
   Add shallots and crab meat. Stir
   over moderately high heat for 1
   minute.
2. Season crab meat mixture with
   salt and pepper. Add ¼ cup
   vermouth and boil rapidly until
   liquid almost evaporates.
3. Put mixture into bowl and set
   aside.

Step II

4. Add ⅓ cup vermouth to skillet
   and boil until reduced to one
   tablespoon. Remove from heat.
5. Blend cornstarch with milk. Add
   cornstarch mixture, cream, and
   seasonings to vermouth. Simmer
   2 minutes, stirring constantly. Add
   Swiss cheese and cook 1
   additional minute.
6. Add one-half of this mixture to
   the crab meat mixture in Step I
   and blend well.
7. Place large spoonful of crab
   mixture on lower third of crêpe
   and roll crêpe into cylindrical
   shape.
8. Arrange crêpes closely together in
   lightly-buttered baking dish.
   Spoon remaining sauce over
   crêpes, sprinkle with cheese and
   dot with butter.
9. Bake in 425° oven for 15 to 20
   minutes in upper third of oven
   until bubbling hot and lightly
   browned.

Temperature: 425°

Time: 15 to 20 minutes

Flounder Marguery

Yield: 4 servings

1 pound flounder
1 cup white wine
½ teaspoon salt
¼ teaspoon pepper
½ cup mushrooms, chopped
3 tablespoons butter
2 tablespoons flour
8 oysters (reserve liquid)
8 shrimp
¼ cup Parmesan cheese

1. Arrange flounder in shallow, buttered baking dish. Pour white wine around and over flounder.
2. Season with salt and pepper. Sprinkle with chopped mushrooms. Bake at 325° for 30 minutes.
3. Melt butter in saucepan and add flour; mix well. Add liquid from oysters, then oysters and shrimp. Cook 4 minutes and add cheese. Pour over fish and return to oven for 5 minutes.
4. Serve immediately.

Temperature: 325°
Time: 30 minutes
        5 minutes

Dilled Flounder

Yield: 4 servings

Butter
2 pounds fresh flounder (8 fillets)
4 teaspoons Dijon mustard
2 teaspoons dried dill
8 green onions, thinly sliced
4 tablespoons bread crumbs
4 teaspoons soy sauce
4 teaspoons lemon juice

1. Butter a 9 x 12 x 2-inch baking dish.
2. Place four flounder fillets on the bottom of the dish. Spread ½ teaspoon mustard on each; sprinkle ¼ teaspoon dill and ⅛ onions on each. Repeat.
3. Sprinkle with bread crumbs, soy sauce, and lemon juice.
4. Bake.

Temperature: 350°
Time: 8 minutes

Baked Stuffed Flounder

Yield: 6 servings

Seafood Dressing

6 tablespoons butter
¼ cup chopped celery
½ cup chopped onion
¼ cup chopped green pepper
½ pound shrimp, cooked and
   diced
1 teaspoon chopped parsley
½ teaspoon paprika
1 teaspoon Worcestershire
   sauce
½ teaspoon seafood seasoning
⅛ teaspoon cayenne pepper
¼ cup dry sherry
1½ cups bread crumbs

Seafood Dressing

1. Melt butter in skillet. Add
   vegetables and saute' until tender.
2. Stir in remaining ingredients,
   except bread crumbs. Cook over
   low heat for 10 minutes.
3. Add bread crumbs.

6 small flounder, boned or 6
   flounder fillets
Salt and pepper to taste
3 tablespoons lemon juice
1 cup fine bread crumbs
¼ cup butter, melted

1. Preheat oven to 375°.
2. Grease shallow baking pan.
3. Stuff each fish with 2 or 3
   tablespoons seafood dressing. Roll
   and fasten each fish with
   toothpicks.
4. Place in pan and season with salt,
   pepper, and lemon juice.
5. Sprinkle bread crumbs over fish
   and pour butter over fish.
6. Bake.

Temperature: 375°
Time: 25 to 30 minutes

Fish Jensen

Yield: 4 servings

4 fish fillets
Juice from 2 oranges
Juice from 2 lemons
2 carrots, cut into large pieces
2 stalks celery, cut into large
   pieces
1 medium onion, cut into
   large pieces
Vegetable oil
Salt and pepper
½ cup dry white wine
Butter
Parsley
Rosemary
Lemon slices

1. Place fish fillets in a 10-inch square baking dish. Squeeze oranges and lemons over fish and allow it to marinate for 15 minutes. Remove fish, leaving juices.
2. Place carrots, celery, and onion in juice in baking dish.
3. Brush each fish fillet with vegetable oil and season with salt and pepper. Arrange fish on top of vegetables and pour white wine over fish. Dot fish with butter, sprinkle with parsley, and add a pinch of rosemary. Garnish with lemon slices.
4. Bake at 375° for about 20 minutes or until fish flakes easily with fork.

Temperature: 375°
Time: 20 minutes

Hint: A thick fillet such as snapper or grouper is best.

Billy's Baked Bass

Yield: 4 to 6 servings

This gives you time to tell tall tales.

½ cup butter
⅔ cup crushed crackers
¼ cup Parmesan cheese
½ teaspoon basil
½ teaspoon oregano
½ teaspoon salt
¼ teaspoon garlic powder
8 bass fillets

1. Melt butter in 9 x 13-inch baking dish.
2. Mix together next six ingredients.
3. Dip fish in cracker batter, breading both sides. Place in baking dish and sprinkle extra crumbs over fish.
4. Bake at 350° for 15 to 20 minutes. To test fish, flake with fork.

Temperature: 350°
Time: 15 to 20 minutes

Poached Kentucky Bass

Yield: 3 servings

1 lemon
6 bass fillets (3 fish)
1 onion, sliced
2 bay leaves
½ teaspoon thyme
½ cup butter, melted
1 tablespoon parsley
Salt
Pepper

1. Squeeze lemon over fillets and set aside.
2. Add onion, bay leaves, and thyme to 2 quarts water in large skillet or roasting pan with cover. Bring to slow boil.
3. Place fish in pan and cover. Reduce heat and simmer until the fish flakes easily with a fork. Do not overcook.
4. Transfer fish to serving dish.
5. Pour butter over fish. Sprinkle with parsley, salt, and pepper to taste.
6. Serve immediately!

Hint: Frog legs are very good cooked this way.

Scalloped Oysters

Yield: 4 servings

Great either as an entree or side dish!

¼ cup butter or margarine

2 cups cracker crumbs

¼ cup oyster liquid

½ cup milk

½ teaspoon Worcestershire
  sauce

Dash of pepper

1 can (8 ounces) oysters

1. Preheat oven to 350°.
2. Melt butter in a small saucepan. Stir in cracker crumbs and set aside.
3. In a measuring cup mix oyster liquid (drained from oyster can), milk, Worcestershire, and pepper.
4. Spread half of crumb mixture in small greased casserole. Top with drained oysters. Pour milk mixture over oysters and top with remaining cracker crumbs.
5. Cover and bake for 30 minutes. Uncover and bake for 10 minutes more.

Temperature: 350°
Time: 30 minutes, covered
       10 minutes, uncovered

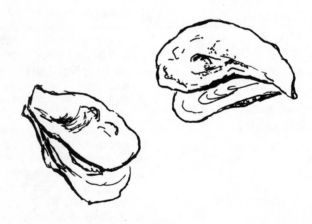

Sweet And Sour Fish

Yield: 6 servings

2 carrots, cut diagonally into
thin slices

½ cup water

1½ to 2 pounds fish fillets, cut
into 1-inch pieces

⅓ cup vinegar

½ cup packed brown sugar

2 tablespoons cornstarch

2 tablespoons soy sauce

1 can (13½ ounces) chunk
pineapple

1 small green pepper, cut into
1-inch pieces

Vegetable oil

Batter

⅔ cup flour

¾ cup water

1¼ teaspoons salt

½ teaspoon baking powder

1. Bring carrots and water to boil.
Cover and cook until barely
tender, approximately 7 to 10
minutes.
2. Rinse and dry fish with paper
towels.
3. Mix vinegar, brown sugar,
cornstarch, and soy sauce in 2-
quart saucepan. Stir in carrots
with liquid, pineapple with syrup,
and green pepper. Bring to a boil,
stirring constantly. Boil and stir 1
minute. Keep warm.
4. Heat oil, 1 to 1½ inches deep, to
360°.
5. Mix batter ingredients.
6. Dip fish in batter, allowing excess
to drip off. Fry until golden brown,
about 1½ minutes on each side.
Drain on paper towels.
7. Arrange fish on platter or in large
bowl. Pour sauce and carrot
mixture over fish. Serve with rice.

*Hint: Fish may be prepared ahead and frozen no longer than
2 weeks. Reheat on ungreased cookie sheet in 400° oven for 8
to 10 minutes.*

Seafood In Shells

Yield: 6 to 7 servings

Bake in individual shells for an elegant appetizer.

1 medium green pepper, finely chopped
1 cup finely-chopped celery
1 medium onion, finely chopped
1 can (6½ ounces) crab meat, shredded
1 can (6½ ounces) shrimp, shredded
½ teaspoon salt
Dash of pepper
1 teaspoon Worcestershire sauce
1 teaspoon lemon juice
1 cup mayonnaise
¾ cup cracker crumbs
2 tablespoons butter

1. Combine first nine ingredients.
2. Mix in mayonnaise.
3. Place in individual shells or lightly-greased casserole dish.
4. Sprinkle cracker crumbs over shells or casserole and dot with butter.
5. Bake.

Temperature: 350°
Time: 30 minutes

Broiled Shrimp With Chili Butter

Different taste for shrimp lovers!

Jumbo shrimp
1 tablespoon chili powder
½ cup melted butter

1. Butterfly the shrimp.
2. Mix chili powder and butter.
3. Dip shrimp in butter mixture and arrange on broiler pan. Bake at 350° on middle rack of oven for 8 minutes. Turn shrimp over and broil 3 to 5 minutes more.
4. Serve with remaining melted butter as a dip.

Temperature: 350°
Time: 8 minutes

Poultry

Poultry

Chicken Pie Supreme

Yield: 6 servings

½ cup chopped onion
⅓ cup margarine or chicken fat
⅓ cup plus 1 tablespoon flour
1½ teaspoons salt
3 cups chicken broth
4 cups coarsely-cut cooked
  chicken
1 can (8 ounces) peas, drained
1 can (8 ounces) mushrooms,
  drained

1. Sauté onions in margarine or chicken fat until tender but not brown.
2. Blend in flour and salt.
3. Gradually stir in broth and cook until thick.
4. Add chicken and vegetables, and cook until bubbling.
5. Pour into 2-quart casserole dish. Top with flaky crust.
6. Bake at 400° for 30 to 40 minutes.

Pastry

1 cup flour
¾ teaspoon baking powder
⅓ cup shortening
3 tablespoons ice water

Pastry

1. Combine dry ingredients and cut in shortening until mixture resembles coarse meal.
2. Add ice water and stir.
3. Turn dough onto lightly-floured board and roll to ¼-inch thickness. Trim to ½-inch larger than casserole dish.

Temperature: 400°
Time: 30 to 40 minutes

Spanish Chicken

Yield: 4 to 6 servings

1 chicken, 2½ to 3 pounds,
  cut up
Salt and pepper to taste
½ cup melted shortening
1 cup chopped onion
½ cup chopped celery
½ cup chopped green pepper
2 cloves garlic, minced
2 tablespoons melted butter
  or margarine
1½ teaspoons salt
1 teaspoon black pepper
1 tablespoon flour
1 can (16 ounces) tomato
  sauce
1½ tablespoons sugar
½ teaspoon thyme
½ teaspoon lemon juice
Cooked rice

1. Sprinkle chicken with salt and pepper and brown in hot shortening in skillet.
2. Remove chicken from skillet and place in a 9x13-inch baking dish.
3. Saute' onion, celery, green pepper, and garlic in butter. Sprinkle over chicken.
4. Combine remaining ingredients except rice in saucepan and simmer over low heat for 10 to 12 minutes. Pour over chicken.
5. Bake uncovered at 350° for one hour.
6. Serve over rice.

Temperature: 350°
Time: 1 hour

Hint: This dish is great to prepare a day ahead.

Javanese Mountain Dinner

Yield: 8 servings

Great for a buffet! Let each guest make his own mountain.

4 whole chicken breasts

1 can (3 ounces) Chow Mein noodles

2 cups chopped fresh tomatoes

4 stalks celery, thinly sliced

20 green onions, thinly sliced

1 can (20 ounces) crushed pineapple, drained

8 ounces Cheddar cheese, grated

½ cup slivered almonds

1 can (3½ ounces) coconut

12 maraschino cherries

2 cups uncooked rice

1. Roast chicken. Skin, bone, and cut into bite-sized pieces. Strain juices and reserve. Store chicken in serving dish.
2. Prepare next nine ingredients as directed, and store in individual serving dishes.
3. Prepare gravy.
4. Cook rice according to package directions.
5. Serve buffet style in the following order; rice, Chow Mein noodles, chicken, gravy, tomatoes, celery, onions, pineapple, cheese, chicken, gravy, almonds, coconut, cherries.

Gravy

¾ cup chicken fat or butter

¾ cup flour

6 cups pan juices and chicken stock

Salt and pepper

Gravy

1. Heat fat. Add flour and stir until blended.
2. Slowly stir in juices and stock. Cook and stir gravy until smooth.
3. Correct seasonings.
4. Cook until thick.

Hint: The key is to keep chicken, gravy, and rice piping hot.

Chicken Paprika

Yield: 8 servings

4 whole chicken breasts, skinned and boned

3 cups chicken broth

1 cup flour

2½ teaspoons paprika

2 teaspoons salt

¼ teaspoon red pepper

¼ teaspoon coarse black pepper

¼ teaspoon ginger (ground)

¼ teaspoon sweet basil

Dash of nutmeg

¼ cup butter

1 pint sour cream

2 tablespoons Worcestershire sauce

3 tablespoons chili sauce

1 clove garlic, minced

½ teaspoon salt

1 can (8 ounces) water chestnuts, sliced

½ pound fresh mushrooms, sliced

2 tablespoons flour

2 tablespoons water

1. Make broth from boiling bones and chicken skins.
2. Roll chicken in flour mixture with seasonings and brown in butter.
3. Transfer chicken to 3-quart baking dish.
4. Prepare sauce by mixing 3 cups broth, sour cream, Worcestershire, chili sauce, garlic, salt, water chestnuts, and mushrooms. Stir over low heat until well mixed.
5. Pour over chicken in casserole dish and cover. Bake at 325° for 1½ hours.
6. Add 2 tablespoons flour and 2 tablespoons water to sauce.
7. Continue to cook at 325° for 30 more minutes.
8. Serve over your favorite rice.

Temperature: 325°
Time: 1½ hours
Time: 30 minutes

Chicken Romano

Yield: 6 to 8 servings

Freshly grated Romano is the secret.

2 whole chickens, cut up, or
   12 to 14 pieces
Salt to taste
½ cup margarine, melted
36 butter-flavored crackers,
   crushed
½ cup grated Romano cheese
1 teaspoon garlic powder

1. Salt chicken pieces and dip in melted margarine.
2. Mix cracker crumbs, cheese, and garlic powder. Roll chicken in this mixture.
3. Place in a shallow pan (15x9x1-inch) and bake.

Temperature: 350°
Time: 1 hour

Hot And Spicy Chicken Kabobs

Yield: 8 servings

2 large whole chicken breasts,
   skinned, boned, and cut
   into 32 (¾-inch) cubes
½ cup oil
1 jar (4 ounces) pimientos,
   drained and pureed
2 tablespoons red wine
   vinegar
2 large shallots, minced
1½ teaspoons salt
½ teaspoon dried red pepper
   flakes
½ teaspoon dried cumin
2 large green peppers cut into
   32 (¾-inch) squares
16 skewers

1. Place chicken pieces in plastic bag.
2. Combine remaining ingredients in bowl and mix thoroughly.
3. Add to chicken and tie bag tightly.
4. Marinate 1 to 2 days in refrigerator, turning bag several times to redistribute marinade.
5. Preheat broiler. Alternate 2 pieces of chicken with 2 pieces of green pepper on skewer.
6. Place in shallow pan and broil 4 inches from heat for about 8 minutes, turning once.
7. Serve immediately with any remaining sauce.

Creamy Chicken Crêpes Yield: 12 servings

Haute cuisine!

Crêpes

1 cup flour, sifted

1½ cups milk

2 eggs

1 tablespoon salad oil

¼ teaspoon salt

Crêpes

1. Combine all ingredients in bowl and beat until smooth.
2. Lightly grease a 6-inch skillet or crêpe pan; heat.
3. Remove from heat; spoon in 2 tablespoons batter and spread evenly. Return to heat and brown on one side only.
4. To remove, invert pan over paper toweling.

Filling

5 tablespoons butter

5 tablespoons flour

1 cup hot milk

1 cup hot chicken broth

4 tablespoons chopped mushrooms

1 tablespoon butter

3 shallots or 4 tablespoons chopped onion

2 cups cooked, diced chicken

3 tablespoons sherry

1 egg yolk

4 tablespoons heavy cream, whipped

Filling

1. Melt 5 tablespoons butter, and stir in flour. Cook roux until lightly browned.
2. Gradually stir in hot milk and chicken broth. Cook over low heat for 20 minutes.
3. Saute' mushrooms in 1 tablespoon butter. Add shallots or onions and cook 2 minutes.
4. Combine with 2 cups chicken, sherry, and ¾ of sauce.
5. Spread crêpes with chicken mixture and roll up. Place in buttered pan.
6. To remaining sauce, add 1 egg yolk beaten with 4 tablespoons whipped cream.
7. Fold remaining whipped cream into sauce and pour over crêpes.
8. Bake at 350° until hot.

Temperature: 350°
Time: 5 minutes

Hint: These may be kept overnight in the refrigerator or frozen.

Chicken Cacciatore

Yield: 4 to 6 servings

1 chicken (3 to 4 pounds)
2 tablespoons butter
2 tablespoons olive oil
1 stalk celery, thinly sliced
1 carrot, thinly sliced
1 onion, diced
1 tablespoon parsley, finely
  cut
1 teaspoon salt
½ teaspoon pepper
2 tablespoons tomato paste
¾ cup dry sherry

1. Cut chicken into serving pieces.
2. Heat butter and olive oil together in heavy skillet.
3. Brown chicken on all sides, about 20 minutes.
4. Add all vegetables, salt, and pepper; cover.
5. Simmer until vegetables are partially cooked, about 15 minutes.
6. Mix tomato paste and sherry, and stir into vegetables.
7. Cover and cook slowly, stirring occasionally to prevent burning, for 30 minutes or until chicken is done. Serve very hot.

Hint: This is delicious served over spaghetti!

Baked Chicken Breasts With Crab

Yield: 6 servings

A wonderful blend of flavors!

6 chicken breast halves, boned
   and skinned

½ cup chopped onion

½ cup chopped celery

3 tablespoons butter or
   margarine

3 tablespoons white wine

1 cup frozen crab meat,
   drained and flaked

½ cup herb-seasoned stuffing
   mix

2 tablespoons flour

½ teaspoon paprika

½ teaspoon sage

5 tablespoons butter

1. Pound chicken to flatten.
2. Saute' celery and onion in butter. Remove from heat.
3. Add wine, crab meat, and stuffing mix. Toss to blend.
4. Place 2 tablespoons of mixture on each flattened chicken breast. Roll up and secure.
5. Combine flour, paprika, and sage.
6. Coat each piece of chicken and place chicken in shallow baking dish.
7. Drizzle with butter and bake uncovered.

Temperature: 325°
Time: 1 hour

Hint: For variation serve baked breasts with your favorite
   Hollandaise sauce to which has been added 2 tablespoons
   white wine and ½ cup grated Swiss cheese.

Chicken Breasts Wellington

Yield: 12 servings

Hats off to the chef!

6 whole chicken breasts, split,
    skinned and boned
Seasoned salt
Seasoned pepper
1 box (6 ounces) long grain
    and wild rice
¼ cup grated orange peel
2 eggs, separated
3 cans (8 ounces each)
    refrigerated crescent
    dinner rolls
1 tablespoon water

1. Pound chicken breasts to ¼-inch thickness. Season with salt and pepper.
2. Cook rice according to package directions. Add orange peel and cool.
3. Beat egg whites until soft peaks form. Fold into rice.
4. On floured surface, roll 2 triangular pieces of dough into a circle. Repeat to make 12 circles.
5. Place a chicken breast half on each circle. Spoon ¼ cup rice mixture and roll up jelly roll fashion. Moisten edges of dough and press to seal.
6. Place breasts seam side down on large baking sheet.
7. Slightly beat egg yolks with water and brush over dough.
8. Bake uncovered. If dough browns too quickly cover loosely with foil.

Temperature: 375°
Time: 45 to 50 minutes

Chicken And Shrimp Potpourri

Yield: 16 servings

3 cans (14 ounces each) artichoke hearts, drained

8 whole chicken breasts, cooked and diced

3 pounds shrimp, cooked and shelled

3 pounds fresh mushrooms, sliced

3 tablespoons butter

2 tablespoons Worcestershire sauce

6 cups white sauce

Salt and pepper to taste

1 cup sherry

½ cup Parmesan cheese, grated

Paprika

Chopped parsley

1. Arrange artichokes in bottom of large buttered casserole dish.
2. Add chicken and shrimp.
3. Saute' mushrooms in butter and add to casserole.
4. Prepare white sauce. Stir in Worcestershire and pour over casserole.
5. Then add salt, pepper, and sherry. Stir gently.
6. Sprinkle top with cheese and paprika. Bake uncovered.
7. Garnish with parsley when served.

White Sauce

¾ cup butter

¾ cup flour

1½ teaspoons salt

¼ teaspoon white pepper

6 cups milk

White Sauce

1. Melt butter in 3-quart saucepan over low heat.
2. Blend in flour, salt, and white pepper.
3. Add milk all at once. Cook quickly, stirring constantly, until mixture thickens and bubbles.

Temperature: 375°
Time: 40 minutes

Chicken Kiev

Yield: 6 servings

½ cup butter, softened
1 tablespoon parsley
1 tablespoon chopped onion
½ teaspoon salt
⅛ teaspoon pepper
6 chicken breasts, skinned
  and boned
Salt and pepper
1 egg
1 tablespoon water
1 cup flour
⅔ cup bread crumbs
¼ cup melted butter

1. Combine first 5 ingredients. Mix well and shape into stick (like butter). Cover and chill about 45 minutes or until firm.
2. Place each chicken breast on sheet of wax paper; flatten to ¼-inch thickness using meat mallet or rolling pin.
3. Cut stick of butter mixture into 6 portions and place a piece in center of each chicken breast.
4. Fold long sides of chicken over butter, then fold ends over and secure with toothpick.
5. Lightly sprinkle each chicken breast with salt and pepper.
6. Combine egg and water, beating well. Dredge each chicken breast in flour, dip in egg mixture, and coat with bread crumbs.
7. Sauté chicken in butter over medium heat until golden brown on all sides.
8. Transfer to a 13x9x2-inch dish and bake.

Temperature: 400°
Time: 20 minutes

Chicken In Orange Sauce

Yield: 6 servings

Delicious served with rice pilaf.

6 chicken breast halves
Salt to taste
¼ cup butter, melted
2 tablespoons flour
¼ teaspoon cinnamon
¼ teaspoon ginger
1½ cups orange juice
½ cup white raisins
1 can (11 ounces) Mandarin
   oranges, drained
¾ cups slivered almonds

Topping

1 can (11 ounces) Mandarin
   oranges, drained
1 jar (10 ounces) orange
   marmalade
¼ cup orange liqueur

1. Salt chicken and brown in butter. Remove from skillet.
2. To drippings add flour, cinnamon, and ginger. Stir in orange juice and cook over medium heat until thick.
3. Add chicken pieces, raisins, oranges, and almonds. Cook over low heat 45 minutes to one hour.
4. Before serving, spoon topping over chicken.

Artichoke-Chicken Mélange

Yield: 6 servings

An elegant party dish.

4 whole chicken breasts,
  boned and skinned
¼ cup oil
3 carrots, cut into 2-inch
  pieces
½ pound fresh mushrooms,
  halved
1 can (14 ounces) artichoke
  hearts, drained and halved
½ cup chopped green onions
½ cup sliced water chestnuts
⅛ teaspoon whole thyme
½ teaspoon salt
⅛ teaspoon pepper
2 cups chicken broth
2 tablespoons corn starch

1. Brown chicken in oil in large
   skillet. Add carrots; cover and
   simmer for 5 minutes.
2. Add mushrooms, artichoke
   hearts, onions, water chestnuts,
   thyme, salt, and pepper; cover
   and simmer for 10 minutes.
3. Combine broth and cornstarch in
   small saucepan. Cook over
   medium heat stirring constantly
   until sauce is thickened.
4. Place chicken and vegetables in a
   greased 13x9x2-inch baking dish.
   Pour sauce over chicken and
   bake at 375° for 45 minutes. Baste
   chicken occasionally with pan
   drippings.

Temperature: 375°
Time: 45 minutes

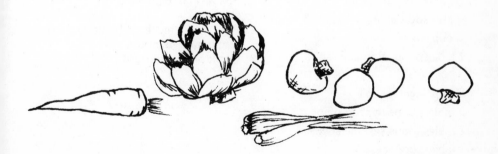

Gourmet Chicken Livers For Two

Yield: 2 servings

¾ pound of chicken livers

2 tablespoons flour

Salt and pepper to taste

3 tablespoons butter

1 large onion, sliced

½ pound fresh mushrooms, sliced in half

¼ cup cooking sherry

1. Dredge chicken livers in seasoned flour and set aside.
2. Melt butter in large skillet. Saute' onions until transparent.
3. Push onions to the side and add chicken livers. Brown on all sides over medium heat.
4. Add mushrooms and toss all ingredients together.
5. Pour sherry over chicken livers. Cover and simmer for five minutes. (Do not overcook. The livers should be slightly pink inside.)

Marinated, Charcoaled Sesame-Chicken

Yield: 6 servings

1 whole chicken, cut up

½ cup soy sauce

¼ cup water

1 tablespoon Worcestershire sauce

½ cup vegetable oil

2 tablespoons minced onion

2 tablespoons sesame seeds

1 tablespoon sugar

1 teaspoon ground ginger

¾ teaspoon salt

1 clove garlic, minced

⅛ teaspoon red pepper

1. Mix all ingredients except chicken.
2. Pour over chicken. Marinate chicken for 12 hours.
2. Cook on outside grill.

Stir-Fried Chicken
And Cashews

Yield: 4 servings

Fun with chop sticks.

3 tablespoons oil

2 raw chicken breasts, boned and diced

1 teaspoon salt

¼ teaspoon pepper

1 to 2 tablespoons soy sauce

1 cup diced celery

1 cup frozen peas

¼ cup diced onions

1 can (4 ounces) button mushrooms

1 cup hot chicken broth

1 tablespoon corn starch

2 tablespoons water

½ cup toasted cashews

Hot rice

1. Heat oil in wok or deep skillet.
2. Stir-fry chicken 3 minutes.
3. Add salt, pepper, soy sauce, celery, peas, onions, and mushrooms. Cook 2 minutes.
4. Stir in broth. Cover and cook over low heat for 5 minutes.
5. Mix corn starch with water; stir into chicken mixture until thickened.
6. Serve over hot rice.
7. Top with cashews.

Hint: Fresh pea pods are a nice substitution for peas.

Crescent Chicken Bundles

Yield: 4 servings

An excellent luncheon dish!

3 ounces cream cheese
2 tablespoons melted butter
2 cups cubed, cooked chicken
¼ teaspoon salt
⅛ teaspoon pepper
2 tablespoons milk
1 tablespoon chopped onion
   or chives
1 tablespoon chopped
   pimiento
1 can (8 ounces) refrigerator
   quick crescent rolls
1 tablespoon melted butter
¾ cup crushed seasoned
   croutons

1. Blend cream cheese and butter until smooth.
2. Add chicken, salt, pepper, milk, onions, and pimientos. Stir.
3. Separate rolls into 4 rectangles. Seal perforations.
4. Spoon ½ cup chicken mixture into center and pull four corners of dough to center and seal.
5. Brush tops with butter and sprinkle on crushed croutons.
6. Bake on cookie sheet.

Temperature: 350°
Time: 20 to 25 minutes

Stuffed Chicken Surprise Yield: 8 servings

Another special for chicken lovers.

8 chicken breast halves,
   boned and skinned

8 slices ham

8 ounces Swiss cheese

24 asparagus spears

1 beaten egg

½ cup evaporated milk

½ cup bread crumbs

Salt to taste

Pepper to taste

Butter

½ cup sherry wine

1. Flatten chicken with meat mallet.
2. Place one slice ham, one slice Swiss cheese, and three asparagus spears in middle of each piece of chicken. Roll up and secure with toothpick.
3. Beat egg and milk together. Dip chicken in mixture and then roll in bread crumbs.
4. Salt and pepper chicken to taste.
5. Arrange in heavily-buttered dish. Bake covered at 350° for one hour.
6. Pour ½ cup sherry over chicken and bake uncovered for 15 minutes.

Temperature: 350°
Time: 1 hour, covered
Time: 15 minutes, uncovered

Creamed Chicken Breasts

Yield: 6 to 8 servings

Enjoy your guests while this is cooking!

10 ounces dried beef

8 chicken breast halves, boned and skinned

8 bacon strips

½ pint sour cream

1 can (10¾ ounces) cream of chicken soup

¼ cup dry white wine

1. Tear beef into pieces and place in a buttered 2-quart oblong baking dish.
2. Roll each chicken breast and wrap with a bacon strip; secure with toothpick.
3. Mix sour cream, soup, and wine. Pour over chicken.
4. Bake covered at 325° for 90 minutes. Remove cover and continue baking for 30 minutes, basting chicken periodically.

Temperature: 325°
Time: 90 minutes, covered
Time: 30 minutes, uncovered

Hint: Thinly-sliced country ham may be substituted for dried beef.

Chicken Fingers

Yield: 6 servings

Oil

3 whole chicken breasts, boned and cut into strips

½ cup flour

¾ teaspoon salt

3 teaspoons sesame seeds

1 egg, beaten

½ cup of water

1. Heat 2 inches of oil in skillet.
2. Make a batter of flour, salt, sesame seeds, egg, and water.
3. Dip chicken in batter and drop into hot oil. Do not crowd pieces. Turn pieces over once. Cook until light brown on both sides, approximately 4 to 5 minutes.

Hint: Prepare in batches and keep warm in oven. These are tasty served with Chinese hot mustard or warmed plum jelly.

Cherry Chicken Flambe′ Yield: 8 servings

Flavorful and beautiful!

4 whole chicken breasts,
  boned and split

Salt

Pepper

1 can (15 ounces) sliced
  pineapple

⅓ cup ground cooked ham

2 tablespoons minced onion

1 tablespoon margarine

¾ cup fresh bread crumbs

3 tablespoons margarine

¾ cup chicken broth

1 tablespoon soy sauce

½ teaspoon ground ginger

2 tablespoons cornstarch

1 cup (17 ounces) pitted, dark
  sweet cherries

⅓ cup brandy

1. Pound each piece of chicken to ¼-inch thickness. Season with salt and pepper.
2. Drain pineapple, reserving juice. Dice one slice of pineapple.
3. Saute′ diced pineapple, ham, and onion in 1 tablespoon of margarine until onion is tender. Add crumbs and mix well.
4. Place one tablespoon ham mixture on each piece of chicken. Fold over and secure with toothpicks.
5. Brown chicken in 3 tablespoons margarine. Add reserved pineapple juice, ½ cup broth, soy sauce, and ginger. Cover and simmer 30 minutes. Remove to serving dish.
6. Add cornstarch, dissolved in remaining ¼ cup broth, to pan juices. Cook, stirring constantly, until thickened and translucent.
7. Add pineapple and cherries. Heat thoroughly and pour over chicken.
8. Warm brandy just before serving. Pour over chicken and ignite.

Cornish Hen Casserole

Yield: 4 servings

An elegant but simple entree.

4 cornish hens, 1 to 1½
  pounds each
⅓ cup butter, softened
½ teaspoon salt
½ teaspoon garlic salt
¼ teaspoon black pepper
4 tablespoons chopped
  parsley
1 cup white wine
3 tomatoes, diced
6 scallions, chopped
1 cup sour cream
Prepared wild rice

1. If using frozen hens, thaw before cooking. Remove giblets and boil giblets in water until tender.
2. Mix soft butter with salts and pepper. Cover birds with mixture.
3. Mash cooked giblets with chopped parsley. Place a generous spoon of mixture into cavity of each bird.
4. Place birds in shallow casserole and roast in 400° oven for 35 minutes.
5. Reduce heat to 350°. Pour white wine over birds. Continue to cook until tender, 30 to 35 minutes, basting once or twice with juices in pan.
6. Add tomatoes and scallions. Cook 10 minutes. Just before serving, blend sour cream into pan gravy and heat thoroughly. Serve at once with wild rice.

Temperature: 400°
Time: 35 minutes
Temperature: 350°
Time: 30 to 35 minutes
  10 minutes

Wine Selection: Fowl recipes mixed with noodles or vegetables should be accompanied with a dry white or even a rose' wine.

Cornish Hens With Brown Rice Dressing

Yield: 6 servings

Guaranteed to bring raves from your guests.

3 cornish hens
¼ cup chopped onion
1 cup chopped celery
Salt
9 slices bacon
1 box (10 ounces) brown rice, cooked according to directions
½ cup milk
1 can (10¾ ounces) cream of chicken soup
1 teaspoon salt
¼ teaspoon sage
¼ teaspoon poultry seasoning
1 can (4 ounces) mushrooms
Butter
Salt
Pepper
Paprika

1. Remove giblets from hens. Simmer giblets with onion and celery in enough salted water to cover until all are tender.
2. Drain giblets and vegetables, reserving the liquid. Chop the giblets and set aside.
3. Fry 6 slices of bacon until crisp; crumble.
4. Cook rice according to directions.
5. In large bowl gradually add milk to soup, stirring until smooth. Add seasonings, giblets, vegetables, bacon, rice, and mushrooms to soup mixture. Mix well.
6. Place dressing in a greased 9x11-inch dish.
7. Cut hens in half; grease well with oil or butter, and season with salt, pepper, and paprika. Place hen halves on top of dressing and cover each with half a strip of uncooked bacon. Cover dish lightly with foil to prevent excess browning.
8. Bake hens and dressing in a 325° oven for 2 hours, basting every half hour with reserved giblet liquid. Remove foil last half hour of cooking.
9. Serve hen halves on platter and rice in separate bowl.

Temperature: 350°
Time: 2 hours

Baked Cornish Hens

Yield: 6 servings

Combination of spices adds an interesting flavor!

3 cornish hens, halved and at
 room temperature
1 teaspoon salt
½ teaspoon nutmeg
½ teaspoon sage
½ teaspoon crushed garlic
½ cup butter
2 tablespoons lemon juice
½ cup orange juice

1. Combine salt, nutmeg, sage, and crushed garlic. Rub over hens both inside and out.
2. Melt butter in 1½ to 2-quart oblong casserole and place hens, skin side down, in casserole.
3. Bake at 350° for 15 minutes.
4. Turn hens and baste with lemon and orange juices. Bake an additional 15 minutes.
5. Check for tenderness. If needed, cook additional 5 to 10 minutes.

Temperature: 350°
Time: 30 to 40 minutes

Hint: Delicious with herbed pasta or brown rice.

Mostaccioli Milano

Yield: 4 servings

2 carrots, thinly sliced
1 clove garlic, crushed
½ cup sliced celery
½ cup chopped onion
3 tablespoons minced parsley
2 tablespoons vegetable oil
2 cups diced, cooked turkey
1 can (12 ounces) tomato
    paste
1 can (2 ounces) sliced
    mushrooms, drained
2 tablespoons white wine
1 teaspoon salt
8 ounces mostaccioli, cooked
    and drained
Grated Parmesan cheese

1. Saute' carrots, garlic, celery,
   onion, and parsley in oil.
2. Add turkey, tomato paste,
   mushrooms, wine, salt, and 2
   cups water to sautéed vegetables.
   Bring to a boil, then cover and
   simmer 20 to 25 minutes, stirring
   occasionally.
3. In serving dish, spoon sauce over
   mostaccioli and sprinkle with
   Parmesan cheese.

Turkey And Rice Delight   Yield: 6 servings

A marvelous use for leftover turkey!

1 box (6 ounces) Uncle Ben's®
  Original Long Grain and Wild
  Rice
½ cup butter
½ cup flour
1 can (4 ounces) mushrooms
1 can (10½ ounces) chicken
  broth
2 cups light cream
2 cups chopped turkey
1 jar (2 ounces) chopped
  pimiento
Slivered almonds

1. Cook rice according to directions
   on box.
2. Melt butter and stir in flour.
3. Add juice from can of
   mushrooms, chicken broth, and
   cream.
4. Stir over low heat until warm and
   creamy.
5. Add rice, mushrooms, turkey,
   and pimiento. Put in 9x13-inch
   casserole. Sprinkle with slivered
   almonds.
6. Bake.

Temperature: 350°
Time: 30 minutes

Breads

Breads

Everlasting Angel Biscuits

Yield: 36 biscuits

Light and fluffy.

2½ cups flour

2 tablespoons sugar

1½ teaspoons baking powder

½ teaspoon salt

½ teaspoon soda

½ cup shortening

1 tablespoon warm water

1½ teaspoons dry yeast

1 cup buttermilk

1. Sift dry ingredients together.
2. Cut shortening into dry ingredients until mixture resembles cornmeal.
3. Dissolve yeast in warm water, then stir into buttermilk.
4. Combine flour mixture and liquid ingredients to make a stiff dough.
5. Roll to ½-inch thickness on floured board.
6. Cut into 2-inch biscuits and bake on greased baking sheet until browned.

Temperature: 450°
Time: 10 minutes

Kentucky Fried Biscuits

Yield: 9 dozen

Unique and surprisingly easy!

2⅔ packages dry yeast

⅔ cup warm water

4 cups milk

½ cup shortening

¼ cup sugar

6 teaspoons salt

7 to 9 cups flour

1. Dissolve yeast in warm water.
2. Scald milk (150°). Add shortening, sugar, and salt. Stir to dissolve shortening. Cool to lukewarm.
3. Combine milk and yeast in large bowl. Stir in flour to make moderately stiff dough.
4. Place in greased bowl, turning once to grease top. Let rise in warm place for 30 minutes.
5. Knead lightly on floured surface. Roll dough to ½-inch thickness; cut with 2-inch biscuit cutter. (Don't let the biscuits rise too high before frying.)
6. Fry in deep fat (deep fryer is ideal), slightly hotter than 350°, until golden brown (about 1 minute).

Hint: Serve these with homemade apple butter.

Indian Cornmeal Cakes

Yield: 6 servings

Fried cornbread in a different and delicate version.

½ cup flour

½ teaspoon salt

½ teaspoon soda

½ teaspoon baking powder

3 teaspoons sugar

1 cup plus 2 tablespoons
   cornmeal

1 egg, beaten

2 tablespoons oil

1 cup buttermilk

Milk to thin batter

1. Sift dry ingredients together and set aside.
2. Mix egg, oil, and buttermilk. Add to dry ingredients, beating well.
3. When mixture is smooth, add enough whole milk to make batter thin.
4. Heat well-greased skillet or griddle until very hot.
5. Dip about ¼ cup batter to form each cake. Fry until bubbly on top and light brown on bottom. Flip and cook until done.

Mother's Coffee Cake Yield: 9-inch coffee cake

Uses ingredients found in any kitchen.

¼ cup soft margarine

¾ cup sugar

1 egg

½ cup milk

1½ cups flour

2 teaspoons baking powder

½ teaspoon salt

1. Cream margarine and sugar; add egg, blending well. Stir in milk.
2. Sift together flour, baking powder, and salt. Add to batter; set aside.

Topping

3 tablespoons melted
   margarine

¾ cup brown sugar

2 teaspoons cinnamon

½ cup chopped nuts

Topping

1. Mix together topping ingredients.
2. In a greased 9x9-inch pan, spread half the batter and sprinkle with half the topping. Add remaining batter and topping.
3. Bake.

Temperature: 375°
Time: 25 to 30 minutes

Sour Cream Coffee Cake

Yield: 9-inch coffee cake

Wonderful texture and taste.

½ cup finely-chopped nuts

1 tablespoon cinnamon

¼ cup sugar

1½ cups sifted flour

1 teaspoon baking powder

½ teaspoon soda

½ cup butter

1 tablespoon vanilla

1 cup sugar

2 eggs, beaten until thick

1 cup sour cream

1. Grease bottom only of 9x9x2-inch cake pan.
2. Mix nuts, cinnamon, and the ¼ cup sugar; set aside.
3. Sift together flour, baking powder, and soda; set aside.
4. Cream butter and vanilla. Add sugar gradually, creaming until fluffy after each addition.
5. Add beaten eggs in thirds, beating thoroughly after each addition.
6. Beating only until smooth after each addition, alternately add dry ingredients in fourths and pour sour cream in thirds. Finally, beat only until smooth; do not overbeat.
7. Turn one half of batter into pan; sprinkle evenly with one-half nut mixture. Turn remaining batter into pan; top with remaining nuts.
8. Bake at 375° for 30 minutes or until cake tester comes out clean. Serve warm; cut in squares.

Temperature: 375°
Time: 30 minutes

Orange-Butter Coffee Cake

Yield: 2 coffee cakes (9 inches each)
Yield: 24 rolls

Light, lovely, and luscious!

2 packages dry yeast

½ cup warm (115°) water

¼ cup sugar

2 eggs, beaten

½ cup sour cream

6 tablespoons melted butter

1 teaspoon salt

3¾ cups sifted flour

⅔ cup sugar

1 cup flaked coconut, toasted

2 tablespoons shredded
   orange peel

2 tablespoons melted butter

1 cup sifted powdered sugar

3 to 4 teaspoons orange juice

1. Soften yeast in warm water.
2. Combine ¼ cup sugar, eggs, sour cream, 6 tablespoons melted butter, and salt in large bowl.
3. Stir in yeast. Gradually add enough flour to form moderately stiff dough, beating well.
4. Cover; let rise until double (about 45 minutes).
5. Combine the ⅔ cup sugar, coconut, and orange peel.
6. Turn dough onto well-floured surface, and knead a few strokes. Divide dough in half.
7. Roll one-half of dough to form a 12x8-inch rectangle; brush with 1 tablespoon melted butter, and sprinkle with ½ cup coconut mixture. Roll up, starting with long side, and cut into twelve 1-inch slices. Place cut side down, in greased 9x1½-inch round baking pan. Repeat for second half.
8. Let rise in warm place until light (30 to 45 minutes). Sprinkle rolls with remaining coconut mixture.
9. Bake at 350° about 30 minutes. Remove from pans; cool right side up.
10. Combine powdered sugar and orange juice; drizzle over cooled cakes.

Temperature: 350°
Time: 30 minutes

235

Cinnamon Twirls

Yield: 18 rolls

Surprisingly easy!

1 package dry yeast

¼ cup lukewarm water

1 cup sour cream

2 tablespoons melted butter

1 teaspoon salt

3 tablespoons sugar

⅛ teaspoon soda

1 egg

3 cups flour

1. Dissolve yeast in warm water; set aside.
2. Heat sour cream to lukewarm. Blend in butter, salt, sugar, and soda. Add unbeaten egg and yeast.
3. Stir in flour and blend well.
4. Knead dough lightly on floured surface. Shape into a ball. Let rest 5 minutes.
5. Roll out to 6x24-inch rectangle.

Filling

2 tablespoons melted butter

⅓ cup brown sugar

2 teaspoons cinnamon

Chopped nuts, optional

Filling

1. Brush dough with melted butter, and sprinkle with mixture of brown sugar and cinnamon. Sprinkle with nuts, if desired.
2. Starting with long side, roll up (as for jelly roll). Cut into 1½-inch slices.
3. Place cut side down in greased muffin pans. Let rise in warm place about 1 hour or until light.
4. Bake.

Icing

2 cups powdered sugar

2 teaspoons melted butter

⅛ teaspoon vanilla

Cream

Icing

1. While rolls bake, mix first three icing ingredients; thin to desired consistency with cream. Drizzle over hot rolls.

Temperature: 375°
Time: 12 to 15 minutes

Cinnamon Crescents

Yield: 64 morsels

Flaky little bites of goodness.

Dough

2 cups flour
1 cup butter
1 egg yolk
¾ cup sour cream

Dough

1. Sift flour into bowl; cut in butter.
2. Mix egg yolk and sour cream; stir into flour mixture.
3. With floured hands, shape dough into ball, sprinkle with flour and wrap in wax paper.
4. Chill several hours or overnight.

Filling

1 cup sugar
1 cup chopped nuts
1 teaspoon cinnamon

Filling

1. Mix filling ingredients.
2. Divide dough into 4 parts. Work with one at a time, refrigerating remainder.
3. Roll each part into an 8-inch circle and sprinkle with one-fourth of the filling mixture.
4. Cut into 16 pie-shaped wedges, and roll up each wedge, beginning at the wide end.
5. Place on greased and floured baking sheet with points underneath.

Glaze

1 tablespoon milk
1 egg white, beaten

Glaze

1. Combine glaze ingredients, and brush mixture on each crescent before baking.
2. Bake.

Temperature: 350°
Time: 20 to 25 minutes

Hint: Allow ample time for chilling dough.

Orange Biscuits

Yield: 10 biscuits

First you make a dough, your own or from a mix.

Dough for 10 biscuits
¼ cup butter
½ cup sugar
½ cup orange juice
2 teaspoons grated orange
  rind
½ cup sugar
½ teaspoon cinnamon

1. Cook butter, ½ cup sugar, juice, and rind for 2 minutes. Pour into greased muffin cups.
2. Roll biscuit dough ½-inch thick. Sprinkle with mixture of ½ cup sugar and cinnamon.
3. Roll up from long side; slice into 10 sections. Place one section into each muffin cup.
4. Bake.
5. Invert on serving plate; serve hot.

Temperature: 375°
Time: 20 to 25 minutes

Pecan Muffins

Yield: 10 muffins

Quickly made and quickly eaten.

1½ cups flour
½ cup sugar
2 teaspoons baking powder
½ teaspoon salt
½ cup chopped pecans
1 egg, slightly beaten
½ cup milk
¼ cup vegetable oil

1. Sift together dry ingredients. Stir in pecans. Make a well in center.
2. Combine egg, milk, and oil. Add to dry ingredients, stirring just until moistened.
3. Fill paper-lined muffin pans ⅔ full.
4. Bake at 400° for 20 minutes. Remove from pan immediately.

Temperature: 400°
Time: 20 minutes

Lemon-Dipped Blueberry Muffins

Yield: 14 muffins (or 48 mini muffins)

Not too tart, not too sweet, just right.

1¾ cups flour

½ cup sugar

2½ teaspoons baking powder

¾ teaspoon salt

¾ cup milk

⅓ cup vegetable oil

1 egg, beaten

1 cup fresh blueberries

2 tablespoons sugar

2 teaspoons grated lemon rind

1. In large bowl combine flour, sugar, baking powder, and salt. Make a well in center of mixture.
2. Combine milk, oil, and egg. Add to dry ingredients, stirring until moistened.
3. Toss blueberries with 2 tablespoons sugar and lemon rind. Fold into batter.
4. Fill muffin papers or greased muffin pans ⅔ full.
5. Bake at 400° for 20 minutes or until golden brown.

Temperature: 400°
Time: 20 minutes

Topping

2 tablespoons melted butter

¼ teaspoon lemon juice

Sugar

Topping

1. While muffins bake, prepare topping by mixing melted butter and lemon juice. Dip warm muffins in butter mixture, then in sugar.

Hint: Batter will keep if refrigerated overnight in paper-lined muffin pans covered with plastic wrap. Just bake, dip, and serve.

Pumpkin Muffins

Yield: 14 muffins
(Do not double recipe.)

Good served with game.

1 cup pumpkin

2 eggs, slightly beaten

½ cup water

½ cup melted shortening

1¾ cups flour

¼ teaspoon salt

1½ cups sugar

1 teaspoon soda

¼ teaspoon baking powder

1 teaspoon cinnamon

½ teaspoon nutmeg

½ teaspoon ginger

¼ teaspoon cloves

1. Blend pumpkin, eggs, water, and shortening in large bowl.
2. Sift together remaining ingredients and add to pumpkin mixture.
3. Fill greased muffin tins about ¾ full.
4. Bake at 350° about 30 minutes or until set when touched.

Temperature: 350°
Time: 30 minutes

Hint: For a sweet muffin, add ½ cup chopped dates and top with lemon sauce or sweetened whipped cream.

Honey Corn Muffins

Yield: 8 muffins

A light, all-purpose muffin.

¾ cup sifted flour

1¼ teaspoons baking powder

½ teaspoon salt

⅓ cup cornmeal

1 egg, well beaten

⅓ cup milk

¼ cup honey

3 tablespoons melted shortening

¼ cup peeled, diced apple

1. Sift flour with baking powder and salt. Stir in cornmeal.
2. Combine egg, milk, honey and shortening. Stir in apple. Add all at once to dry mixture, stirring only until moistened.
3. Fill greased muffin pans ¾ full.
4. Bake at 400° for 20 minutes or until golden brown.

Temperature: 400°
Time: 20 minutes

Ever-Ready Bran Muffins   Yield: 54 muffins

How satisfying to have on hand!

4 cups whole bran cereal

2 cups crushed shredded
   wheat biscuits

2 cups boiling water

1 cup shortening

4 cups buttermilk

4 eggs, beaten

5 cups flour

2 cups sugar

1 tablespoon baking powder

1 tablespoon soda

2 teaspoons salt

1 cup chopped dates, optional

1. In large bowl combine cereals.
2. Stir in boiling water, then stir in shortening until melted.
3. Add buttermilk and eggs, mixing well.
4. Sift together dry ingredients. Add all at once to cereal mixture, stirring just until moistened.
5. Add dates, if desired.
6. Spoon into greased muffin tins, filling ⅔ full.
7. Bake at 400°for 20 to 25 minutes or until browned.

Temperature: 400°
Time: 20 minutes

Hint: Place leftover dough in refrigerator in tightly-covered container. It will keep up to 4 weeks.

Cheese Muffins   Yield: 12 muffins

Very rich and extraordinarily good!

2 cups sifted flour

4 teaspoons baking powder

1 tablespoon sugar

½ teaspoon salt

1 egg

1 cup milk

3 tablespoons butter, softened

1½ cups shredded sharp
   Cheddar cheese

1. Sift together dry ingredients and set aside.
2. Beat egg, milk, and butter until smooth. Stir in cheese. Add to dry ingredients, mixing only until moistened.
3. Fill greased muffin tins ⅔ full.
4. Bake.

Temperature: 350°
Time: 30 to 35 minutes

Hint: Four ounces of cheese equals 1½ cups shredded cheese.

241

Bourbon Pecan Bread
Yield: 1 medium loaf

For really mellow flavor, resist until the next day.

2 cups flour

1 teaspoon baking powder

¾ teaspoon soda

¼ teaspoon salt

½ cup butter, softened

⅓ cup firmly-packed dark
  brown sugar

½ cup maple syrup

2 eggs

½ cup buttermilk

1 cup chopped pecans

3 tablespoons Kentucky
  bourbon

1. Preheat oven to 350°.
2. Generously grease an 8½ x 4½ x 2½-inch loaf pan; line with wax paper.
3. Sift together flour, baking powder, soda, and salt. Set aside.
4. Cream butter and sugar. Add syrup and eggs; beat at medium speed until light and fluffy.
5. On low speed add dry ingredients alternately with buttermilk, beating well after each addition.
6. Stir in pecans and bourbon. Pour batter into pan.
7. Bake 55 minutes. Let cool in pan 10 minutes.
8. Remove and discard wax paper; cool completely before serving.

Temperature: 350°
Time: 55 minutes

Beat-The-Clock Banana Bread
Yield: 1 loaf

Think it's too easy to be good? Just try it!

3 very ripe bananas

¾ cup sugar

Pinch salt

1 egg, beaten

¼ cup butter, melted

1 teaspoon soda

1 tablespoon water

2 cups flour

1. Mash bananas with fork.
2. Blend in sugar, salt, and egg.
3. Stir in melted butter.
4. Dissolve soda in water and add to mixture.
5. Blend in flour.
6. Pour into greased and floured 9 x 5 x 3-inch loaf pan.
7. Bake; cool partially before removing from pan.

Temperature: 350°
Time: 1 hour

Spicy Nut Bread

Yield: 2 small loaves

Make ahead — give the spices time to do their thing.

3 cups sifted flour

1 teaspoon baking powder

1 teaspoon salt

1 teaspoon soda

¾ teaspoon nutmeg

¾ teaspoon ginger

½ teaspoon cinnamon

2 large eggs

1 cup firmly-packed light
 brown sugar

1½ cups melted butter, cooled

½ cup dark molasses

1 cup chopped walnuts

1¼ cups milk

1 teaspoon vinegar

1. Sift together first 7 (dry) ingredients; set aside.
2. In large mixing bowl, beat eggs until light and fluffy. Gradually beat in brown sugar until mixture begins to thicken. Stir in butter, molasses, and nuts.
3. Stir together milk and vinegar.
4. Alternately add flour mixture and milk to egg mixture, stirring only enough to blend.
5. Pour into 2 well-greased and floured 7½ x 3¾ x 2¼-inch loaf pans.
6. Bake at 350° for 1 hour or until edges are lightly browned.
7. Cool in pans on rack for 10 minutes. Turn out and cool completely.

Temperature: 350°
Time: 1 hour

Hint: For easier slicing, wrap in foil or plastic wrap and store overnight.

Apple Crunch Bread

Yield: 1 loaf

The topping makes it different.

½ cup butter

1 cup sugar

2 eggs

2 cups flour

½ teaspoon salt

1 teaspoon soda

2 tablespoons buttermilk

1 teaspoon vanilla

2 cups peeled, diced apples

1. Cream butter and sugar. Beat in eggs. Add flour and salt.
2. Dissolve soda in buttermilk. Add to batter, mixing well.
3. Stir in vanilla and apples.
4. Spoon into greased and floured 9 x 5 x 3-inch loaf pan.

Topping

2 tablespoons butter

2 tablespoons sugar

2 tablespoons flour

1 teaspoon cinnamon

Topping

1. Cream butter and sugar; cut in flour and cinnamon to consistency of coarse crumbs. Sprinkle over batter.
2. Bake.

Temperature: 325°
Time: 70 minutes

Sweet Caraway Bread

Yield: 1 large loaf or
2 medium loaves

Add this accent to a light luncheon.

3 cups sifted flour

4 teaspoons baking powder

½ teaspoon salt

⅓ cup butter

1¼ cups sugar

2 eggs

1¼ cups milk

4 teaspoons caraway seeds

1 teaspoon vanilla

1. Sift flour, baking powder, and salt; set aside.
2. Cream butter and sugar until light and fluffy. Add eggs, beating well.
3. Alternately add flour mixture and milk, blending well after each addition.
4. Add caraway seeds and vanilla.
5. Pour batter into greased and floured loaf pan (1 large 9 x 5 x 3-inch or 2 medium 8½ x 4½ x 2½-inch).
6. Bake at 350° for about 1 hour or until cake tester comes out clean.
7. Cool in pan on rack 30 minutes. Remove from pan and cool completely before slicing.

Temperature: 350°
Time: 1 hour

Serving suggestion: Slice, butter, wrap, and heat through.

Granola Bread

Yield: 1 loaf

Chewy and oh, so good for you.

3 to 3¼ cups flour

1 package dry yeast

1 cup granola

¼ cup brown sugar

1 cup warm water (120°)

2 tablespoons oil

1 egg

1. Combine 1½ cups of flour with remaining ingredients. Beat 3 minutes.
2. Stir in the rest of the flour. Knead 5 to 8 minutes.
3. Place in greased bowl, cover, and let rise for 1 hour.
4. Punch down, form into loaf, and place in greased loaf pan. Let rise until double (about 1 hour).
5. Bake.

Temperature: 375°
Time: 30 to 35 minutes

Challah

Yield: 2 braided loaves

Delicious Jewish braided bread (pronounced "holla").

2 tablespoons yeast

½ cup warm water (110°)

¾ cup milk

¼ cup butter or margarine

2 tablespoons sugar

2 teaspoons salt

4½ to 5 cups unbleached flour

2 eggs, beaten

Glaze

1 egg yolk

1 tablespoon water

Poppy seeds

1. Dissolve yeast in warm water. Set aside.
2. In saucepan mix milk, butter, sugar, and salt. Cook over low heat until sugar and salt have dissolved.
3. Pour mixture into large bowl. Cool to lukewarm.
4. Stir in 2 cups flour, beating well.
5. Add yeast and eggs, beating well.
6. Add enough remaining flour to make a soft dough (does not stick to fingers when kneaded).
7. Knead on floured surface until smooth and elastic (8 to 10 minutes).
8. Place ball of dough in greased bowl, turning to grease both sides. Cover and let rise until double (about 1 hour). Punch down; let rest 10 minutes.
9. Divide dough into two equal parts. Cover one while working with the other.
10. Divide one of the parts into two pieces, one about ¾ of the dough and the other about ¼ of the dough.
11. Divide the large piece into 3 equal parts. Roll each of the 3 pieces into a rope about 18 inches long. Lay the ropes side by side and braid together starting in the middle. Pinch ends to seal.
12. Divide the small piece into 3 equal parts. Roll each into a slender 18-inch rope. Braid and place on top of large braid, sealing the ends together. Place on greased baking sheet.

Challah, continued

13. Repeat with remaining dough to form second loaf.
14. Beat together water and egg yolk. Brush loaves with mixture. Sprinkle with poppy seeds.
15. Cover and let rise until double (about 1 hour).
16. Bake.

Temperature: 375°
Time: 45 to 50 minutes

Hint: To test rising bread for double in size, press the tips of two fingers lightly and quickly ½-inch into the dough. If the dent stays, it is double.

Wheaten Bread

Yield: 2 loaves

Simplicity and goodness, hallmark of the Shakers.

1 cup milk

1 tablespoon salt

3 tablespoons butter

4 tablespoons honey or maple syrup

¾ cup water

1 package active dry yeast

¼ cup warm water (110°)

2 cups sifted flour

4 cups whole wheat flour

1. Scald milk. Add salt, butter, honey, and water. Stir well, cool to lukewarm.
2. Dissolve yeast in warm water. Add to milk mixture.
3. Gradually stir in flours.
4. On floured surface, knead until smooth and elastic (8 to 10 minutes).
5. Place in buttered bowl, brush top with softened butter. Cover and let rise in warm place until double.
6. Knead lightly, shape into loaves, place in 2 greased 9 x 5 x 3-inch loaf pans.
7. Brush with softened butter, cover and let rise until double.
8. Bake.

Temperature: 350°
Time: 40 to 50 minutes

Maple Syrup Braided Bread

Yield: 2 loaves

Maple syrup adds a subtle sweetness to this delicious bread.

1 package active dry yeast
¼ cup warm water (110°)
¾ cup milk
¾ cup maple syrup
½ cup cooking oil
2 teaspoons salt
4½ to 5 cups flour
1 egg
1 egg yolk

Glaze

1 egg white, slightly beaten
1 tablespoon water

1. Dissolve yeast in water. Set aside.
2. Scald milk; pour into large bowl. Add syrup, oil, and salt.
3. Stir in 2 cups flour. Beat 2 minutes.
4. Blend in yeast, egg, and egg yolk.
5. Stir in remaining flour to make a soft dough. On lightly-floured surface, knead until smooth and elastic (10 minutes).
6. Shape into a ball and place in greased bowl, turning to grease all sides. Cover and let rise in warm place until double (about 2 hours).
7. Punch down, divide into 6 equal pieces. Cover and let rest 10 minutes.
8. Roll each piece on floured surface with hands to make 20-inch rope. Pinch together the ends of 3 ropes, braid tightly, and pinch strands together at other end.
9. Repeat with remaining 3 strands to make second loaf.
10. Place loaves on greased baking sheet at least 2 inches apart. Cover and let rise until double.
11. Bake at 325° for 35 minutes.

Maple Syrup Braided Bread, continued

12. Combine glaze ingredients. Brush loaves with glaze. Continue baking at least 15 minutes or until loaves sound hollow when thumped on the bottom. If loaves brown too fast, cover with aluminum foil.

Temperature: 325°
Time: 35 minutes
     15 minutes

Hint: To vary the taste, you may substitute for the ¾ cup of maple syrup, either:

¼ *cup maple syrup and*   or   ¼ *cup regular pancake syrup and*
½ *cup white corn syrup*   ½ *cup white corn syrup*

Poppy Seed Bread   Yield: 6 small loaves

Delicate, sweet bread.

3 cups flour

1½ teaspoons salt

1½ teaspoons baking powder

3 eggs

1½ cups milk

1⅛ cups oil

2 cups sugar

1½ teaspoons each: almond, vanilla, and butter flavorings

1½ tablespoons poppy seeds

1. Combine all ingredients in large bowl of electric mixer. Beat at medium speed for 2 minutes.
2. Pour into 6 lightly-greased 4½ x 2½ x 1¾-inch loaf pans.
3. Bake. Cool 5 minutes in pans.

Temperature: 350°
Time: 45 minutes

Frosting

¼ cup orange juice

¾ cup sugar

½ teaspoon each: almond, vanilla, and butter flavorings

Frosting

1. Combine frosting ingredients. Mix until smooth.
2. Drizzle frosting over the loaves. Let stand 5 more minutes, then remove from pans.

Whole Wheat Bread

Yield: 1 loaf

This breadmaker grinds her own flour, since freshness is important.

2 packages active dry yeast

2 tablespoons warm water (110°)

4 tablespoons honey (or 2 tablespoons sugar)

3 cups whole wheat flour

1 cup milk (or potato water)

1 tablespoon butter (or margarine)

½ teaspoon salt

1. Dissolve yeast in water. Add honey.
2. Place flour in large bowl and make a well in the center.
3. Pour yeast mixture into center of flour. Cover with wax paper and folded tea towel; allow to foam 10 minutes.
4. Scald milk (or heat potato water); stir in butter. Pour into center of flour; add salt around edge. Allow to foam 20 minutes.
5. Work flour into center to mix thoroughly. Cover and let rise until double.
6. On lightly-floured surface, knead until smooth and elastic (8 to 10 minutes).
7. Shape into loaf; place in greased 9 x 5 x 3-inch loaf pan. Cover and let rise again until double.
8. Bake.

Temperature: 400°
Time: 45 minutes

Hint: To make potato water, boil pared and diced medium potato in 1½ cups water until tender, about 20 minutes.

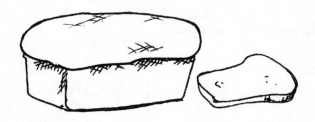

Italian Bread

Yield: 2 loaves

Make this ahead; remove from refrigerator an hour before serving.

4½ to 5½ cups unsifted flour

1 tablespoon sugar

1 tablespoon salt

2 packages active dry yeast

1 tablespoon softened butter
   or margarine

1¾ cups very warm tap water
   (120° to 130°)

Cornmeal

Peanut oil

1 egg white, slightly beaten

1 tablespoon cold water

1. In a large bowl thoroughly mix 1½ cups flour, sugar, salt, and undissolved yeast.
2. Add butter.
3. Gradually add water and beat 2 minutes at medium speed of electric mixer, scraping bowl occasionally.
4. Add ¾ cup flour. Beat at high speed 2 minutes, scraping bowl occasionally.
5. Stir in enough additional flour to make a stiff dough.
6. On lightly-floured surface, knead until smooth and elastic (8 to 10 minutes). Cover with plastic wrap then a towel. Let rest 20 minutes.
7. Divide dough in half. Roll each half into an oblong 15 x 10 inches. Roll tightly from wide side; pinch seam to seal. Taper ends by rolling gently back and forth.
8. Place on greased baking sheets sprinkled with cornmeal. Brush dough with oil.
9. Cover loosely with plastic wrap. Refrigerate 2 to 24 hours.
10. Remove from refrigerator. Uncover dough carefully. Let stand at room temperature 15 to 20 minutes.
11. Make 3 or 4 diagonal cuts on top of each loaf with a sharp knife.
12. Bake 20 minutes. Remove from oven and brush with mixture of egg white and water. Bake until golden brown.

Temperature: 425°
Time: 20 minutes
      5 to 10 minutes longer

Golden Puffs

Yield: 2 to 3 dozen

A quick and easy drop doughnut.

2 cups flour

¼ cup sugar

1 teaspoon salt

3 teaspoons baking powder

1 teaspoon mace or nutmeg

¼ cup oil

¾ cup milk

1 egg, beaten

Powdered sugar, optional

1. Sift together dry ingredients.
2. Add liquid ingredients, and stir with fork until thoroughly mixed.
3. Drop by teaspoonful into deep hot fat (370°). Fry until golden brown, about 3 minutes.
4. Sprinkle with powdered sugar while still hot.

Hint: These keep well, freeze, and reheat well in microwave.

Kentucky Spoon Bread

Yield: 4 to 6 servings

A classic southern dish.

3 cups milk

1 cup cornmeal

1 teaspoon sugar

1 teaspoon butter

1 teaspoon salt

3 egg yolks, beaten

3 egg whites, well beaten

1. Heat milk in double boiler.
2. Add cornmeal slowly. Cook 5 minutes (or to consistency of heavy cream), stirring constantly.
3. Remove from heat and add sugar, butter, and salt. Blend well.
4. Add beaten egg yolks.
5. Fold in beaten egg whites.
6. Pour into buttered 2-quart baking dish. Bake.

Temperature: 350°
Time: 45 minutes

Hint: Serve with lots of butter as a meal accompaniment. It's also marvelous spooned into a soup bowl and covered with Venison Stew.

Herb Popovers

Yield: 7 popovers

Popovers do such spectacular things!

1 cup sifted flour
½ teaspoon salt
1 large clove garlic, crushed
½ teaspoon thyme
2 teaspoons finely-snipped
  parsley
2 tablespoons melted butter
1 cup milk
3 eggs, slightly beaten

1. Grease seven 5-ounce ovenproof custard cups with cooking oil.
2. Sift flour and salt into mixer bowl.
3. Stir garlic, thyme, and parsley into melted butter. Beat butter and milk into beaten eggs.
4. Make a well in center of dry ingredients, and pour in the egg-milk mixture. Beat at medium speed until batter is smooth.
5. Half-fill custard cups with batter.
6. Bake at 475° for 10 minutes. Reduce heat to 350° and bake 30 minutes. Turn off heat; leave popovers in oven 10 minutes longer.

Temperature: 475°
Time: 10 minutes

Temperature: 350°
Time: 30 minutes

Hint: Muffin tins may be used. Alter baking times to 475° - 8 minutes and 350° - 20 minutes.

Corn Fritters

Yield: 6 servings

A special treat served with honey butter.

3 eggs, separated
1⅔ cups corn, drained
½ teaspoon salt
⅛ teaspoon pepper
¼ cup flour

1. Beat egg yolks well.
2. Add corn, salt, pepper, and flour.
3. Fold in stiffly-beaten egg whites.
4. Drop by tablespoonfuls on hot greased skillet or griddle. Cook each side until golden brown.

Spoon Rolls

Yield: 24 rolls

Exceptionally easy and better made ahead.

2 cups warm water

1 envelope dry yeast

¼ cup sugar

¾ cup butter, melted

1 egg, beaten

4 cups self-rising flour

1. Dissolve yeast in warm water. Set aside.
2. Mix sugar and butter in large bowl. Add egg. Alternately add flour and yeast mixture.
3. Refrigerate batter in air-tight bowl several hours or overnight. It will keep for a week or more.
4. To serve, stir batter thoroughly and spoon into greased muffin tins filling ⅔ full. Bake at 400° about 20 minutes or until brown.

Temperature: 400°
Time: 20 minutes

Hint: 1 cup self-rising flour = 1 cup all purpose flour + 1½ teaspoons baking powder + ¼ teaspoon salt.

Corn Sticks

Yield: 24 corn sticks or
16 muffins or
1 pan or skillet

Enjoy the true taste of cornbread.

1 egg

2 cups thick buttermilk

2 cups plain white cornmeal

1 teaspoon salt

1 teaspoon soda

1. Preheat oven to 500° (450° for pan or skillet). Place well-greased pans inside to heat.
2. Beat egg slightly; mix in buttermilk.
3. Mix dry ingredients thoroughly and add to milk, stirring only until blended.
4. Spoon into hot pans. Bake for 15 to 20 minutes (30 minutes for pan or skillet).

Temperature: 500° (or 450°)
Time: 20 (or 30) minutes

Yeast Rolls

Yield: 24 rolls

One of life's little pleasures.

1 package dry yeast
1 tablespoon warm water
1 tablespoon sugar
1¼ cups milk
3 tablespoons butter
¼ cup sugar
1 teaspoon salt
1 egg white, beaten
4 cups sifted flour

1. Dissolve yeast in warm water. Add 1 tablespoon sugar. Set aside.
2. Scald milk. Remove from heat and stir in butter, sugar, and salt. Cool to lukewarm.
3. Add egg white and yeast mixture.
4. Stir in about 3½ cups of flour to make a soft dough. Turn out on floured surface; knead heavily (8 to 10 minutes) working in remaining flour.
5. Place in greased bowl, turning once to grease top. Cover and let rise in warm place until double (about 1 hour).
6. Turn out onto floured surface and knead gently. Divide dough in half; divide each half into 12 equal pieces, and form each piece into a smooth round ball. Place balls in 2 greased 8-inch round cake pans, brush with melted butter. Let rise until double (about 1 hour).
7. Bake.

Temperature: 400°
Time: 10 minutes

Hint: Let bread rise in the oven over a pan of hot water.

Brown And Serve Rolls

Yield: 60 rolls

Make these a day ahead or weeks ahead.

1 cup shortening

1 cup boiling water

2 packages dry yeast

½ cup warm water

2 eggs, beaten

¾ cup sugar

2 teaspoons salt

1 cup cold water

7½ cups flour

Melted butter

1. In a large bowl, stir shortening into boiling water until melted. Cool to lukewarm.
2. Dissolve yeast in warm (110°) water.
3. Beat together eggs, sugar, and salt; stir in cold water.
4. Add egg and yeast mixtures to shortening. Sift in flour, stirring well.
5. Cover and refrigerate overnight.
6. On floured surface, roll dough ½-inch thick and cut with floured cutter (or use pizza cutter for neat square rolls).
7. Place close together in greased pans. Brush tops with butter (or dip in butter). Cover and let rise 2 to 3 hours.
8. Bake.

Temperature: 275°
Time: 30 minutes

Temperature: 400°
Time: 8 to 10 minutes (until brown)

Hint: To use as brown and serve, refrigerate or freeze after first cooking time.

256

Crusty Hard Rolls

Yield: 20 rolls

Neat, impressive, good, and easy!

2 cups warm (115°) water

1 envelope dry yeast

1 tablespoon sugar

2 teaspoons salt

6 cups flour (approximately)

Soft shortening

1 egg white, unbeaten

1. Measure water into large bowl; sprinkle yeast over it, stirring until dissolved.
2. Add sugar, salt, and 3 cups flour. Stir to mix; beat until smooth.
3. Stir in 3 cups of flour.
4. Turn dough onto lightly-floured surface; knead until smooth and elastic (about 10 minutes).
5. Place in large, greased bowl, and brush top with soft shortening. Cover and let rise in warm, draft-free place until doubled in bulk (about 1 hour).
6. Punch down; turn onto lightly-floured surface. Divide dough in half; form each into roll about 10 inches long. Cover and let rest 5 minutes.
7. Cut each roll into 10 equal pieces, and form into small balls. Place about 3 inches apart on lightly-greased baking sheet. With scissors, make a cross ½ inch deep on top of each roll by making two snips at right angles to each other. Cover and let rise until doubled.
8. Bake at 425° for 15 to 20 minutes. Remove from oven; brush each roll with egg white, and return to oven for 2 minutes.

Temperature: 425°
Time: 15 to 20 minutes
2 minutes

Heavenly Yeast Bread

Yield: 5 loaves

Versatile, bountiful, and basic.

2 packages active dry yeast

1 cup warm water (110°)

1 cup boiling water

⅓ cup sugar

3 teaspoons salt

⅓ cup shortening

1 can (14 ounces) sweetened condensed milk

2½ cups cold water

4 to 4½ pounds flour

1. Dissolve yeast in warm water. Set aside.
2. In large bowl stir together boiling water, sugar, salt, and shortening until shortening melts.
3. Add milk, cold water, and yeast mixture.
4. Stir in 4 cups flour and beat until smooth. Add enough additional flour to make a slightly stiff dough.
5. On floured surface knead until smooth and elastic (8 to 10 minutes).
6. Divide dough, placing one-half in each of 2 ungreased bowls. Cover with damp towel and let rise in warm place until double.
7. Punch down, knead lightly, and shape into 5 loaves.
8. Place in greased 9 x 5 x 3-inch loaf pans, cover with damp towel and let rise until double.
9. Bake.

Temperature: 350°
Time: 45 minutes

Hint: Freeze some of the loaves, or use part of the dough for dinner or sweet rolls.

Sweets

Sweets

Black Bottom Cups

Yield: 24 cupcakes

An elegant cupcake.

1 package (8 ounces) cream
   cheese
1 egg
⅓ cup sugar
⅛ teaspoon salt
1 package (6 ounces) semi-sweet
   chocolate chips
1½ cups flour
1 cup sugar
¼ cup cocoa
1 teaspoon baking soda
½ teaspoon salt
1 cup water
⅓ cup vegetable oil
1 tablespoon vinegar
1 teaspoon vanilla

1. Beat together cream cheese, egg,
   sugar, and salt. Stir in chocolate
   chips. Set aside.
2. In large bowl, sift together flour,
   sugar, cocoa, baking soda, and
   salt. Add water, oil, vinegar, and
   vanilla. Beat well.
3. Fill muffin cups ⅓ full with
   chocolate batter. Top with one
   heaping teaspoon cream cheese
   mixture. Bake.

Temperature: 350°
Time: 30 to 35 minutes

261

Dutch Apple Cake

Yield: 16 servings

2 eggs
1 cup sugar
1 cup brown sugar
1½ cups vegetable oil
3 cups flour
1 teaspoon baking soda
1 teaspoon cinnamon
¼ teaspoon salt
3 cups chopped apples
1 cup chopped nuts
1 teaspoon vanilla

1. Beat eggs; add sugars and oil. Beat 3 minutes.
2. Sift together flour, baking soda, cinnamon, and salt. Add slowly to creamed mixture.
3. Add apples, nuts, and vanilla. Beat well.
4. Bake in greased tube pan.

Temperature: 350°
Time: 1 hour

Glaze

½ cup brown sugar
2 tablespoons margarine
2 tablespoons milk

Glaze

1. Mix together brown sugar, margarine, and milk and heat to boiling. Boil 2 to 3 minutes over medium heat.
2. Spread over warm cake.

Apple-Date-Pecan Cake
Yield: 10-inch cake

Prepare this a day ahead as taste improves with age.

2 cups sugar

1½ cups oil

3 eggs

2 teaspoons vanilla

2½ cups sifted flour

1 teaspoon soda

½ teaspoon salt

1 teaspoon cinnamon

3 cups chopped apples

1 cup chopped pecans

1 cup chopped dates

1. Blend together first eight ingredients.
2. Add apples, pecans, and dates.
3. Bake in 10-inch greased and floured tube or bundt pan.

Temperature: 300°
Time: 1 hour 25 minutes

Hint: Serve with a spoonful of whipped cream.

Turtle Cake
Yield: 13 x 9-inch cake

Delightful served warm with whipped cream.

1 box (1 pound 2 ounces) German chocolate cake mix

1 package (14 ounces) caramels

½ cup butter

1 can (5.33 ounces) evaporated milk

1 cup chopped pecans

1 cup semi-sweet chocolate chips

1. Mix cake according to directions on box. Pour half of batter into prepared 13 x 9-inch pan. Bake 15 minutes.
2. Melt caramels with butter and milk. Pour over cake.
3. Sprinkle pecans and chocolate chips over caramel layer.
4. Cover with rest of batter and bake 15 to 20 minutes longer.

Temperature: 350°
Time: 15 minutes
15 to 20 minutes

Chocolate Bourbon Cake

Yield: 12 servings

2 cups flour
1 teaspoon baking soda
¼ teaspoon salt
1¾ cups prepared coffee
¼ cup Kentucky bourbon
5 ounces unsweetened
    chocolate
1 cup butter
2 cups sugar
2 eggs
1 teaspoon vanilla
Cocoa

Topping

2 cups whipped cream
¼ cup white crème de cacao

1. Sift flour, baking soda, and salt together. Set aside.
2. Heat coffee and bourbon in double boiler for 5 minutes. Add chocolate and butter. Stir constantly until melted and smooth. Remove from heat and add sugar. Cool for 3 minutes.
3. Add flour mixture to chocolate mixture, ½ cup at a time, and beat at medium speed. Continue to beat for 1 minute.
4. Slightly beat eggs. Add eggs and vanilla to batter and beat until smooth.
5. Butter 9-inch tube or bundt pan and dust with cocoa. Pour batter into pan and bake.
6. Let cake cool completely before serving with whipped cream flavored with crème de cacao.

Temperature: 275°
Time: 90 minutes

Coconut Pound Cake   Yield: 12 to 15 servings

2 cups sugar

1 cup shortening

5 eggs

2 cups flour

1½ teaspoons baking powder

1 teaspoon salt

1 cup buttermilk

1½ teaspoons coconut
   flavoring

1 can (3¼ ounces) coconut

1. Cream together sugar and shortening. Add eggs, one at a time, beating well.
2. Sift together flour, baking powder, and salt three times.
3. To sugar mixture, add buttermilk alternately with dry ingredients. Mix well. Add coconut flavoring and coconut.
4. Grease and flour 10-inch bundt pan. Pour cake batter into bundt pan and bake. Let stand in pan for 15 minutes after removing from oven.

Temperature: 325°
Time: 1 hour

Glaze

½ cup sugar

¼ cup hot water

½ teaspoon coconut flavoring

Glaze

1. Stir sugar and water over low heat until mixture reaches low boil. Add coconut flavoring.
2. Pour over cooled cake after it has been removed from pan.

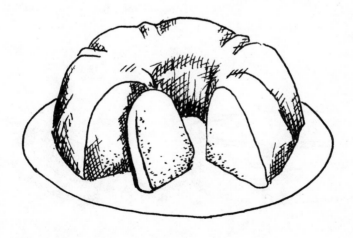

265

Chocolate Cheese Cake

Yield: 10 to 12 servings

1⅓ cups chocolate wafer
  crumbs
2 tablespoons sugar
¼ teaspoon ground cinnamon
¼ cup butter, softened
1½ cups semi-sweet chocolate
  chips
2 eggs
½ cup sugar
2 teaspoons rum
8 ounces sour cream
2 packages (8 ounces each)
  cream cheese, cubed and
  softened
2 tablespoons butter, melted
Whipped cream

1. Combine wafer crumbs, sugar, cinnamon, and ¼ cup butter; mix well.
2. Firmly press into bottom of 10-inch springform pan; set aside.
3. Melt chocolate chips over hot water in double boiler; set aside.
4. Combine eggs, sugar, rum, and sour cream in electric blender and process for 15 seconds.
5. Continue blending and gradually add chocolate and cream cheese. Add melted butter and blend well.
6. Pour cheese mixture into chocolate crust and bake until cheese cake is set in center.
7. Cool at room temperature for at least 1 hour, then chill at least 6 hours.
8. Remove sides of springform pan and garnish with whipped cream.

Temperature: 325°
Time: 45 minutes

Bavarian Cheese Cake Yield: 10 servings

Crust

1¾ cups graham cracker
   crumbs
¼ cup finely-chopped walnuts
1 teaspoon cinnamon
½ cup butter or margarine,
   melted

Filling

2 eggs, well beaten
2 packages (8 ounces each)
   cream cheese, softened
1 cup sugar
¼ teaspoon salt
2 teaspoons vanilla
1 teaspoon almond extract
2 cups sour cream

Crust

1. Mix all ingredients together.
2. Reserve 3 tablespoons of mixture. Press the remainder of mixture into bottom and 2½ inches up sides of 9-inch springform pan or pie plate.

Filling

1. Combine eggs, cream cheese, sugar, salt, vanilla, and almond extract. Beat until smooth.
2. Blend in sour cream and pour mixture into crust.
3. Sprinkle with reserved graham cracker crumbs.
4. Bake.
5. Cool and then chill for 6 hours.

Temperature: 375°
Time: 35 to 40 minutes

Hint: Make the day before serving. Keeps for 3 to 5 days.

Chocolate Chip-Cream Cheese Squares

Yield: 16 servings

This is a simple cake composed of two batters.

First Batter

8 ounces cream cheese,
  cubed and softened
½ cup sugar
1 egg
½ teaspoon salt
6 ounces chocolate chips

Second Batter

1½ cups flour
¼ cup cocoa
½ teaspoon salt
½ cup vegetable oil
1 cup sugar
1 teaspoon vanilla
1 teaspoon baking soda
1 cup water
1 tablespoon vinegar

First Batter

1. Place all ingredients in bowl except chocolate chips and beat with electric mixer until smooth.
2. Stir in chocolate chips and set bowl aside.

Second Batter

1. Blend all ingredients together with spoon (the batter will be thin).
2. Pour into 9 x 13-inch greased and floured pan.
3. Drop first batter by spoonfuls over second batter in pan. Swirl batter together slightly to create a marbled effect. Do not swirl all of top.
4. Bake.
5. Cool; cut into squares and refrigerate.

Temperature: 350°
Time: 50 minutes

Georgia Lee's Pumpkin Roll

Yield: 8 servings

A spicy delight!

3 eggs

1 cup sugar

⅔ cup pumpkin

1 teaspoon lemon juice

¾ cup flour

½ teaspoon salt

2 teaspoons cinnamon

1 teaspoon ginger

1 teaspoon baking powder

½ teaspoon nutmeg

½ cup chopped pecans

Filling

1 cup powdered sugar

6 ounces cream cheese, softened

4 tablespoons margarine

½ teaspoon vanilla

1. Beat eggs at high speed for 5 minutes. Add sugar a little at a time.
2. Stir in pumpkin and lemon juice.
3. Mix remaining ingredients, except nuts, and add to pumpkin mixture.
4. Pour into greased and floured 15½ x 13½-inch jelly roll pan. Sprinkle nuts on top.
5. Bake at 375° for 15 minutes.
6. When cake is done, remove from pan to towel sprinkled with powdered sugar. Roll cake. Cool.
7. Combine all filling ingredients and beat until smooth.
8. When cake has cooled, unroll and spread with filling; roll again.
9. Slice to serve.

Temperature: 375°
Time: 15 minutes

Hint: Decorate with sprigs of holly and serve at Christmas.

Early American Pumpkin Spice Cake

Yield: 12 to 16 servings

Not too spicy!

Cake

1 cup shortening
3 cups sugar
3 eggs, beaten
2 cups pumpkin
1 teaspoon vanilla
1 teaspoon butter flavoring
½ teaspoon coconut flavoring
3 cups flour
¼ teaspoon salt
½ teaspoon baking powder
1 teaspoon baking soda
1 teaspoon nutmeg
1 teaspoon allspice
1 teaspoon cloves
1 teaspoon cinnamon
1 cup chopped nuts or 1 cup
   raisins

Cake

1. Cream shortening and sugar. Add eggs, pumpkin, and flavorings.
2. Sift next eight dry ingredients; add to creamed mixture. Stir in nuts.
3. Pour into greased and floured tube pan.
4. Bake at 350° for 1 hour and 15 minutes.
5. Cool cake for 15 minutes and remove from pan.

Temperature: 350°
Time: 1 hour and 15 minutes

Glaze

1 cup brown sugar
½ cup sour cream

Glaze

1. Combine glaze ingredients and cook over medium heat until sugar dissolves.
2. Bring to a boil and simmer for one minute.
3. Cool for 5 minutes.
4. Drizzle glaze over cooled cake.

Hint: To serve, top each slice with a dollop of whipped cream sweetened with brown sugar, and add a drizzle of glaze.

Christmas Jam Cake

Yield: 16 servings

Moist and rich!

Cake

1 cup shortening or butter

2 cups sugar

4 eggs

1½ teaspoons soda

2 cups buttermilk

1½ cups blackberry jam

3½ cups flour

1 teaspoon allspice

1 teaspoon nutmeg

1 teaspoon cinnamon

1 teaspoon salt, if shortening
  is used

1 cup chopped nuts, optional

1 cup chopped raisins,
  optional

Cake

1. Grease three 9-inch pans and line with greased wax paper. Dust with flour.
2. Cream butter (or shortening) and sugar until fluffy.
3. Add eggs, one at a time, beating until creamy after each.
4. Dissolve soda in buttermilk and mix in jam.
5. Add buttermilk mixture to egg mixture.
6. Sift flour with spices and add salt, if necessary.
7. Gradually beat flour mixture into first mixture.
8. Fold in nuts and raisins.
9. Pour batter into prepared pans and bake at 350° for 25 minutes or until layers shrink from pan sides.
10. Allow to rest 5 minutes in pans then turn on racks.

Temperature: 350°
Time: 25 minutes

Caramel Icing

1 cup butter

2 cups brown sugar

½ cup milk

2 teaspoons vanilla

5 cups sifted powdered sugar

1 cup chopped nuts

Icing

1. Melt butter in saucepan. Add brown sugar and bring to boil.
2. Add milk and bring to boil again.
3. Remove from heat and add vanilla and enough of sugar to make it spreading consistency.
4. Beat several minutes and frost cooled cake.
5. Press chopped nuts into sides of cake while still soft.

Nellie's Orange Cake
Yield: 12 to 16 servings

Topping

2 cups sugar
1 cup orange juice
2 tablespoons grated orange
   rind

Cake

1 package (7¼ ounces)
   chopped dates
1 cup chopped pecans
1 cup shortening
2 cups sugar
4 eggs, separated
4 cups flour
1 teaspoon soda
1⅓ cups buttermilk
2 tablespoons grated orange
   rind

Topping

1. Mix all ingredients.
2. Stir occasionally to dissolve sugar.

Cake

1. Dredge dates and nuts in small amount of flour.
2. Cream shortening; add sugar gradually, mixing well. Add well-beaten egg yolks.
3. Sift flour three times.
4. Dissolve soda in buttermilk.
5. Add flour alternately with buttermilk mixture.
6. Fold in dates, nuts, and orange rind.
7. Fold in stiffly beaten egg whites.
8. Pour mixture into large, greased tube pan which has been lined with wax paper.
9. Bake.
10. Remove cake from the oven and punch with an ice pick to make holes all over the top.
11. Slowly pour topping over the cake a small amount at a time, allowing it to soak in. Cover and serve next day.

Temperature: 300°
Time: 1½ hours

Hint: This needs to be prepared a day ahead to allow for full expansion of flavors.

Kentucky Bourbon Fruit Cake

Yield: 12 to 15 servings

Best made 6 weeks before serving.

1 pound candied cherries, halved

½ pound chopped dates

2 cups of Kentucky bourbon

1½ cups butter, softened

2 cups sugar

1 cup brown sugar

6 eggs, separated

5 cups flour

1 pound pecans, chopped

2 teaspoons ground nutmeg

1 teaspoon baking powder

1. Soak cherries and dates in bourbon overnight.
2. Line greased 10-inch tube pan or 3 greased 4½ x 8½ x 2½-inch loaf pans with greased brown paper.
3. Cream butter and sugars until fluffy; add egg yolks and beat well.
4. Stir in soaked fruit and bourbon.
5. Mix ½ cup flour with pecans.
6. Add remaining flour, nutmeg, and baking powder to creamed mixture. Mix thoroughly.
7. Beat egg whites until stiff peaks form, and fold into batter. Gently mix in floured pecans.
8. Spoon batter into prepared pans and bake as directed.
9. Cool in pans, then peel off paper and wrap in bourbon-soaked cheese cloth. Wrap tightly in foil and store in refrigerator.

Temperature: 250°
Time: 3½ hours

Hint: A wonderful Christmas gift!

Apple Cobbler

Yield: 6 to 8 servings

Pastry for 1 pie shell
7 cups peeled, sliced apples
¾ cup sugar
¼ teaspoon nutmeg
⅛ teaspoon salt
1 tablespoon lemon juice
½ teaspoon grated lemon rind
¼ teaspoon cinnamon
2 tablespoons butter

1. Place apples in 8 x 12-inch or 9 x 9-inch baking dish.
2. Sprinkle apples with remaining ingredients and dot with butter.
3. Top with rolled pie crust. Pierce with knife and bake.

Temperature: 350°
Time: 1 hour

Fresh Cherry Cobbler

Yield: 6 to 8 servings

Bright red and wonderful!

1 quart fresh cherries, pitted
   or frozen sour cherries
1 cup sugar
1 tablespoon tapioca
1 teaspoon vanilla
½ cup butter or margarine
1 cup flour
1 cup sugar
½ cup milk
1¼ teaspoons baking powder

1. Bring cherries to boil.
2. Remove from heat and add 1 cup sugar, tapioca, and vanilla.
3. Melt butter in 8 x 12-inch or 9 x 9-inch baking dish in 350° oven.
4. Mix together flour, sugar, milk, and baking powder; pour batter on top of melted butter.
5. Spoon cherries on top of batter and bake.

Temperature: 350 °
Time: 35 minutes

Peach Cobbler

Yield: 6 servings

½ cup self-rising flour
½ cup milk
½ cup sugar
5 peaches, peeled and sliced
1 cup sugar
⅓ cup butter

1. Mix first three ingredients and place in 8 x 8-inch baking dish.
2. Add peaches and the additional cup sugar.
3. Dot with butter and bake.

Temperature: 325 °
Time: 1 hour

Old-Fashioned Blackberry Cobbler

Yield: 6 servings

1 cup sugar
1½ tablespoons cornstarch
1 cup water
2 to 3 cups fresh or frozen blackberries, drained
2 tablespoons butter
Cinnamon
3 tablespoons shortening
1 cup self-rising flour
½ to ¾ cup milk

1. In saucepan, mix sugar and cornstarch. Stir in water. Bring mixture to boil and boil for one minute or until mixture is clear.
2. Stir in blackberries; pour into 1½-quart baking dish.
3. Dot with butter and sprinkle lightly with cinnamon.
4. Cut shortening into flour with pastry blender until dough resembles coarse cornmeal. Add milk and mix well. Pour batter or drop by spoonfuls over hot fruit.
5. Bake.

Temperature: 400 °
Time: 25 to 30 minutes

Hint: Reserved juice from drained blackberries may be heated and served over cobbler.

275

Dent-The-Diet Pie

Yield: 1 pie (9-inch)

A rich and gooey favorite in Kentucky!

1 unbaked pie shell (9-inch)
6 tablespoons white sugar
2 tablespoons brown sugar
½ tablespoon flour
½ cup butter
2 eggs
½ teaspoon vanilla
½ cup white syrup
½ cup chocolate chips
½ cup pecans

1. Mix sugars and flour. Blend in butter.
2. In another bowl, mix eggs, vanilla, and syrup; add to sugar mixture.
3. Add chocolate chips and pecans.
4. Pour into 9-inch unbaked pie shell and bake until almost firm.

Temperature: 350 °
Time: 45 minutes

Fudge Pie

Yield: 1 pie (9-inch)

Super easy and great!

1 unbaked pie shell (9-inch)
½ cup margarine
3 ounces semi-sweet
   chocolate
3 eggs
3 tablespoons flour
1 cup sugar
1 teaspoon vanilla
1 cup pecans, chopped

1. Melt margarine and chocolate in double boiler; pour into mixing bowl.
2. Add eggs, flour, sugar, and vanilla; beat until smooth.
3. Mix in pecans; pour into pie shell and bake until firm when shaken.

Temperature: 350°
Time: 35 to 45 minutes

Hint: Let pie set for 2 hours before serving.

Orange-Coconut Chess Pie

Yield: 1 pie (9-inch)

Serve this quick and easy dessert warm!

1 unbaked pie shell (9-inch)
6 tablespoons melted butter
1½ cups sugar
3 eggs, well beaten
¼ cup orange juice
1 cup frozen coconut

1. Combine butter, sugar, eggs, orange juice, and coconut.
2. Pour into pie shell and bake.

Temperature: 350°
Time: 35 to 45 minutes

Strawberry Sour Cream Pie

Yield: 1 pie (9-inch)

Tastes like a strawberry cobbler.

1 unbaked pie shell (9-inch)
1 quart fresh strawberries
1¼ cups sugar
1 cup sifted flour
¼ teaspoon salt
1 cup sour cream
2 tablespoons sugar

1. Sort, rinse, drain, and hull strawberries. Cut berries in halves, and pour into pie shell (glass dish preferable).
2. Sift sugar, flour, and salt together; add gradually to sour cream.
3. Pour sour cream mixture over strawberries.
4. Sprinkle remaining 2 tablespoons sugar evenly over top of sour cream. Bake until firm and lightly browned.

Temperature: 450 °
Time: 15 minutes, then

Temperature: 350 °
Time: 50 to 60 minutes longer

Hint: This recipe is also good with blackberries or peaches.

Coffee Angel Pie

Yield: 1 pie (9-inch)

Out of this world!

Filling

2 egg whites
½ teaspoon vanilla
¼ teaspoon salt
¼ teaspoon cream of tartar
½ cup sugar
½ cup finely-chopped pecans
1 pint coffee ice cream
1 pint vanilla ice cream

Filling

1. Beat together egg whites, vanilla, salt, and cream of tartar until soft peaks form.
2. Gradually add sugar and continue beating until stiff peaks form and sugar is dissolved.
3. Fold in nuts.
4. Spread in a well-buttered 9-inch pie plate, building up sides to form a shell.
5. Bake in very slow oven (275°) for 1 hour.
6. Turn off oven after one hour; let meringue cook in oven for another hour with door closed.
7. Pile scoops of coffee and vanilla ice creams into cooled shell and freeze.
8. Let stand 20 minutes at room temperature before serving with caramel sauce.

Temperature: 275 °
Time: 1 hour

Sauce

3 tablespoons butter
1 cup brown sugar
⅔ cup evaporated milk
Dash of salt
1 teaspoon vanilla

Sauce

1. In small saucepan, melt butter.
2. Stir in brown sugar, milk, and salt.
3. Cook and stir over medium-low heat until mixture boils.
4. Remove from heat, and add vanilla. Cool slightly before pouring onto pie.
5. Serve immediately.

Hint: May be made ahead and sauce reheated before serving.

Lemon Luscious

Yield: 1 pie (9-inch)

Pastry

1½ cups flour
1 teaspoon salt
1 teaspoon baking powder
¾ cup shortening
¼ cup cool water

Pastry

1. Sift flour with salt and baking powder.
2. Cut in shortening with pastry blender.
3. Add water and toss with fork until mixture holds together.
4. Roll out onto floured surface. Place in 9-inch pie pan, flute edges, and prick bottom with fork.
5. Bake.

Temperature: 450 °
Time: 15 to 20 minutes

Filling

1½ cups sugar
⅓ cup cornstarch
¼ teaspoon salt
1½ cups water
4 egg yolks, slightly beaten
2 tablespoons grated lemon rind
2 tablespoons butter
¼ cup lemon juice

Filling

1. Combine sugar, cornstarch, and salt in heavy saucepan, and stir in water.
2. Bring to boil, stirring constantly.
3. Boil one minute, then remove from heat and add egg yolks and rind.
4. Cook, stirring constantly until mixture boils. Boil one minute longer, then remove from heat and add butter and lemon juice.
5. Pour into baked pie shell and cool.

Apple-Pecan Crumb-Top Pie

Yield: 1 pie (9-inch)

An easy, delightful dessert!

1 unbaked pie shell (9-inch)

Filling

¼ cup chopped pecans
1 cup sugar
2 tablespoons flour
¼ teaspoon nutmeg
½ teaspoon cinnamon
6 cups thinly sliced tart apples
2 tablespoons butter or
  margarine

Filling

1. Sprinkle pecans on bottom of pie shell.
2. Mix sugar, flour, nutmeg, and cinnamon. Toss thoroughly with apples.
3. Heap apples into pie shell. Dot with butter.

Topping

½ cup packed brown sugar
¼ cup butter or margarine,
  softened
⅓ cup flour, sifted
¼ teaspoon cinnamon
¼ cup chopped pecans

Topping

1. Combine brown sugar, butter, flour, and cinnamon with fork until topping is crumbly.
2. Stir in pecans. Spread evenly over pie filling. Bake.

Temperature: 425°
Time: 10 minutes

Temperature: 350°
Time: 40 to 50 minutes

Kentucky Pie

Yield: 1 pie (10-inch)

1 unbaked pie shell (10-inch)
½ cup butter
5 eggs
3 cups packed brown sugar
½ cup cream or milk
1 teaspoon vanilla
Pinch of salt

1. Cream butter, eggs, and sugar. Add remaining ingredients. Mix until smooth.
2. Pour into pie shell. Bake.

Temperature: 450°
Time: 5 minutes, then

Temperature: 325°
Time: 25 to 40 minutes

Pineapple Meringue Pie

Yield: 1 pie (9-inch)

1 baked pie shell (9-inch)

Filling

1 can (20 ounces) crushed
  pineapple
2 tablespoons cornstarch
½ teaspoon salt
½ cup sugar
3 egg yolks, beaten
2 teaspoons lemon juice

Filling

1. Bring pineapple to a boil. Combine cornstarch, salt, and sugar. Stir into hot pineapple.
2. Reduce heat and cook 10 minutes, stirring occasionally.
3. Add egg yolks and lemon juice slowly. Cover and cook 5 minutes.
4. Cool; spoon into baked pie crust.

Meringue

3 egg whites
¼ teaspoon cream of tartar
6 tablespoons sugar
½ teaspoon vanilla

Meringue

1. Beat egg whites with cream of tartar until frothy.
2. Gradually beat in sugar and continue beating until stiff. Beat in vanilla.
3. Pile meringue onto pie filling, being careful to seal the meringue onto edge of crust to prevent shrinking. Bake.

Temperature: 400°
Time: 8 to 10 minutes

281

Black Bottom Pie With Bourbon

Yield: 1 pie (9-inch)

Delicious! Different! Dazzle your guests!

1 baked pie shell (9-inch)
1 envelope unflavored gelatin
¼ cup cold water
1 cup sugar, divided
3 tablespoons cornstarch
2 cups milk
4 large eggs, separated
3 tablespoons Kentucky
    bourbon
1½ ounces unsweetened
    chocolate, melted
1 teaspoon vanilla
¼ teaspoon cream of tartar

1. Sprinkle gelatin into cold water.
2. In saucepan, stir together ½ cup sugar and cornstarch. Gradually stir in milk. Add egg yolks.
3. Cook over medium heat, stirring constantly until mixture becomes as thick as mayonnaise. Remove from heat.
4. Reserve one cup of mixture. Into remaining hot mixture, stir gelatin and bourbon. Refrigerate until cooled thoroughly (about 30 minutes).
5. Stir chocolate and vanilla into reserved one cup of mixture. Spread over bottom of pie shell. Refrigerate.
6. When refrigerated mixture is cooled, beat egg whites with cream of tartar; gradually add remaining ½ cup sugar, beating until soft peaks form.
7. Fold into chilled gelatin mixture. Spoon over chocolate layer in pie shell. Refrigerate at least 3 hours before serving.

Praline Ice Cream Pie

Yield: 1 pie (9-inch)

A fantastic dessert! Well-worth the effort!

1 baked pie shell (9-inch)
½ cup packed brown sugar
½ cup whipping cream
2 tablespoons butter
1 cup chopped pecans
1 teaspoon vanilla
1½ quarts vanilla ice cream
3 egg whites
¼ teaspoon cream of tartar
½ teaspoon vanilla
⅓ cup sugar

1. In medium skillet, heat brown sugar over medium-low heat just until sugar melts, stirring constantly.
2. Gradually blend in cream; cook 2 to 3 minutes longer, or until smooth.
3. Remove from heat; stir in butter, pecans, and vanilla. Cool.
4. Stir ice cream just enough to soften. Quickly fold into praline mixture. Pour into pie shell. Freeze.
5. Just before serving, beat egg whites. Add cream of tartar and vanilla; gradually add sugar and beat until stiff peaks form.
6. Spread meringue over ice cream, sealing to edges. Bake until lightly browned. Serve immediately with rum sauce.

Temperature: 475°
Time: 4 to 5 minutes

Rum Sauce

2 egg yolks, beaten
½ teaspoon grated lemon peel
¼ cup lemon juice
¼ cup sugar
4 tablespoons butter
3 tablespoons light rum

Rum Sauce

1. In small saucepan, combine egg yolks, lemon peel, lemon juice, sugar, and butter. Cook until mixture thickens, stirring constantly.
2. Stir in rum. Let cool to about room temperature before serving over pie.

Hint: Brown sugar melts quickly and will get hard, so do not heat too long. Do not let ice cream become too soft.

Pearl's Pecan Pie

Yield: 1 pie (9-inch)

Simple and superb!

1 unbaked pie shell (9-inch)
3 eggs, beaten
2 tablespoons butter, melted
1 cup sugar
½ cup dark corn syrup
½ cup light corn syrup
1½ teaspoons vanilla
⅛ teaspoon salt
2 cups pecan halves

1. Preheat oven to 400°.
2. Combine eggs, butter, sugar, corn syrups, vanilla, and salt. Mix well.
3. Stir in pecans. Pour into pie shell. Bake.

Temperature: 400°
Time: 15 minutes, then

Temperature: 350°
Time: 35 to 40 minutes

Creamy Peach Pie

Yield: 1 pie (9-inch)

A nice departure from plain peach pie.

1 unbaked pie shell (9-inch)
4 fresh peaches, peeled and
  sliced
⅓ cup butter
1 scant cup sugar
1 egg
⅓ cup flour
¼ teaspoon vanilla

1. Place peach slices in unbaked shell.
2. Cream butter and sugar until smooth.
3. Add remaining ingredients and mix well.
4. Pour custard mixture over peaches.
5. Bake.

Temperature: 300°
Time: 1 hour

Hint: For a more elegant look, use peach halves instead of slices.

Choco-Pecan Treats

Yield: 24 cookie bars

For a special touch, top with whipped cream.

1¾ cups flour, divided

½ teaspoon cinnamon

¼ teaspoon baking powder

1 cup firmly-packed light brown sugar, divided

¾ cup butter, softened

3 eggs

1 cup dark corn syrup

2 ounces semi-sweet chocolate, melted and cooled

1½ teaspoons vanilla

¼ teaspoon salt

1½ cups coarsely-chopped pecans

1. Sift 1½ cups flour, cinnamon, and baking powder into large bowl.
2. Stir in ½ cup brown sugar.
3. Cut in butter with pastry blender until mixture is crumbly.
4. Press into greased 13 x 9 x 2-inch baking pan.
5. Bake at 350° for 10 minutes.
6. Beat eggs, ½ cup brown sugar, corn syrup, ¼ cup flour, chocolate, vanilla, and salt in large bowl until well-blended.
7. Pour this mixture over dough layer in baking pan.
8. Sprinkle with nuts.
9. Return to oven and continue baking for 30 minutes.
10. Cool on wire rack and then cut into bars.

Temperature: 350°
Time: 10 minutes
     30 minutes

Alex's Brownies

Yield: 3 dozen

1 cup butter
4 ounces unsweetened
   chocolate
4 eggs
2 cups sugar
1½ cups flour
Dash of salt
2 teaspoons vanilla
1½ cups chopped pecans
1 cup semi-sweet chocolate
   chips

1. Melt butter and chocolate in a
   double boiler.
2. Beat eggs and sugar together.
3. Add chocolate mixture, flour,
   and salt to eggs and sugar. Mix
   well.
4. Stir in vanilla, pecans, and
   chocolate chips.
5. Pour brownie mixture into a 15½
   x 10½ x 1-inch greased and
   floured pan and bake.

Temperature: 350°
Time: 15 to 20 minutes

Frosting

¾ cup sugar
¾ cup brown sugar
¾ cup milk
2 ounces unsweetened
   chocolate
1 teaspoon vanilla
½ cup semi-sweet chocolate
   chips

Frosting

1. In a saucepan bring sugar, brown
   sugar, and milk to a boil. Continue
   boiling and stirring for 4 to 5
   minutes until mixture reaches
   220°.
2. Stir in chocolate and vanilla.
3. Beat until thick, adding chocolate
   chips.
4. Spread over cooled brownies.

Double-Frosted Bourbon Brownies

Yield: 30 brownies

Brownies

¾ cup sifted flour
¼ teaspoon soda
¼ teaspoon salt
½ cup sugar
⅓ cup shortening
2 tablespoons water
1 package (6 ounces) semi-
   sweet chocolate chips
1 teaspoon vanilla
2 eggs
1½ cups chopped walnuts
4 tablespoons Kentucky
   bourbon

Brownies

1. Sift together flour, soda, and salt. Set aside.
2. Combine sugar, shortening, and water in saucepan. Bring just to boil, stirring constantly. Remove from heat.
3. Stir in chocolate chips and vanilla, stirring until smooth.
4. Beat in eggs, one at a time.
5. Add dry ingredients and nuts and mix well.
6. Bake in 9-inch square greased pan.
7. Remove from oven and sprinkle with bourbon. Cool.

Temperature: 325°
Time: 30 minutes

White Icing

½ cup butter, softened
1 teaspoon vanilla
2 cups powdered sugar

White Icing

1. Combine butter and vanilla, beating until creamy.
2. Gradually add powdered sugar, beating until smooth.
3. Spread over cooled brownies.

Chocolate Glaze

1 tablespoon shortening
1 package (6 ounces) semi-
   sweet chocolate chips

Chocolate Glaze

1. Melt together shortening and chocolate in double boiler over hot water.
2. Spread over iced brownies.

Bit O' Chocolate Cookies   Yield: 2½ dozen

Great to nibble on between sit-ups!

1½ cups semi-sweet chocolate
   chips, divided

¼ cup butter or margarine

¾ cup sugar

1 egg

1½ teaspoons vanilla

½ cup flour

½ teaspoon salt

¼ teaspoon baking powder

½ cup chopped walnuts

1. In small saucepan over low heat, melt 1 cup chocolate chips. Cool.
2. In small bowl, cream butter and sugar. Add egg and vanilla, beating well.
3. Blend in melted chocolate.
4. Sift together flour, salt, and baking powder. Add to creamed mixture and mix well.
5. Stir in remaining chocolate chips and walnuts.
6. Drop by teaspoonfuls on lightly-greased cookie sheet two inches apart. Bake.

Temperature: 350°
Time: 8 to 10 minutes

Hawaiian Coconut Fruit Squares
Yield: 25 squares

2 eggs

¾ cup sugar

¾ cup flour

1 teaspoon baking powder

¼ teaspoon salt

½ cup crushed pineapple,
   drained

½ cup chopped nuts

½ cup chopped dates

½ cup coconut

Powdered sugar

1. Cream eggs and sugar. Set aside.
2. Sift together flour, baking powder, and salt. Add to creamed mixture, stirring until well mixed.
3. Stir in pineapple, nuts, dates, and coconut. Pour into well-greased 9 x 9 x 2-inch pan. Bake.
4. Cut into squares and roll in powdered sugar while warm.

Temperature: 350°
Time: 30 to 35 minutes

Swedish Ginger Cookies

Yield: 8 dozen

Decorate with sugar sprinkles or icing.

1 cup butter or margarine

1½ cups sugar

1 egg

1½ tablespoons grated orange peel

2 tablespoons corn syrup or molasses

1 tablespoon water

3¼ cups flour

2 teaspoons soda

2 teaspoons cinnamon

1 teaspoon ginger

½ teaspoon ground cloves

1. Cream butter and sugar. Add egg to this mixture and beat until fluffy.
2. Stir in orange peel, corn syrup or molasses, and water. Mix well and set aside.
3. Sift together flour, soda, cinnamon, ginger, and cloves. Stir into creamed mixture.
4. Chill one hour.
5. Roll dough to ⅛-inch thickness on lightly-floured surface. Cut dough into desired shapes with floured cookie cutter.
6. Place cookies one inch apart on ungreased cookie sheet.
7. Bake. Remove from cookie sheet while still warm.

Temperature: 375°
Time: 7 to 8 minutes

Sour Cream Cookies

Yield: 4 dozen

Add nuts or chocolate chips for a change.

2 cups sugar

1 cup butter, softened

3 eggs

1 cup sour cream

3½ cups flour

Dash salt

1 heaping teaspoon baking
  powder

1 teaspoon vanilla

½ teaspoon nutmeg

1. Cream sugar and butter. Mix in eggs and sour cream. Set aside.
2. Sift flour, salt, and baking powder together. Add to first mixture.
3. Add vanilla and nutmeg.
4. Drop by rounded teaspoonfuls onto lightly-greased cookie sheet.
5. Bake at 375° for 8 to 10 minutes until lightly browned.

Temperature: 375°
Time: 8 to 10 minutes

Frosting

2 cups powdered sugar

½ teaspoon vanilla

¼ cup butter

Light cream

Frosting

1. Mix powdered sugar, vanilla, and butter together.
2. Add cream until frosting is speading consistency.
3. Frost cooled cookies.

Hint: For Christmas, frost with red and green icing.

Aunt Izzie's Italian Pizzelles

Yield: 2 dozen 4-inch pizzelles

Children love to help make and eat these!

3 eggs, beaten
¾ cup sugar
¾ cup margarine, melted
1¾ cups flour
1 teaspoon baking powder
2 teaspoons vanilla
1 teaspoon anise extract
Powdered sugar, optional

1. Mix all ingredients together in the order listed.
2. Drop by rounded tablespoons onto center of a preheated electric pizzelle iron. Close lid and clip the handle together. Cook until the steaming stops.
3. Remove with fork and allow to cool on towels.
4. May be shaped, while hot, into a shell to hold custard. To do this, mold around a round-bottomed glass.
5. The pizzelles may be stored for up to 3 weeks in tightly closed container. They also freeze well.
6. To eat while fresh, dip in powdered sugar.

Time: 30 to 40 seconds, each

Hint: Pizzelle irons may be purchased in the housewares department of many stores.

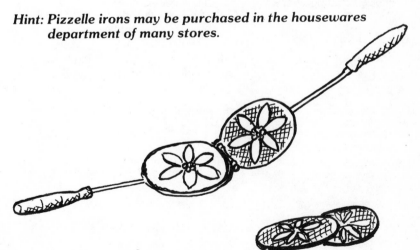

Frosted Pumpkin Spice Cookies

Yield: 5 dozen

These brighten up the cookie jar.

½ cup shortening
1 cup packed brown sugar
2 eggs
1 cup canned pumpkin
2 cups flour
1 tablespoon baking powder
1 teaspoon salt
2 teaspoons cinnamon
½ teaspoon nutmeg
¼ teaspoon ginger

1. Cream shortening until light and fluffy. Gradually add brown sugar, mixing well.
2. Add eggs, one at a time, beating well after each addition.
3. Stir in pumpkin.
4. Combine flour, baking powder, salt, cinnamon, nutmeg, and ginger into pumpkin mixture. Chill dough.
5. Drop by teaspoonfuls onto lightly-greased baking sheet.
6. Bake. Cool.

Temperature: 400°
Time: 10 minutes

Icing

½ cup margarine
4 to 4½ cups sifted powdered sugar
¼ cup boiling water
Pecan or walnut halves, optional

Icing

1. In saucepan, heat margarine until light golden brown.
2. Add powdered sugar and boiling water. Beat until mixture is smooth.
3. Frost each cookie and top with pecan or walnut half, if desired.

Appetizing Apricot Bars

Yield: 2 dozen

Rich and tasty.

2 packages (6 ounces each)
   dried apricots
1¾ cups sugar, divided
¾ cup butter, softened
2 cups flour
½ teaspoon soda
½ teaspoon salt
1 can (3 ounces) coconut
½ cup chopped pecans

1. Cover apricots with water and simmer for 20 minutes.
2. Drain apricots, reserving ¼ cup of liquid. Chop the apricots and set aside.
3. Combine the reserved liquid with ¾ cup sugar in saucepan. Simmer for 5 minutes, then stir in apricots. Set aside.
4. Cream butter and 1 cup sugar, beating until fluffy.
5. Combine flour, soda, and salt. Add to creamed mixture, blending until crumbly.
6. Stir in coconut and pecans.
7. Pat ¾ of this mixture into 9 x 13 x 2-inch greased pan. Bake at 350° for 10 minutes.
8. Remove from oven and spread apricot mixture over crust. Sprinkle with remaining crust mixture.
9. Bake an additional 30 minutes.

Temperature: 350°
Time: 10 minutes
         30 minutes

Hint: Freeze these for a special occasion.

Fibber McGee Cookies

Yield: 5 dozen

Shamefully good!

1 cup butter
1⅓ cups sugar
1⅓ cups brown sugar
2 eggs
1 teaspoon vanilla
1¾ cups flour
1 teaspoon soda
3½ cups quick-cooking oats
1½ cups salted peanuts or pecans
1 package (6 ounces) chocolate chips

1. Cream together butter and sugars.
2. Beat in eggs.
3. Stir in vanilla.
4. Add flour and soda.
5. Stir in oats, nuts, and chocolate chips.
6. Drop onto ungreased cookie sheet by teaspoonfuls.
7. Bake as directed.

Temperature: 350°
Time: 12 minutes

Hint: Mailable and freezable.

Forgotten Cookies

Yield: 2½ dozen

2 egg whites, at room
   temperature
⅔ cup sugar
Pinch salt
1 teaspoon vanilla
1 cup chopped pecans
1 cup semi-sweet chocolate
   chips

1. Preheat oven to 350°.
2. Beat egg whites until almost stiff.
3. Gradually add sugar and beat until egg whites are stiff.
4. Mix in salt and vanilla.
5. Fold in pecans and chocolate chips.
6. Drop by teaspoonfuls onto greased, foil-covered cookie sheet.
7. Place cookies in oven and immediately turn off oven.
8. Leave cookies in closed oven all night.

Temperature: 350°
Time: Overnight

Pan Lebkuchen

Yield: 32 pieces

Cookie

2 cups flour
1 tablespoon pumpkin pie
   spice
½ teaspoon salt
1 egg
2 tablespoons oil
½ cup packed brown sugar
½ cup honey
½ cup dark molasses
½ cup chopped almonds
½ cup mixed candied fruits
   and peels, finely chopped

Cookie

1. Sift together flour, pumpkin pie spice, and salt. Set aside.
2. Beat together egg and oil. Add brown sugar and beat until fluffy.
3. Stir in honey and molasses.
4. Add dry ingredients to molasses mixture. Beat until well blended.
5. Add nuts, fruits, and peels.
6. Spread in greased 15 x 10 x 1-inch pan.
7. Bake until done. Immediately score in squares with sharp knife. Glaze while still warm.

Temperature: 350°
Time: 15 to 20 minutes

Lemon Glaze

1 egg white
1½ cups sifted powdered sugar
½ teaspoon finely-shredded lemon
   peel
1 tablespoon lemon juice

Lemon Glaze

1. Slightly beat egg white.
2. Add sugar, lemon peel, and lemon juice. Beat until smooth.
3. Brush on Lemon Glaze while cookies are still warm. Garnish each square with candied pineapple, if desired.
4. When cool, cut through completely into squares.

Hint: Begin preparing glaze five minutes before cookie is finished baking.

Scotch Shortbread

Yield: 4 dozen

You'll hear bagpipes!

1 cup butter
¾ cup powdered sugar, divided
1 teaspoon vanilla
2 cups cake flour
¼ teaspoon salt
¼ teaspoon baking powder

1. Cream butter thoroughly. Gradually add ½ cup powdered sugar, beating until mixture is creamy and light.
2. Add vanilla.
3. Sift flour, salt, and baking powder together. Stir into above mixture, blending thoroughly.
4. Chill dough.
5. Preheat oven to 350°.
6. Roll dough to ¼-inch thickness. Cut into squares and prick dough all over with fork.
7. Cover baking sheet with foil and place the squares on it.
8. Bake until shortbread just begins to color.
9. Sift remaining powdered sugar over hot cookies.

Temperature: 350°
Time: 15 to 20 minutes

Hint: The less you work the dough, the lighter the cookies.

Caramel Parfait Delight

Yield: 15 servings

A light frozen filling in a delicious crust!

Crust

½ cup butter, softened
2 tablespoons sugar
1 cup flour

Crust

1. Combine butter and sugar. Do not cream.
2. Add flour and mix until dough forms.
3. Reserve one-third of mixture in small baking pan for crumb topping.
4. With well-greased fingers, press remaining mixture into 9 x 13-inch pan. Bake the crumbs and the crust. Remove from oven and cool.

Temperature: 375°
Time: 12 to 15 minutes

Hint: Stir the crumbs often to prevent burning.

Filling

18 caramels
⅓ cup milk
⅔ cup sugar
½ cup water
1 egg white, unbeaten
1½ teaspoons vanilla
1 teaspoon lemon juice
1 cup whipping cream

Filling

1. Melt caramels and milk in double boiler. Cool slightly and set aside.
2. In small bowl, combine sugar, water, egg white, vanilla, and lemon juice. Beat on high speed for 3 to 5 minutes.
3. Whip the cream, then fold into egg white mixture.
4. Pour ½ of filling over crust. Dribble caramel syrup mixture over filling. Repeat, using remaining filling and syrup. Cut through with knife to give marbled appearance.
5. Sprinkle with reserved crumbs. Freeze for at least 5 to 6 hours before serving.

Stupendous Fruit Pizza

Yield: 12 servings

Very unusual! Everyone loves this!

Crust

¾ cup margarine
3 tablespoons powdered
  sugar
1½ cups flour

Crust

1. Melt margarine. Add sugar and flour and mix well.
2. Pat crust into 12-inch round pizza pan.
3. Bake until golden brown. Remove from oven and cool.

Temperature: 350°
Time: 10 to 15 minutes

Filling

8 ounces cream cheese,
  softened
⅓ cup sugar
½ teaspoon vanilla
Fruit: bananas, blueberries,
  kiwi, grapes, strawberries,
  or peaches

Filling

1. Cream together cream cheese, sugar, and vanilla.
2. Spread over cooled crust.
3. Slice a variety of fruits and arrange artistically in concentric circles on filling.

Glaze

½ cup sugar
1 tablespoon cornstarch
⅛ teaspoon salt
½ cup orange juice
2 tablespoons lemon juice

Glaze

1. Combine all ingredients in small saucepan.
2. Boil until thickened.
3. Cool.
4. Spoon cooled glaze over fruit, covering completely.
5. Chill.
6. Serve in wedges.

Peaches With Amaretto Sauce

Yield: 4 servings

An easy and delicious summertime dessert!

2 packages (3 ounces each)
  cream cheese, softened
½ cup plain yogurt
¼ cup amaretto liqueur
3 tablespoons sugar, divided
3 medium to large or 6 small
  fresh peaches
1 tablespoon orange juice
Fresh mint leaves for garnish
  (optional)

1. In medium bowl, beat together cream cheese, yogurt, Amaretto liqueur, and 2 tablespoons of sugar until blended. This makes one and one-half cups of sauce.
2. Cover and chill overnight.
3. Shortly before serving, peel and pit peaches. Slice fairly thin.
4. Toss with remaining sugar and orange juice. Refrigerate.
5. At serving time, divide peaches among four dessert dishes. Spoon Amaretto sauce over fruit. Garnish with mint leaves.

Old-Fashioned Boiled Custard

Yield: 5 to 6 (8 ounce) servings

This is well worth the time it takes.

1 quart milk
3 whole eggs
⅜ cup sugar
1 teaspoon vanilla, optional

1. Scald milk.
2. Beat eggs thoroughly and strain.
3. Add sugar to eggs.
4. Beat small amount of hot milk into egg mixture.
5. Add egg mixture to milk slowly and cook on low heat, stirring constantly until spoon is coated.
6. Add vanilla, if desired.
7. Strain and refrigerate.

Hint: Milk is scalded when it makes a coating on the spoon — before it boils.

Old-Fashioned Banana Pudding

Yield: 16 servings

A delicious all-time favorite!

1½ cups sugar
4 tablespoons cornstarch
½ teaspoon salt
4 cups milk
2 eggs, beaten
2 teaspoons vanilla
4 tablespoons butter
5 to 6 bananas
1 box (7¼ ounces) vanilla
  wafers

1. In large saucepan, combine sugar, cornstarch, and salt. Gradually add milk.
2. Cook over medium heat until thick, stirring frequently. After mixture thickens, cook 2 minutes longer, stirring. Remove from heat.
3. In small bowl, stir small amount of hot mixture into the beaten eggs. Return egg mixture to the hot mixture and cook additional 2 minutes, sitrring often.
4. Remove from heat; stir in vanilla and butter.
5. In 2½-quart oblong casserole, layer bananas, pudding, and wafers.

Hint: This dessert is delicious topped with your favorite meringue recipe or with wafer crumbs.

All New Chocolate Mousse

Yield: 6 servings

Rich chocolate flavor!

1 cup semi-sweet chocolate
  chips
2 eggs
3 tablespoons strong, hot
  coffee
2 tablespoons orange or coffee
  liqueur
¾ cup milk, scalded
Whipped cream

1. Combine all ingredients except cream in a blender.
2. Cover and mix well until smooth and chocolate is melted.
3. Pour into individual serving dishes and chill 3 to 4 hours.
4. Serve with whipped cream.

Refrigerator Poppy Seed Torte

Yield: 12 servings

Very attractive! Tastes delicious!

Crust

1 cup graham cracker crumbs
1 cup flour
½ cup butter, melted
½ cup chopped pecans

Crust

1. Mix together graham cracker crumbs, flour, butter, and nuts. Pat into 10 x 14-inch pan. Bake until brown.

Temperature: 325°
Time: 10 to 15 minutes

Hint: Crust may be made ahead and frozen.

Filling

1½ cups milk
1½ cups sugar, divided
5 eggs, separated
¼ cup poppy seeds
¼ teaspoon salt
2 tablespoons cornstarch
1½ tablespoons gelatin
¼ cup cold water
½ teaspoon vanilla
½ teaspon cream of tartar
1 cup heavy cream, whipped

Filling

1. Combine milk, 1 cup sugar, and egg yolks in double boiler; beat until sugar dissolves.
2. Add poppy seeds, salt, and cornstarch and cook until thickened.
3. Dissolve gelatin in ¼ cup cold water. Add to cooked mixture. Cool.
4. Fold vanilla into cooled mixture.
5. Beat egg whites until stiff; add cream of tartar and remaining ½ cup sugar. Fold into cooled filling.
6. Pour filling into crust. Refrigerate. Serve with whipped cream.

Chocolate Refrigerator Cake

Yield: 8 servings

A very rich and delicious dessert!

18 lady fingers
2 tablespoons water
1 package (6 ounces) semi-
   sweet chocolate chips
½ cup butter
½ cup powdered sugar
4 eggs, separated
1 teaspoon vanilla
Whipped cream
Shaved chocolate

1. Split lady fingers. Line bottom and sides of 9 x 5 x 3-inch loaf pan (or 6-inch spring-form pan) with wax paper. Arrange lady fingers against sides and along bottom of pan. Save remaining to use between filling.
2. Add 2 tablespoons water to chocolate and melt over hot water. Stir until smooth. Cool.
3. Cream butter; add powdered sugar.
4. Beat egg yolks until thick. Add to the butter and sugar mixture. Add chocolate and vanilla.
5. Beat egg whites until stiff; gently stir into chocolate mixture.
6. Alternate layers of filling and lady fingers in lined pan. Chill overnight.
7. Garnish with whipped cream and shaved chocolate.

Rosy Apple Dumplings

Yield: 8 servings

This pastry is special!

1 cup plus 3 tablespoons
   shortening
3 cups sifted flour
3 teaspoons salt
1 egg, beaten
⅓ cup water
2 tablespoons vinegar
8 apples, peeled and cored
1 cup red hot candies, divided
1½ cups sugar, divided
2 cups water
5 tablespoons plus 1 teaspoon
   butter, divided

1. Cut shortening into flour and salt.
2. Beat egg with water and vinegar. Stir into flour mixture.
3. Divide dough into 8 parts. Roll each into 8-inch square.
4. Place one apple in each square. Fill each center with red hot candies, 1 tablespoon sugar, and ½ teaspoon butter. Seal pastry around each apple.
5. Combine 1 cup sugar, 2 cups water, 4 tablespoons butter, and ⅓ cup red hot candies and boil three minutes.
6. Place apples in baking pan and pour syrup around dumplings.
7. Bake.

Temperature: 425°
Time: 40 minutes

Nutty Caramel Corn

Yield: 6 quarts

Children love this snow day treat!

6 quarts popped popcorn
1 cup packed brown sugar
½ cup butter
½ cup dark corn syrup
1 teaspoon soda
Peanuts, optional

1. Combine brown sugar, butter, and syrup. Bring to boil over medium heat and cook for 5 minutes.
2. Add soda and stir.
3. In roasting pan, pour syrup mixture over popcorn. Stir until popcorn is well-coated. Bake, stirring every 15 minutes.

Temperature: 200°
Time: 1 hour

Apple Beignets

Yield: 8 to 10 servings
Sauce Yield: 1¾ cups

A dessert with that continental touch.

Crème Fraîche Sauce

⅓ cup sour cream

1 cup whipping cream, unwhipped

⅓ cup powdered sugar

1 teaspoon amaretto

1 tablespoon plus 2 teaspoons cream cheese, softened

Sauce

1. Blend all sauce ingredients in processor until thickened. Chill.

Beignets

6 cooking apples

½ cup sugar

¼ teaspoon cinnamon

½ cup brandy or rum

1¾ cups flour

⅛ teaspoon salt

2 eggs, separated

¾ cup milk

⅔ cup flat beer

2 tablespoons butter, melted

Powdered sugar

Beignets

1. Peel and core apples. Cut into ¼-inch slices.
2. Sprinkle slices with sugar and cinnamon, then pour brandy over them. Refrigerate at least 1 hour.
3. In processor, combine flour, salt, egg yolks, milk, beer, and butter. Beat until smooth. Let rest for 1 hour.
4. When ready to cook, strain liquid from apples and beat into batter. Fold in beaten egg whites.
5. Pour batter over apple slices in bowl, coating both sides.
6. Drop slices into hot (375°) oil. Cook until lightly browned, turning frequently. Drain completely on paper towels.
7. Serve hot with sauce or sprinkle with powdered sugar.

Hint: This isn't a make-ahead item.

Chocolate Madeleines

Yield: 8 servings

Serve with ice cream for a yummy dessert.

2 eggs, separated
½ cup sugar
½ cup cocoa
½ cup flour, sifted
1 teaspoon baking powder
Pinch of salt
½ cup butter, softened
2 teaspoons coconut flavoring
Powdered sugar (optional)

1. Beat egg yolks, sugar, and cocoa together. Stir in flour, baking powder, and salt. Add softened butter and coconut flavoring; mix well.
2. Beat egg whites with electric mixer until stiff. Fold into cocoa mixture.
3. Brush Madeleine molds with melted butter. Fill each mold ⅔ full.
4. Bake in 425° oven for 12 minutes until Madelines have risen and are firm. Turn out immediately. Sprinkle with powdered sugar. Makes 22 Madeleines.

Temperature: 425°
Time: 12 minutes

Chocolate Sauce

Yield: 2 cups sauce

Delicious over ice cream or cream puffs!

2 squares (1 ounce each) unsweetened chocolate
¾ cup sour cream
1 cup sugar

1. Melt chocolate in double boiler.
2. Mix melted chocolate, sour cream, and sugar. Cook for one minute until creamy.

Plum Pudding

Yield: 8 to 10 servings

1½ cups sugar, divided
1 egg
1½ cups plus 2 tablespoons
    flour
Dash of salt
1½ cups plums, drained
    (reserve juice)
1 cup pecans
½ teaspoon soda
½ teaspoon baking powder
½ cup brown sugar
1 cup plum juice

1. Combine 1 cup sugar, egg, flour, salt, plums, pecans, soda, and baking powder. Mix well. Batter will be stiff.
2. Pour batter into 9x12-inch glass baking dish. Bake at 350° for 45 minutes.
3. Combine brown sugar and ½ cup white sugar in saucepan. Gradually add plum juice, mixing well. Cook until thickened. Pour over warm pudding before serving.

Temperature: 350°
Time: 30 to 45 minutes

Frozen Lemon Mousse

Yield: 8 to 10 servings

Vanilla wafer crumbs
6 eggs, separated
1¼ cups sugar
½ cup lemon juice
½ pint whipping cream,
    whipped

1. Cover bottom of buttered 9-inch square pan with vanilla wafer crumbs.
2. Beat egg whites until stiff, adding sugar gradually. Add egg yolks, one at a time, beating well after each addition. Add lemon juice and beat well.
3. Fold whipped cream in with mixture and turn into crumb-lined dish. Cover top with crumbs. Freeze.

Strawberries In Sherry Cream

Yield: 8 servings

A light and pretty dessert.

3 pints whole, fresh
   strawberries
5 egg yolks
1 cup sugar
1 cup dry sherry
½ pint whipping cream

1. Wash, cap, and chill strawberries.
2. Beat egg yolks until thick and lemon-colored. Beat in sugar and sherry. Cook over low heat until thickened. Cool.
3. Before serving, whip cream and fold carefully into sauce. Alternate strawberries and sauce in parfait glasses.

Frosty, Frozen Charlotte Russe

Yield: 10 servings

For a special treat.

2 packages lady fingers or
   pound cake, thinly sliced
6 eggs, separated
1 cup sugar
1 pint whipping cream
Pinch of salt
1 teaspoon vanilla
Strawberries or peaches for
   topping

1. Line a spring mold pan with split lady fingers covering the bottom first, then sides.
2. Beat egg yolks until thick and lemon-colored. Add sugar gradually and beat until light.
3. Beat whipping cream until thick. Fold into egg mixture.
4. Add salt to egg whites and beat until stiff. Fold into cream mixture, adding vanilla.
5. Pour mixture into lined pan of lady fingers and freeze immediately. Top with fresh or frozen fruit to serve.

Chocomint Freeze

Yield: 12 to 16 servings

Nice for a "special dessert," especially at Christmas time.

1¼ cups crushed vanilla
   wafers
12 tablespoons butter or
   margarine, melted, divided
1 quart peppermint stick ice
   cream
2 ounces unsweetened
   chocolate
3 eggs, separated
1½ cups sifted powdered
   sugar
½ cup chopped pecans
1 teaspoon vanilla

1. Mix crushed vanilla wafers and 4 tablespoons butter. Reserve ¼ of crumb mixture and press remaining into 9 x 9 x 2-inch glass dish.
2. Spread softened ice cream over crumb mixture and freeze.
3. Melt ½ cup butter and chocolate over low heat.
4. Beat egg yolks; gradually stir into chocolate mixture. Add powdered sugar, nuts, and vanilla. Cool thoroughly.
5. Beat egg whites until stiff peaks form.
6. Beat cooled chocolate mixture until smooth, then fold in egg whites. Pour over ice cream.
7. Top with reserved crumbs and freeze.

Cappucino Ice Cream

Yield: 2 quarts

Coffee lover's delight!

1¼ cups double-strength
   coffee or Espresso-blend
   coffee, cooled
¾ cup sugar
½ cup dark corn syrup
2 tablespoons dark rum
½ teaspoon cinnamon
2 cups heavy cream

1. In medium bowl, mix coffee, sugar, corn syrup, rum, and cinnamon. Stir until sugar dissolves. Blend in cream.
2. Freeze mixture in 2-quart ice cream freezer.

"Six-Three" Ice Cream

Yield: 2 quarts

3 bananas, mashed
Juice of 3 oranges
Juice of 3 lemons
3 cups sugar
3 cups cream
3 cups milk
1 can (8 ounces) crushed
    pineapple (optional)

1. Mix all ingredients and freeze in ice cream freezer.

Lemon Cake-Top Pudding

Yield: 8 servings

For the real lemon lovers—very lemony and tart!

3 tablespoons butter
1 cup sugar
4 eggs, separated
3 tablespoons flour
⅓ cup fresh lemon juice
2 teaspoons grated lemon rind
¼ teaspoon salt
1 cup milk
⅓ cup slivered almonds,
    toasted

1. Cream butter, adding sugar gradually; cream together until light and fluffy.
2. Add egg yolks and beat well.
3. Add flour, juice, rind, and salt; mix well.
4. Stir in milk, then blend in ¼ cup almonds.
5. Beat egg whites until stiff and fold into mixture.
6. Pour into 9 x 5-inch loaf pan and set in pan of hot water.
7. Bake as directed. Increase temperature and continue baking.
8. Sprinkle with the remaining almonds and serve warm or chilled.

Temperature: 325°
Time: 40 minutes then

Temperature: 350°
Time: 10 minutes

Kentucky Bourbon Balls
Yield: 3½ dozen

3¼ cups powdered sugar
½ cup butter, softened
8 teaspoons 100 proof
   Kentucky bourbon
¾ cup chopped pecans
1 to 1½ pounds semi-sweet
   chocolate chips

1. Cream sugar, butter, and bourbon until smooth.
2. Add nuts and mix well. Form into ¾-inch balls. Add additional sugar . if balls are too soft.
3. Place on metal tray and chill for 1 to 1½ hours.
4. Melt chocolate chips in top of double boiler over hot water. Bring just to boiling, stirring slowly.
5. Remove from heat and cool until warm. Keep warm while dipping candies.
6. Dip balls in chocolate and cool on foil.
7. Refrigerate when cool.

Hint: Eat these when the Christmas season starts getting to you.

Pralines
Yield: 3 dozen

A family favorite.

2 cups sugar
1 teaspoon soda
1 cup buttermilk
Pinch of salt
2 tablespoons butter
3 cups pecan halves

1. Cook sugar, soda, buttermilk, and salt over high heat five minutes or to 210°, stirring constantly.
2. Add butter and pecans. Cook, stirring constantly, five minutes more or to 230°.
3. Remove from heat, cool one to two minutes, then beat until thick and creamy.
4. Drop by spoonfuls onto buttered marble slab, buttered cookie sheet, or wax paper.

Hint: May be stored in tin in freezer.

Microwave Marble Fudge Yield: 24 squares

1 package (12 ounces) semi-
sweet chocolate chips
1 package (12 ounces)
butterscotch chips
1 cup peanut butter
1 package (10½ ounces)
miniature marshmallows
1 cup salted nuts

Microwave instructions

1. Combine chocolate, butterscotch,
and peanut butter in large glass
mixing bowl.
2. Microwave on medium for about
10 minutes, then stir until melted.
3. Add marshmallows and nuts, then
spread in buttered 13 x 9 x 2-inch
pan.
4. Refrigerate until set. Cut into
squares.

Conventional

1. Melt chocolate, butterscotch, and
peanut butter in top of double
boiler.
2. Add marshmallows and nuts, then
spread in 13 x 9 x 2-inch pan.
3. Refrigerate until set. Cut into
squares.

Texas Millionaires Yield: 3 dozen

Easy and delicious.

1 package (14 ounces)
caramels
3 tablespoons water
2 cups chopped pecans
3 tablespoons melted paraffin
2 large (1.45 ounces each)
plain chocolate bars

1. Melt caramels with water in top of
double boiler.
2. Add pecans and drop by
teaspoonfuls onto greased wax
paper.
3. Refrigerate until firm enough to
remove from wax paper.
4. Melt paraffin and chocolate bars in
top of double boiler.
5. Dip caramels into chocolate
mixture and place on buttered wax
paper. Do not refrigerate.

Irresistible Caramels

Yield: 24 to 48 pieces

These are just too tempting!

2½ cups sugar
2 cups white corn syrup
1 cup sweetened condensed
   milk, divided
1 cup margarine or butter
1 inch cube paraffin
1 tablespoon vanilla
3 cups chopped nuts

1. Combine sugar, corn syrup, and ½ cup milk in large heavy saucepan. Bring to boil and boil hard for four minutes, stirring constantly.
2. Add remaining milk and continue cooking and stirring until mixture reaches firm ball stage (246°-252°).
3. Add margarine or butter, paraffin, and vanilla and stir until well blended.
4. Stir in nuts and pour into buttered 9-inch square pan (for thicker caramels) or 9 x 13-inch pan (for thinner caramels).
5. Refrigerate for twenty-four hours. Cut and wrap individually.

Hint: A candy thermometer comes in handy for these.

Chocolate-Peanut Butter Bars

Yield: 20 bars

Kids love these ... and easy too!

1 cup margarine, softened
1 cup peanut butter
1 box (16 ounces) powdered
   sugar
1½ cups graham cracker
   crumbs
1 bag (12 ounces) semi-sweet
   chocolate chips

1. Mix margarine, peanut butter, sugar, and graham cracker crumbs; press into buttered 9 x 13-inch pan.
2. Melt chocolate chips in double boiler, then spread on top of peanut butter mixture.
3. Chill.
4. Remove from refrigerator awhile before cutting or chocolate will crack.

312